The Internet and Society

The Internet and Society

James Slevin

Polity Press

First published in 2000 by Polity Press in association with
Blackwell Publishers Ltd

Editorial office:
Polity Press
65 Bridge Street
Cambridge CB2 1UR, UK

Marketing and production:
Blackwell Publishers Ltd
108 Cowley Road
Oxford OX4 1JF, UK

Published in the USA by
Blackwell Publishers Inc.
Commerce Place
350 Main Street
Malden, MA 02148, USA

ISBN 0–7456–2086–8
ISBN 0–7456–2087–6 (pbk)

A catalogue record for this book is available from the British Library.

Library of Congress Cataloging-in-Publication Data
Slevin, James.
    The internet and society / James Slevin.
      p. cm.
    ISBN 0–7456–2086–8 (plpc : alk. paper). — ISBN 0–7456–2087–6 (pbk. : alk. paper)
      1. Internet (Computer network)—Social aspects. 2. Computers and civilization. 3. Information society. I. Title.
    HM851.S58   2000
    303.48′33—dc21
                                        99–39729
                                          CIP

Typeset in 10 on 11.5pt Sabon
by Graphicraft Limited, Hong Kong
Printed in Great Britain by MPG Books, Bodmin, Cornwall

This book is printed on acid-free paper.

Contents

Preface

In conversations I have been deeply struck by the differences in opinions people hold about the internet and its consequences for our lives. Some think that the internet is trivial and at best a marginal phenomenon. Others see it as a very exciting development with almost unfathomable opportunities. Yet others think it sinister, frightening and even dangerous. Sometimes rather contradictory and diverse thoughts are voiced by one and the same person.

While a clash of competing views is healthy, and certainly so in intellectual life, more can be said about the nature of this debate. One important reason for the wide diversity of opinion is of course that the internet, both as a network and as an interactive medium, brings together a wide range of different people who might otherwise never have met, let alone conversed. A less obvious reason for these different interpretations of the consequences of the internet is that the debates are often carried on with little reference to the contexts in which the internet is used, or that such contexts are somehow cancelled out. Once we are online, we seem to enter and become submerged in a different world where, as some would have it, we can be whoever we like. From this point of view this 'different world' appears not just open to interpretation, but to be interpreted any way we like. Such an attitude is encouraged by the emerging literature on internet culture which is mostly about 'culture online', quite divorced from the people who produced it and from the socially structured contexts in which they are situated. In this book, I try to address this problem. Not by claiming that culture online is irrelevant, but by insisting that we can only understand the impact of the internet on modern culture if we see that symbolic content and online interaction are embedded in social and historical contexts of various kinds.

It is not surprising in the face of divergent opinion and the vagueness of 'life online' that a great many of us adopt an attitude of resignation – computers were never much fun anyway. Yet the risky and uncertain conditions of modern life often call on us to sort out many of our problems ourselves, without the help of institutions, and even to help others to do the same. This explains why so often we can feel torn between avoiding its use and the need to know more about the internet because it might be beneficial to us. I hope that this book contributes to an exciting but also more down to earth view of the consequences of the internet, a medium which creates both new options and new burdens.

My analysis of the internet and society would not be possible without those whose work I have drawn on heavily and directly. First, John Thompson, whose work in *Ideology and Modern Culture* and *The Media and Modernity* is fundamental to my study. Although he stops short of addressing the possible impact of new technologies such as the internet, my work has benefited greatly from his cultural approach to communication media, together with the arguments, concepts and ideas that he has developed. Second, Anthony Giddens is clearly a major influence in my writing. I do not discuss his theory of structuration directly, yet many of his concepts and arguments, particularly those presented in *The Constitution of Society*, are never far from the surface of my work. They continue to help us understand the changes that are going on in our world. The relevance for an analysis of the internet of his more recent work, for example *Beyond Left and Right* and *The Third Way* – concerning the future of radical politics – has not yet been widely noticed or remarked on: I demonstrate how much it has to offer in this field. An analysis of the internet drawing on John Thompson's theory of cultural transmission and the work of Anthony Giddens cannot shun a critical engagement with views and scenarios that are often labelled as 'postmodern'. Therefore, the third writer whose work I draw on heavily and directly is Zygmunt Bauman. Considered as *the* theorist of postmodernity, his books *Intimations of Postmodernity*, *Life in Fragments* and *Postmodernity and its Discontents* have allowed me to attend to this issue in a significant way. Given the strong presence of these theorists, I consider my own contribution to be one of drawing these works together and critically applying them to the study of the internet. More modestly I hope that this endeavour may feed back into the further development of their perspectives. On a more personal note, I am very grateful to Anthony Giddens for suggesting that I should write this book. I must also especially thank John Thompson for not only encouraging me to do so but also for his critical reading of my work and for his valuable comments as it progressed.

Working on this book, I also benefited from the comments and criticisms of Neal Woodcock who served as my sounding board and contributed substantially to the production of this text. Among others who helped me a great deal are Marisca Milikowski, Carin Mulié-Velgersdijk, Josien Huizinga, and many of my students at the University of Amsterdam. In addition I should like to thank Jan van Cuilenburg and Holli Semetko who helped me create time to work on this book within the Amsterdam School of Communications Research (ASCoR). I am also grateful to Ann Bone who carefully read and copy-edited the book and the many people at Polity who have contributed to its production and circulation. Finally, I should like to thank my family and friends.

Many of the websites mentioned in this book, together with many of the sources that I have used and found to be available via the internet, may be accessed through the following webpage: http://www.xs4all.nl/~giotto/slevin.html.

Introduction

Although we may hold very different ideas about the nature of society, communication and technological media, it would not take long for most of us to agree that communication media are pervasive features of modern everyday life. As John Thompson argues, the development of the media have transformed in a profound and irreversible way the nature of communication in contemporary society.[1] No matter where we are or what time of day it is, a vast number of different media, from newspapers to television and from telephones to pagers, allow individuals to experience events outside their immediate social surroundings. Now the rise of new media, spearheaded by the internet, is beginning to contribute significantly to the complexity of these channels of communication in an already uncertain modern world. If we wish to understand the transformations taking place in modern societies, then we must recognize the central role such media play and be aware of the impact they have.

Compared to the rise of other electronic media, the internet has expanded at a phenomenal rate, integrating various modes of conventional communication, including radio and television, into a vast interactive network. Its use has already reshaped the conditions of mediated experience for many millions of individuals and many thousands of organizations around the world. Given its enormity, it is difficult to imagine that such an important technological transformation will have anything other than a profound impact as a means of cultural transmission. Indeed, some commentators, most notably Manuel Castells, argue that the new communication networks have a cultural dimension all of their own. They do not, he claims, facilitate 'a new culture, in a traditional sense of a system of values, because the multiplicity of subjects in the network and the diversity of networks reject such unifying network culture'.

Instead, he continues, new communication networks are 'made of many cultures, many values, many projects, that cross through the minds and inform the strategies of the various participants'.[2] The Media Lab prophet at the Massachusetts Institute of Technology (MIT), Nicholas Negroponte, also sees the advent of a 'radically new culture', one in which 'your right and left cuff links or earrings may communicate with each other by low-orbiting satellites and have more computer power than your present PC. . . . The digital planet will look and feel like the head of a pin.'[3]

These observations are very exciting ones. Yet while Castells and Negroponte are right to point out that new communication networks are opening up new opportunities for human intervention and new ways of doing things together, such technologies also create new uncertainties. Moreover, these new technologies are spreading the consciousness that the world we live in today is a highly risky and unpredictable environment.

Dependent as we are on information to actively decide how to live, what to do, what to be and who we are, we are now being confronted with how difficult it is to deal with the consequences of new forms of network communication such as the internet. In *Close to the Machine*, for example, Ellen Ullman gives an account of a computer consultant grappling with the world of information and network communication. She writes:

> I recognize my virtual colleagues by their overattention to little interactions with waiters and cashiers, a supersensitivity that has come from too much time spent alone. We've been in a machine-mediated world – computers and e-mail, phones and faxes – and suddenly we're in a world where people lumber up and down the steps of buses, walk in and out of stores, have actual in-person conversations. *All this has been going on while I was in another universe*: that's what comes to us with a force like the too-bright sun or a stiff wind off the bay. . . . Sometimes I think about taking a real job, with a real company. So what if my virtual company in its trendy loft is what everyone imagines is a perfect life?[4]

In much the same way, Clifford Stoll also describes the culture of network communication in terms of 'an unreal universe, a soluble tissue of nothingness'. He writes and asks: 'Perhaps our networked world isn't a universal doorway to freedom. Might it be a distraction from reality? An ostrich hole to divert our attention and resources from social problems? A misuse of technology that encourages passive rather than active participation?'. He continues: 'While the internet beckons brightly, seductively flashing an icon of knowledge-as-power, this nonplace lures us to surrender our time on earth. A poor substitute it is, this virtual reality where frustration is legion and where – in the holy names of Education and Progress – important aspects of human interactions are relentlessly devalued.'[5]

In *Disconnected*, William Wresch on his part is not so much interested in those who participate in network communication but rather in those who are excluded from it. Describing the life of Negumbo Johannes who lives on the northern outskirts of Windhoek, in South Africa, Wresch contrasts the opportunities of the information-rich with those of the information-poor. Negumbo Johannes's life is

> everyone's nightmare about the information age. Johannes wakes every morning at six. He sleeps on the floor of a friend's house in Wanaheda. The house is a concrete block rectangle about the size of a one-car garage in the United States. . . . His street is gravel. Water and electricity are planned, but neither has arrived yet. . . . His life has become almost an obsession with finding a job. . . . What he does not know is that his situation is getting worse. The information age has arrived in Africa and new systems are being established. Those systems totally exclude him. . . . Newspapers cost N$ 1.50 – 10 percent of his daily wage on days when he has a wage. So he doesn't buy them. Television is broadcast by the state, but few of his neighbors have a TV, and broadcasts are in English, a language he doesn't know. Radio has one channel broadcasting in Oshiwambo, his only source of news. Professional information excludes him because he has no profession. . . . Organizational information bypasses him as well. None of his employers take the time to inform him of their future directions, their future prospects. . . . His personal information is virtually nonexistent. . . . He has travelled nowhere but Windhoek and his village in the north, so he knows nothing of the world. . . . As for the great wired future, he will never in his life see a computer, much less use one to communicate or learn.[6]

However, while such critical observations might fuel our attempts at being on our guard against euphoric interpretations and the excesses of futurology, we must equally be careful not to shift our analysis to the other extreme and present an overly dismal account of the transformations taking place. The unpredictable information environment which we live in today clearly demands that we deal with it in an active way.[7] Ullman, Stoll and Wresch may well elaborate certain trends that configure society in the early twenty-first century, yet they do so in a way that offers little help for anyone seeking to sketch a way out of the problems they describe. And isn't a more active engagement with these issues the only way in which it might be possible to avert some of the perverse and unintended consequences of networked social interaction? If we are to develop positive ways of using the internet, we need to develop a more informed understanding and a firmer grasp of what it amounts to.

Three complicating factors have stood in the way of gaining a more informed understanding of new media up till now. The first is the term *new media* itself, often used as a convenient label for referring to technologies like the internet. In some ways, the term new media is a misleading one.

It suggests, for example, that we may begin our understanding of the interactional impact of the internet as if we are able to make a fresh start. In fact, we must approach this phenomenon much like any other: critically using existing theories and knowledge.

The second complicating factor is that despite the growing significance of communication media, they were for far too long unfairly neglected in the literature of social and political theory. As Thompson argues, until relatively recently there were no adequate frameworks to help us understand and assess the importance of the development of mediated communication for the cultural transformations associated with the rise of modern societies. This is in part due to the legacy of early social and political thought. The writings of Marx, Weber and Durkheim set the agenda for many of our contemporary theoretical debates, and they did not give the development of communication media the prominence they deserve.[8]

The third complicating factor has to do with the specialist literature in the field of communications. Many mass communication researchers have overlooked the area of computer-mediated communication altogether.[9] Computers were seen to be firmly within the realm of 'nerds' and 'geeks', who were believed to communicate very little with anyone. The few attempts at studying the internet as a cultural phenomenon invariably adopt a limited and uncritical concept of culture. Such accounts are more interested in what is happening on the net, confining themselves to analysing and classifying so-called 'virtual communities',[10] or elucidating 'textual cyberspace'.[11] While online exchanges are indeed worthy of study, to proceed in this way is to make many of the same mistakes made by those studying the mass media. As Thompson points out, this amounts to ignoring how information and symbolic content are embedded in the social contexts within which, and by virtue of which, they are produced and received.[12]

As a consequence of these complicating factors, both the literature of social theory and the specialist literature in the field of communications have, as yet, neglected to study comprehensively the development of the internet and the way it enmeshes with the cultural transformations associated with modern societies. The issue of its impact remains fraught with many anxieties as well as scarred by conflicting opinions. At the same time, there is a growing realization that communication technologies such as the internet are not incidental to our lives but fundamental to the way we live now.

One of my central aims in this book is to elaborate some conceptual issues which might help us come to terms with the theoretical and practical implications of the impact of the internet on modern culture. I shall pursue this aim in three steps. First, I shall link the emergence of the internet to the developments that have transformed modern societies, organizations and the lives of individuals. Second, I shall draw out some conceptions that might help us understand the interactional impact of the internet. Lastly, I shall describe ways in which individuals and their broader institutional contexts might respond proactively to the challenges which the internet undoubtedly brings.

The emergence of the internet and the transformation of modern societies

In the first step, I shall start out from three important developments that have transformed modern societies. These are described by Giddens as the *intensification of globalization*, the *detraditionalizing of society* and the *expansion and intensification of social reflexivity*. Together, these developments have resulted in the acceleration of manufactured uncertainty in our late modern world.[13] It was not by accident that the internet originated under such conditions. Its emergence can only be understood if all these developments are seen to interlock.

As with the conditions of its development, the consequences of internet use come out of the tense, contradictory shoving and tugging of different technical and social conditions. Continuing the first step, I shall want in particular to tease out the ambivalent potential of the internet as a medium of cultural transmission. The world of the early twenty-first century may well be a world of 'intensified reflexivity', yet a world of clever people does not necessarily mean a world of greater autonomy of action. The 'Beards and Birkenstocks'[14] who think that the internet will almost by its very nature further the cause of libertarian and utopian counterculture are already being disappointed. Like any other media of communication, the internet introduces a new dialectic of empowerment and powerlessness into social relations. This observation will spark off a number of critical questions which I believe to be relevant to all those studying and using the internet. I base these on central issues contained in Giddens's framework for radical politics:[15]

1 To what extent might the internet facilitate an advance in intelligent relationships between organizations, groups and individuals which are ordered through dialogue rather than through existing patterns of domination?
2 How might the internet allow organizations, groups and individuals to make things happen rather than to have things happen to them, in the context of overall social goals?
3 In what way might the internet offer the basis for new forms of solidarity, bringing together organizations, groups and individuals who were hitherto geographically and socially far apart, and in what

way might it contribute to the production of new forms of social disintegration?

4 In what way might the internet create new ways of limiting the damaging consequences of new kinds of uncertainty in modern life, for example those arising from new areas of network violence and conflict? The internet allows people to cross paths with others whose views and interests may differ from their own. Network violence might involve verbal abuse, the spreading of computer viruses, computer hacking, etc.

Conceptualizing the internet as a modality of cultural transmission

It is much easier to call attention to the internet as a contextualized social phenomenon than it is to deal with any of these four questions satisfactorily. In order to examine these issues constructively, we must shift our perspective to a different level. This is the second step in pursuing the aim of this book. Here my concern is to draw out and provide some conceptions which might help us make this necessary shift and spell out, albeit theoretically, how we might go about understanding the interactional impact of the internet. My account is based first and foremost on Thompson's reworking of conceptions of culture and my attempt to follow through his arguments and conceptualize the internet as a modality of cultural transmission.

Recent developments in social theory, particularly evident in the work of Thompson,[16] attempt to redress its neglect of mass communication and offer in my view a suitable starting point for developing such a constructive approach to the study of the internet. Traces of systematic attempts to develop a social theory of mass communication can be found from the early 1960s onwards, when those studying communication and society began to allot a more central place to the concept of culture.[17] Three traditions of contemporary social and cultural theory have been particularly influential in the development of Thompson's approach. The first tradition is concerned with the contextual interpretation of symbolic forms, and is associated with the work of Clifford Geertz. The second tradition is that of the so-called media theorists, exemplified in the writings of Harold Innis which concern the relationship between media of communication and the organization of power. The third tradition is that of critical theory, in particular, Habermas's account of the emergence and transformation of the public sphere.

Thompson's theory of cultural transmission, informed by ideas drawn critically from these three traditions, is concerned with both the mean-

ingful character of the content of communication and with the production, storage and circulation of material which is meaningful for the
individuals who produce and receive it. The 'technical' features of communication media, which facilitate communication and the flow of information, are not obscured from view, but are considered as part of
the broader contexts of social life. Such an approach allows us to avoid
technological determinism while opening up new horizons for understanding how communication technologies 'can be used to affect, to
alter, and in some cases control our social process'.[18] However, Thompson
has stopped short of elaborating a theoretical framework which enables
us to understand the distinctive characteristics of new media such as the
internet.

In order to overcome this deficiency I shall follow through Thompson's
arguments, concepts and ideas in a study of the internet. I shall argue
that any full analysis of the impact of the internet on society, organizations and individual life must also be fundamentally 'cultural'. This means
that we must build on a conceptual framework which does more than
simply map out the internet as an alternative means of distributing information and communication. It must also provide us with the means
for analysing the way in which internet use involves the creation of new
forms of action and interaction. Such a framework will increase our
awareness that, in a fundamental way, the internet is contributing to the
transformation of the spatial and temporal organization of social life
which began with the advent of telecommunication. The internet has
the potential to enable individuals and organizations to interact with
distant others on an unprecedented scale, creating new modes of exercis-
ing power and new modes of underwriting the legitimate use of that
power. When individuals publish information on the world wide web or
send and receive e-mail, they enter into forms of interaction which differ
in many respects not only from face-to-face interaction but also from
conventional forms of mediated communication. Consequently, I shall not
only be concerned with what is happening on the net. I shall also want
to explore how organizations, groups and individuals using the internet
are continuously and routinely engaged in negotiating the boundaries
between real and virtual time-space. When they are online they have a
foot in both worlds. We must therefore try to understand how these
discontinuous experiences interlock. Without real people and real organizations, 'virtual communities' and 'textual cyberspace' would not exist.
Applying Thompson's theory of cultural transmission to the internet will
also involve revisiting some of the major sources he has used in order to
develop his approach. The new burdens and opportunities created by the
internet, I would argue, call for some of these to be considered in a new
light.

How we might respond to the impact of the internet

The final step in pursuing the aim of this book involves demonstrating how the process of rethinking conceptual issues, in particular Thompson's theory of cultural transmission, can be placed in the service of illuminating some concrete issues of internet praxis. My aim here is to look afresh at the problems faced by organizations, groups and individuals using the internet, and to demonstrate how these users might brace themselves generatively to meet the challenges it poses rather than to stress the disorientation and uncertainty they may feel. I firmly believe that if organizations, groups and individuals are to cope under the conditions of late modernity, they need to approach these challenges head on and not shy away from them. While I do not pretend to resolve conclusively any of the questions and issues I raise, I do hope to contribute positively to this debate. While Zygmunt Bauman's work helps me define some of the challenges we face, the work of Anthony Giddens helps me structure my ideas concerning possible responses to them.

The chapters that follow are intended to cast light on some of the consequences of the internet for the mediazation of modern culture. In chapter 1, I shall set out some of the developments which some eminent social thinkers consider to be constitutive of late modern culture. I do not mean to communicate by this cultural approach that the technical features of the internet are somehow unimportant, but rather that they must first of all be understood as contextualized social phenomena.

Against this backdrop, I trace in chapter 2 the development of the internet and describe some of its principal technological and institutional features. I also begin to pursue some of the ways in which internet use might have an impact on the mediazation of modern culture for the purpose of elaborating the need for a systematic theoretical reflection.

Chapter 3 represents a preliminary contribution to a social theory of the internet. I shall take as my starting point Thompson's analysis of some basic concepts of culture and demonstrate how Thompson's rethinking of the concept of culture may help us to better understand the internet and the way it affects organizations, groups and individuals. Some commentators argue that the internet somehow cancels out the importance of time-space. I find such a stance very misleading, and want to elaborate on the reordering of space and time that the development of the internet brings. In following through Thompson's argument in studying the impact of the internet, I shall focus on the kinds of interactional situations it creates.

In chapter 4, I shift the analysis on to a number of themes, not only exploring the impact the internet is starting to have, but also taking as objects of study concrete problems and debates. The first of the six themes to be discussed concerns the rise of 'virtual communities'. The internet provides individuals with a variety of arenas for communication and interaction, such as internet relay chat, newsgroups, e-mail and the world wide web. I shall argue that in order to understand the significance of these arenas as opportunities for establishing new forms of human association, it is necessary to embed them in the broader social contexts in which participants are situated. The remaining themes will be discussed in the chapters that follow.

In chapter 5, I shall explore some of the ways in which the internet is affecting organizations and institutions of social life. It makes sense to examine the role the internet plays in modern organizational culture, particularly in view of Giddens's claim that our modern world is a world of organizations.[19] I shall argue that the internet is contributing to the acceleration and intensification of reflexivity in modern culture by allowing organizations to both alter and intensify their modes of surveillance, information collation and retrieval. I want also to focus on the general question of what the consequences of the internet are for traditional forms of social life. Here I shall argue that the internet, as Thompson argues for mass communication, is affecting the mediazation of tradition by endowing it with a new life, and also by exposing it to new sources of critique. The internet presents organizations with a range of new options but also new burdens. I therefore also discuss a number of traits of internet use which may help them steer a careful path between their newly acquired options and autonomy and the responsibilities arising from the practical and situated contexts in which the internet is used.

In chapter 6, I shall examine the ways in which the internet is affecting the daily lives of individuals. The internet not only extends the individual's capacity to experience distant events, but also provides new ways for participating in their creation. I am particularly interested in new mechanisms of self-formation, but will also examine how the internet is bound up with the tremendous increase in the mediation of the experience of organizations and institutions, now intruding deeper into our lives than ever before.

In the last three chapters I shall discuss briefly three related themes which arise from my discussion of 'virtual communities'. In chapter 7, I shall again focus on some of Thompson's concepts to analyse how the internet might be understood as facilitating a new concept of publicness, one in which openness and visibility is shifting from being non-dialogically mediated to being dialogically mediated. As such, the internet offers some interesting opportunities for the renewal of politics and moral-practical thinking. I shall examine to what extent the internet allows individuals to be endowed with the status of knowledgeable agents, capable of participating as competent members in the formation of opinion in modern political society. The development of the internet, however, has not just changed the nature of openness and visibility, it has fundamentally transformed it on an unprecedented scale. In chapter 8, I shall follow through some of Giddens's and Thompson's arguments and seek to show how the internet has interwoven with the globalization of communication. In chapter 9, I am concerned to analyse how the internet is challenging the ways we seek to manage openness and visibility in modern culture. Existing forms of media regulation are proving inadequate and have unintendedly resulted in either the intensification of struggles for visibility or in the dispersal of certain groups. I shall focus on the question of what opportunities regulators have to intervene effectively.

In the final chapter, I want to draw together the threads of my argument regarding the consequences of the internet as a new modality of cultural transmission. Should we take seriously Jean-François Lyotard's claim that we now stand at the opening of a new era and that new media such as the internet are beginning to take us beyond modernity?[20] Is the internet contributing unquestionably to the emergence of the 'information society' and to a shift towards postmodern culture? I shall attempt to argue that this is far from the case. Rather than facilitating our entry into a period of postmodernity, I shall draw on Giddens's work and argue that the internet is contributing instead to a shift into a period in which the consequences of modernity are becoming more radical, and more universal than ever before.

1

Some developments that have transformed modern societies

It is argued by many that the emergence of the internet signals the coming of a new era in the history of cultural transmission. Indeed, a baffling array of terms are now in use relating the birth of a new kind of society to the consequences of modern communication.[1] There is, for example, talk of an information technology revolution leading to an information society.[2] Yet the importance of the internet and the consequences of its use are clearly not beyond controversy. In order to begin to properly understand the impact of the internet on the mediazation of modern culture we must focus on its characteristics and reconstruct its development. The internet may well be creating a new technical scenario, but the varied and complex social and technological transformations we are experiencing today have roots which can be traced back in time. The challenge is to understand how all these developments interlock.

The term *new media* suggests that the internet is somehow a sudden invention, governed solely by conditions internal to its own technological development. In fact, none of our modern communication technologies has ever simply mysteriously appeared out of a bag of independently given technological opportunity.[3] Like all modern communication technology, the internet is closely interwoven with the wider development of mediated communication, a process which has gone hand in hand with the expansion of economic organizations and with the development of the modern nation-state.[4] On a different level, the transmutations introduced by modern organizations interlace in a direct way with the nature of day-to-day individual life. As such, the development of the internet is at once a purposive and an unintended result of human endeavour. It can therefore best be understood as a result of the tensionful, contradictory technical and social conditions, and the consequences of its use no less so.

Taken together, the first two chapters of this book constitute the first step in elaborating some conceptual issues which might help us come to terms with the theoretical and practical implications of the impact of the internet on modern culture. As such, they prepare the ground for the rest of this book. My aim in this first chapter is to socially contextualize the advent of the internet by examining a series of developments that have transformed modern societies.

To begin with I shall draw on the work of some of today's most eminent social theorists. In the light of their ideas, I shall attempt to clarify the main lines of social transformation, paying particular attention to three sets of developments: the influence of intensifying globalization, the emergence of a post-traditional social order, and the expansion of social reflexivity. I shall relate these developments to what Giddens has described as the acceleration of the production of manufactured uncertainty in late modernity.[5]

Then I shall focus on the way these developments interlace with the changes taking place in modern organizations and with the changes taking place in the lives of individuals. Our uncertain world demands an active engagement, one which has both extensional and intentional dimensions. Drawing on a wide range of writers, I shall tease out a number of ideal-typical interests and projects which are gradually emerging among various institutional and cultural contexts which, I claim, constitute a move toward a more positive and active approach to the management of risk.

Modern societies and manufactured uncertainty

Modern societies that are stretched over wide expanses of time-space have always been interwoven in complex ways with the development of technologies enabling the 'control of far-flung activities'.[6] The invention of electronic media has provided the means to radically increase the scope for nation-states, commercial enterprises and other forms of social organization to monitor their production and reproduction in time-space. Electronic media have also provided the means to radically increase the scope for individuals to appropriate information and to monitor the differing ideas of others. This has opened up ways for them to participate more competently in the formation of opinion and in the making of decisions which affect their own lives and the lives of others.

The introduction of electric telegraphy in the 1830s was the first of many key innovations that gave rise to new kinds of interconnectedness in the modern world.[7] The significance of the development of the telephone, radio and television, and later, the new forms of information processing based on digital systems, is often expressed via the notion of time-space convergence. Studies of early postal communication show that it was slow and unreliable.[8] In modern telephone communication, however, there is only a small difference in speed and efficiency between placing a local call and placing one across many thousands of miles.[9] Technological progress, it is argued, has allowed for an almost complete time-space convergence in the world, pitching the administrative unity within economic organizations and nation-states to a higher degree than ever before.[10] Well before the advent of the internet Marshall McLuhan wrote, 'After three thousand years of specialist explosion and of increasing specialism and alienation in the technological extensions of our bodies, our world has become compressional by dramatic reversal. As electrically contracted, the globe is no more than a village.'[11]

Although we can use these observations to emphasize the fact that communication media are important for the organization of power, few would claim seriously that the kind of electronically mediated world we live in today is one subject to tight control. A one-way view of social and technological change projected by a crude conceptualization of time-space convergence is untenable. It ignores the material conditions and consequences of communication and the social constraints which are imposed on and flow from it. While the advances in the collation, storage and retrieval of information have undoubtedly created vastly greater opportunities for organizations and their worldwide spread, there is also a sombre side to this development, one which is becoming ever more apparent. Even McLuhan argued that we now live in an 'Age of Anxiety for the reason of the electric implosion that compels commitment and participation, quite regardless of any "point of view" '.[12] Over a decade later, Ulrich Beck claims that 'in advanced modernity the social production of wealth is systematically accompanied by the social production of risks.'[13] Anthony Giddens also points to 'manufactured uncertainty' as 'the outcome of the long-term maturation of modern institutions'.[14] New kinds of risk feature as both unacknowledged conditions and unintended consequences in the process of connecting the local and the global by means of modern communication technology. The manufacture of uncertainty is therefore elusive, varied and extremely complex. Let me dwell on this issue for a moment by considering several related aspects of manufactured uncertainty which illustrate the complexity of this process, and by explaining how this process has accelerated over the past four or five decades.

Interaction stretched across time-space acquires an additional normative complexity

When the exchange of information in the social world takes place in contexts of mediated interaction between individuals who do not share a common locale, their interaction acquires an additional normative complexity. This first aspect of manufactured uncertainty is explained by Zygmunt Bauman, who writes,

> what we and other people do may have profound, far-reaching and long-lasting consequences, which we can neither see directly nor predict with precision. Between the deeds and their outcomes there is a huge distance – both in time and in space – which we cannot fathom using our innate, ordinary powers of perception – and so we can hardly measure the quality of our actions by a full inventory of their effects.[15]

We may, for example, find a bargain at a local retail store and not realize that in buying it we are perpetuating poor labour conditions in another part of the world. The consequences of our actions often materialize out of sight, rendering much of our moral imagination impotent. Jürgen Habermas also sets out how the stretching of interaction across time and space can result in anxieties. These anxieties, he says, 'function as catalysts for a feeling of being overwhelmed in the view of the possible consequences of processes for which we are morally accountable – since we do set them in motion technically and politically – yet for which we can no longer take moral responsibility – since their scale has put them beyond our control'.[16] As Giddens suggests, some of the most encompassing of such risks are to do with the consequences of ecological disaster and the possibility of nuclear war.[17]

Abstract systems of communication relieve uncertainty but also create new areas of vulnerability

One response to the complexity of stretching communication across extended reaches of time-space is the increasing importance given to so-called abstract systems of communication. These are meant to stabilize the outcome of complex social transactions and make them less risky. Both Habermas and Giddens analyse such systems and point to three in particular: symbolic tokens, expert systems and generalized forms of communication.

Symbolic tokens   Symbolic tokens are used in innumerable exchanges taking place all the time by individuals who neither meet nor talk. Money is a prime example. It provides, writes Giddens, 'for the enactment of transactions between agents widely separated in time and space'.[18] As Habermas explains, abstract media, such as money, 'encode a purposive-rational attitude toward calculable amounts of value and make it possible to exert generalized, strategic influence on the decisions of other

participants while bypassing processes of consensus-oriented communication'.[19] Given the scale and complexity of modern economies, it would
be difficult to envisage coordination of exchanges involving only dialogue
between participants or some other form of high-level information input.[20]
Most attempts at central economic planning on a grand scale, for example,
have indeed proved to be impossible.

Expert systems   Expert systems allow for more complex exchanges than
symbolic tokens but, like them, work to relieve uncertainty and reduce
the expenditure of communication. Giddens describes them as 'systems
of technical accomplishment or professional expertise that organize large
areas of material and social environments in which we live today'.[21] For
example, we very rarely talk to professionals such as doctors, broadcasters, architects, bankers, airline pilots or tram-drivers in person, yet
we are all continuously involved in systems into which their expertise is
integrated. Like abstract media, expert systems provide 'guarantees' of
expectations we have of them without us having to communicate and
negotiate directly with all those involved. We do not have to ask a tram-
driver whether they know the way to the next stop, or whether they are
in possession of the right documents proving they have the competence
to drive the vehicle safely.

Generalized forms of communication   Generalized forms of communication involve mediated communication produced for an indefinite, or
at least a large range of potential recipients. Habermas cites the mass
media as ultimate examples of this kind of information exchange.
He writes: 'they free communication processes from the provinciality of
spatiotemporally restricted contexts and permit public spheres to emerge,
through establishing the abstract simultaneity of a virtually present
network of communication contents far removed in space and time
and through keeping messages available in manifold contexts.'[22] When
we switch on our televisions and switch between channels we are fairly
confident that broadcasters may be called upon to account for the accept-
ability of their actions within certain parameters of good taste.

However, while symbolic tokens, expert systems and generalized forms
of communication are meant to relieve uncertainty and reduce the
expenditure of communication, they also unintendedly contribute to
the creation of new forms of uncertainty and risk. Both Giddens and
Habermas articulate with particular acuity the inability of abstract systems of communication to uncouple communication from the lifeworld
context of shared cultural knowledge altogether. As Habermas writes,
generalized forms of communication 'do not replace reaching agreement
in language'.[23] Giddens sets out how mechanisms such as symbolic

tokens and expert systems depend on active trust and how attitudes of trust are influenced by communication.[24] Consequently, abstract systems of communication place new burdens on individuals, organizations and representatives of expert systems to display their integrity and so maintain and develop trust. We must therefore conclude that while symbolic tokens, expert systems and generalized forms of communication open up new areas of social opportunity, they also open up new areas of vulnerability and make modern communication no less precarious.

The intermingling of feelings of security and uncertainty in modern life is thus not only an issue of moral accountability and responsibility, but also a disturbing feature which is linked to the standardized influences of abstract systems of communication. Although these contribute to routine and continuance by filtering the diversity of options, they also produce outcomes which may be experienced as arbitrary and unacceptable. This can result in marginalization and disappointment in all sectors of social life. To complicate matters further, abstract systems are also seen to play an important role in the deskilling of day-to-day life.[25] All this makes it difficult for individuals to cope under the stresses and strains placed on them.

Feelings of security and uncertainty can be particularly acute during what Giddens calls 'fateful moments'. These are occasions when individuals 'are called on to take decisions that are particularly consequential for their ambitions, or more generally their future lives'.[26] Making a decision, for example, to invest time in a period of study can be particularly complicated, often involving a wide range of 'experts' and 'authorities' advising a wide range of different trajectories of action. There are no taken-for-granted solutions and the individual has to develop skills in order to gather together and process this information, weighing up the likely risks and certainties related to different outcomes. Modern everyday life is rife with such moments.

Modern communication technology can radically alter the degree of control participants have over the transmission process

While face-to-face interaction commonly involves significant differentials of power and resources, contexts of mediated interaction acquire additional complexity in this respect. This is a third aspect of manufactured uncertainty. The nature of mediated interaction often transforms opportunities for reflexivity and reciprocity, and calls on participants to mobilize sophisticated technologies and skills.

Mass media, for example, involve predominantly one-way communication from the producer to the recipient. They draw their audiences into what Richard Sennett has dubbed 'crowd silence'.[27] Members of a television audience cannot talk back to their TV; any response they make is an inaudible one; television does not allow its audience to interrupt, for they have to remain silent to be spoken to. Producers of TV programmes are most likely to be large-scale international organizations. In order to understand the complex relationship between manufactured uncertainty and the extension of communication, we must therefore be aware of considerable variations and asymmetries of economic and political power. Uncertainty and risk depend on the kinds of skills and power that individuals and organizations can bring to bear in the exchange of information. The modern world is more risky and uncertain for some than for others. As Dougan writes: even now as we enter a new millennium 'more than half the people on earth have yet to make their first phone call.'[28]

Reflexive modernization and the accelerated manufacture of risk

In the light of this exploration it would be hard to deny the ambivalence of the potential of modern communication. It is clearly capable of both unifying and fragmenting our social world. While opening up new possibilities for control, it also facilitates the creation of new kinds of risk. Such an observation is more important now than ever before because, as Giddens argues, the advance of manufactured uncertainty has accelerated and intensified over the past four or five decades. We would seem to be entering into a new stage of modernization, moving from simple to radicalized modernity, with the consequences of modernity becoming more pronounced than ever before. Such a view is supported by Scott Lash and John Urry, who claim that we are moving not into a period of 'radical refusal of modernism, but its radical exaggeration. It is more modern than modernism.'[29] Beck, Giddens and Lash refer to this period as the stage of 'reflexive modernization'.[30]

Giddens sees the radicalization of modernity as the result of three related sets of developments. These are the *influence of intensifying globalization*, the *emergence of post-traditional forms of organization* and the *expansion and intensification of social reflexivity*. These developments affect particularly the industrialized countries, but are increasingly worldwide in their impact.[31] All three relate in a direct way to the nature of modern communication technology.

Influence of intensifying globalization Giddens defines the influence of intensifying globalization as an intensification of 'action at distance'. The activities of nation-states, economic organizations and individuals, facilitated by modern communication media, increasingly interlace with events happening in distant locales. Globalization in his view consists of a complex variety of processes which are often contradictory, and which produce an array of conflicts, new forms of social stratification and, above all, new forms of uncertainty.

Emergence of post-traditional forms of organization   Related to the influence of intensifying globalization, we are witnessing the emergence of post-traditional forms of organization. This process might seem to be rather odd, since we have come to think of modern society as already being post-traditional. However, Giddens, much like Beck,[32] believes that tradition continued to play an important role in modernity in that it remained the main source of the legitimization of power. It helped stabilize the definition of truth and seemed at least to reduce the risk of decision-making.

However, Giddens writes that today 'modernity has been forced to "come to its senses".'[33] Detraditionalization he argues, involves all forms of authority being reflexively challenged, having to explain themselves and to open themselves up to critical questioning. In culturally cosmopolitan societies and in open and informed organizations, the solutions to problems are no longer taken as given and acted on as a matter of course. They are continually redecided and subjected to critique. While authorities such as governments or management teams remain influential, they become decentred and dependent on a broader system of authority being enacted from a multiplicity of sources. Manufactured uncertainty has entered into all forms of life which have been opened up to decision-making in this way.

Expansion and intensification of social reflexivity   Related both to the influence of intensifying globalization and the detraditionalizing of society is the expansion and intensification of social reflexivity. This involves nation-states, organizations and individuals having to deal with vast amounts of information relevant to the course of their everyday activities. Here, Giddens seems to support Habermas's claim that we are now experiencing an 'overburdening of the communicative infrastructure'.[34] However, Giddens carries Habermas's concern further by pointing out that it is the dislocation between knowledge and control rather than the abundance of information itself which is the fundamental source of manufactured uncertainty. Thompson also writes, 'the problem that confronts most people and organizations today is a problem of symbolic dislocation: in a world where the capacity to experience is no longer linked to the activity of encountering, how can we relate mediated experiences to the practical contexts of our day-to-day lives?'[35]

Reflexive modernization as expressed through these three developments, Giddens, Beck and Lash claim, is undercutting conventional ways of dealing with risk and uncertainty.[36] Uncertainty associated with late modernity can no longer be managed in accordance with conventional institutionalized standards that treat uncertainty as if it were quantifiable and measurable. Risk today has become more risky and therefore demands our active engagement in dealing with it. Although many of us may seem to live in a disconnected world, we live today increasingly in one world, one in which uncertainty impinges on our lives in ways from which there is no escape. But at the same time there has been a rise of new ways of coping with risk. It is in terms of the developments that have transformed modern societies that we should expect to examine the reshaping of the conditions of mediated experience. What is it like to live and work in a world increasingly permeated by manufactured risk? What new dynamics are being introduced into our lives? Let us now look more concretely at some of the ways in which these developments interact with changes taking place in modern institutions and in individual lives; processes in which the rise of the internet is centrally involved.

Organizational contexts in the late modern age

Everywhere we look in late modernity, radical changes are taking place in organizational contexts. In a fundamental way, many of our organizations have simply become inadequate to the tasks we expect them to perform. In this section, I shall focus in particular on the nation-state and economic organizations as specific brands of organization, but I shall also look briefly at the shake-up of traditional forms of social organization as they attempt to cope with the changing demands we put on them. For my purposes it will suffice to discuss a few key issues.

The nation-state confronting manufactured risk

Over the past four or five decades, nation-states have been confronted by a series of problems to do with matters such as the rationale underpinning state activity, the grounding of order, the interpretation of democracy, the accountability of state decision-making, and questions concerning the legitimacy of state rule.[37] As Castells explains, the nation-state has become increasingly exposed to 'competition from sources of power that are undefined, and sometimes, undefinable. These are networks of capital, production, communication, crime, international institutions, supranational military apparatuses, non-governmental organizations, transnational religions, and public opinion movements. And below the state, there are communities, tribes, localities, cults and gangs.'[38] Habermas and Offe have also set out how central state authorities are finding it increasingly difficult to cope properly with the contradictory demands arising from these problems.[39]

The response of governments to such a situation has been complex and by no means coherent. The dwindling success of the traditional directive intelligence of the state has, for example, resulted in governments taking a new look at radical free market philosophies. These suggest that the successful organizational integration of modern nation-states depends increasingly on low-level input, such as that provided in the economic market.[40] Governments have accordingly taken steps to trim back state intervention in economic life. They have done so, for example, by cutting the provision of state-run services and welfare resources, and by encouraging competitive capitalism. Yet governments also increasingly find themselves caught up in an endless process of damage control and repair regarding a wide range of issues. These include the safety of food, the quality of health care, the reliability of financial services, the safety of public transportation, the control of pollution, the curbing of crime and the safeguarding of national security. Each of these issues places new demands on surveillance and administrative power, and therefore on the communicative infrastructure of the nation-state. The current problems of nation-states are thus very much a crisis in the management of risk.

In spite of a great cultural diversity in approaches with respect to the reshaping and renewal of intelligence-led governance, there is a degree of coincidence in some fundamental points. In late modernity, nation-states are attempting to initiate policies to cope more actively with the 'uncertainization' of modern life.[41] They are, for example, increasingly drawing on and further encouraging *deliberative democracy*, *generative politics* and *new forms of solidarity*, involving attempts at forging new strategic alliances in order to strengthen their administrative control.[42] Let us look at each of these in turn.

Deliberative democracy   Governability and the maintenance of organizational integrity cannot depend only on the expansion of surveillance and administrative power, and on the low-level informational input of market forces. Modern government must also invest heavily in the continuing responsiveness of government to the preferences of its citizens. Restoring trust in the rule of government involves a conscious push towards the decentralizing of administrative power and the bringing of government closer to its citizens.[43] Governments are thus looking to promote deliberative democracy and a greater transparency of their activities, thereby seeking to mobilize active trust in their performance through discussion and the interchange of views with diverse individuals and organizations. This phenomenon also extends into areas other than that of the formal political sphere. Nation-states have much to gain from advances in the discursive spaces of other forms of social organization.

Such groups might then express their views and contribute more readily to the heightened reflexivity of political activity in contemporary societies.

Generative politics   The challenges facing traditional forms of directive intelligence cannot be equated with the inevitable demise of the nation-state. Castells writes: 'what really matters is that the new power system is characterized . . . by the plurality of sources of authority . . . the nation-state just being one of these sources.'[44] Rather than keeping other organizations or even individuals in subordination, central nation-state authorities are finding it necessary to decentralize power in exchange for their own durability. They are doing this not only by letting lower levels of governance take more responsibility for managing the issues of everyday life, but more generally by seeking ways to empower other organizations and individuals in society to 'make things happen, rather than have things happen to them, in the context of overall social concerns and goals'.[45]

New forms of solidarity   In the age of late modernity, nation-states are invariably finding themselves caught between two extremes. On the one hand, they are finding it necessary to defend their sovereignty, yet on the other they are increasingly finding themselves in the position of having to share it out. Within these parameters, nation-states are struggling to carve out some tenable level of sovereignty and control. In so doing, they have little other choice than to seek out cooperation and new forms of strategic alliances and band together with major national and international political and economic players. At the same time, they are continually and actively involved in looking for ways to overcome any form of historical mistrust.

The economic organization confronting manufactured risk

In late modernity, economic organizations, like nation-states, are experiencing a crisis of the traditional model of organization. Larry Hirschhorn and Thomas Gilmore write:

> In the traditional company, boundaries were "hardwired" into the very structure of the organization. The hierarchy of occupational titles made manifest differences in power and authority. . . . Company boundaries functioned like markers on a map. By making clear who reported to whom and who was responsible for what, boundaries oriented and coordinated individual behavior and harnessed it to the purposes of the company as a whole. The problem is that this traditional organizational map describes a world that no longer exists.[46]

Under post-traditional conditions, and with intensified reflexivity and globalization, the weaknesses of the classical functionally organized enterprise are becoming increasingly apparent. The vertical organization with its oligopolistic style of control cannot properly cope with the uncertainty related to the rapidly changing business environment and highly diverse market dynamics. Like the nation-state, modern organizations are experiencing a crisis in the management of risk.

The response of economic organizations to these changes is complex. However, the political and economic restructuring of the past four or five decades has induced several interrelated transformations in economic organizations which seem to show a marked departure from traditional modes of organization. Let us look at three such trajectories. In late modernity, economic organizations are increasingly drawing on and further encouraging a series of generative policies involving the promotion of *new forms of institutionalized deliberation, decentralized initiative* and *increased teamwork and interfirm networking.*[47] Each of these trajectories runs parallel and merges into the changes associated with the transformations of the nation-state. They are also related to processes of change which are pushing aside the traditional organizational model in all modern forms of social organization.

New forms of institutionalized deliberation   An important organizational trend emphasized by business analysts in recent years has been the move to promote new forms of institutionalized deliberation.[48] Evidence of this may be found throughout business chains and in many economic sectors, but probably nowhere more so than in so-called market-based organizations. Here, organizational resources are aligned in a very direct way to serve customers – a process involving both the horizontal and vertical integration of organizational practices. 'Fundamental to this seamless form of enterprise', writes Vincent Barabba, 'is an understanding of industries, customers, and community based on decision-making networks informed by knowledge developed from listening, learning, and leading. . . . This knowledge and the decision-making networks are the ties that bind the otherwise disconnected pieces of the enterprise.'[49] So while governments are looking to promote deliberative democracy within the political domain, economic organizations are seeking to mobilize active trust in their performance through discussion and the interchange of views with individuals and groups both within and outside the confines of the organization.

Decentralized initiative   A second trend in economic organizations concerns efforts to facilitate various forms of decentralized initiative, organized around core processes rather than hierarchically structured departments. The aim is to recognize and muster a greater degree of autonomy of action and, in so doing, unleash the creative potential of individuals within organizations. Creating the conditions which allow for more autonomy on the part of those working in business projects is an objective that organizations need to pursue in order to survive in a universe of high reflexivity. In the same vein, organizations are also attempting to empower their customers to participate more actively in the shaping of products and services they may wish to have.

Increased teamwork and interfirm networking   A third trend in organizational transition is the steady growth of a variety of strategic alliances. These involve not only creative modes of interlinking within the organization in the shape of teamwork, but also cooperative agreements between organizations. The latter often do not preclude continuing competition in areas outside the agreement. Interfirm network initiatives are important competitive weapons in helping economic organizations survive in the late modern age. 'The arrogance', writes Castells, 'of the IBMs . . . or the Mitsuis of the world has become a matter of cultural history.'[50] This trend coincides closely with the way in which nation-states are attempting to forge new strategic alliances in order to strengthen their administrative control.

The reconstruction of traditional forms of social organization

In an important sense, the contours of traditional forms of organization, for example traditional family life and religion, like those of nation-states and economic organizations, are also undergoing a radical reconstruction in late modernity. Such traditions have by no means disappeared. For Habermas the growing interest in 'the revaluation of the particular, the natural, the provincial, of social spaces that are small enough to be familiar, of decentralized forms of commerce and despecialized activities, of segmented pubs, simple interactions and dedifferentiated public spheres' are all attempts to revitalize communication as uncertainty penetrates to the core of everyday life.[51] We see all around us the redefinition and revival of family values, religion, nationalism and ethnic identity as different cultural groups and social movements search for new forms of identity. It is in this context that Giddens refers to 'the establishment of "new traditions"'.[52] Thus, while it may be true to say that traditional institutions of society have become weakened as sources of authority, they are still very much relevant as sources of meaning and protection. Moreover, these diverse groupings are pre-eminently concerned with finding ways to facilitate what Thompson calls the 're-mooring of tradition', by which he means the renewal and extension of tradition, and its re-embedding in spatial units which often exceed the bounds of face-to-face interaction.[53]

Coping with the 'uncertainization' of modern life which I have been discussing here is not just an extensional dimension. The transformations taking place in nation-states, economic organizations and other forms of social organization also interlace in a direct way with the life and self-development of individuals.

The self in the late modern age

In late modernity, the self, writes Giddens, 'like the broader institutional contexts in which it exists, has to be reflexively made'.[54] Reflexive modernization for individuals means that they are faced with unprecedented levels of openness in their daily lives. In contexts in which information is coming from a diversity of sources, individuals have to make sense of such information and use it to choose among alternative courses of action. Even if they choose to follow traditional routines, traditional ways of life still have to be contemplated, defended and decided upon with an awareness that there are a variety of other ways of getting things done. Under these conditions, new mechanisms of self-identity are beginning to emerge. These involve how individuals negotiate the strategic decisions they make, and the way in which they deal with new parameters of risk and uncertainty.

The new mechanisms of self-identity which are shaped by – yet also shape – all forms of social organization in the modern age are dazzlingly complex. However, in the light of the transformations described so far, let me tease out and consider some matching transformations in the lifestyles and practices of individuals. I shall focus on the negotiation of experience, the reacquisition of knowledge and skills, and the forging of commitment and mutuality.

The negotiation of experience   Rather than having things happen to them, in the context of overall social concerns and goals, individuals are being confronted by the incapacity of authorities such as nation-states, economic organizations and other organizational forms to solve their problems. In response, individuals are having to continually monitor and assess claims made by a complex array of rival sources of authority as their own expertise is fed by radical doubt. They are also having to seek ways to make their own views heard. Seizing opportunities to communicate their specific wants and expectations to others allows them to achieve a greater reflexive control over their self-identity. To this effect they contribute to a variety of deliberative arrangements. These provide platforms which allow them to react creatively and interpretatively to the standardized influences of commodification, institutionalized politics and managerial directives. Critical movements and special-interest groups have used such platforms to place new issues on the political agenda, while others have sought to revaluate more traditional ways of life.

Women, children, gays and members of minority groups, for example, have had to put up a considerable struggle in order to obtain visibility for views which were once dismissed as unreasonable or irrelevant.

The reacquisition of knowledge and skills   In late modernity, individuals are not involved in a one-way process of deskilling in their encounters with expert systems. New skills are being created and acquired all of the time. In a world without final authorities, individuals are continually engaged in the reappropriation of knowledge and control.[55] This often involves offsetting feelings of powerlessness by drawing on non-local knowledge to create greater autonomy of action locally and at a distance. However, gaining control may also involve the revaluation of local knowledge and the exclusion of those who lack it.

The forging of commitment and mutuality   In modern social conditions, individuals are engaged in a diversity of contexts of interaction and are caught up in encounters which cut across a diversity of cultural settings. Individuals, therefore, actively seek to forge commitment and mutuality with others in an attempt to restrict the experiences they have to sample in order to develop a coherent self-identity and successfully fulfil the projects in which they are engaged. In a world of rival sources of authority, commitment increasingly depends on an individual's ability to build on active trust in other individuals, groups and organizations. Individuals are thus routinely engaged in accessing information which often stems from distant sources, and in making information available to distant others in an attempt to unify and make sense of their own involvement and the involvement of others.[56]

New dynamics in risk, compulsion and fundamentalism

As new forms of dialogue, empowerment and solidarity gather weight and replace the old ties that bind organizations and individual life together, these changes also create new challenges. The movement towards these ideals is often messy and conflictual. For nation-states, attempts at coming to grips with the problems of governability and the management of risk result in a very unstable mix of contradictory consequences. These open up new opportunities to them in some areas, yet paralyse their ability to act in others. Measures to promote deliberative democracy, for example, may flounder given the scale and complexity of modern societies and the growing interconnectedness of the modern world. Such arrangements have also been criticized as tools for opinion management and window-dressing. New kinds of risk also emerge as generative politics erodes the effectiveness of vertical bureaucratic surveillance. When nation-states have to engage in intense negotiations and liaise with powerful national and international lobbies, their capacity to intervene may be inhibited or even brought to a halt.

For economic organizations, institutionalized deliberation and reflexive engagements may well deliver new opportunities and benefits. Yet some business analysts also refer to the general lack of permanent expectations which seems to pervade modern organizational culture when communication shifts to becoming more relational rather than mere routine.[57] The advancement of self-reliance and relationships governed by interdependency rather than dependence within business also creates new kinds of uncertainty. As traditional bureaucratic directives give way to organizational forms which are 'dominated by tentative principles rather than fixed rules', the outcome of such procedures is no longer pre-set.[58] New kinds of conflict emerge as formerly disengaged individuals and groups within organizations meet. Resolving such conflict through deliberative arrangements and the interchange of views rather than by arbitrary administrative fiat of one sort or another places new burdens on organization.[59]

For individuals, the opening up of decision-making procedures often serves to heighten their awareness of the limits of their ability to answer back. There are still many instances where individuals have to engage in considerable struggle so as not to be helplessly engulfed by events. Even when they have access to the necessary information, they may not be empowered to act on it. In order to survive such conditions, individuals must revitalize their communication; however, in the very complexity of this process, the meshing of intended and unintended consequences often contributes further to the fragmentation of their social life. Failure to reconstruct and promote a degree of integration in their personal experiences can become a new and potent source of anxiety.

Yet, as Giddens explains, even greater dangers loom, for the new dynamics introduced by reflexive modernization can best be summarized as pushes and pulls between autonomy of action and compulsiveness on the one hand, and between cosmopolitanism and fundamentalism on the other.[60] Compulsiveness refers to an individual's 'inability to escape from the past'.[61] As an extensional dimension, fundamentalism may be understood as 'an assertion of formulaic truth without regard to consequences'.[62] However, even though many individuals and organizations, despairing of the uncertainty of late modernity, would like to resurrect the apparent certainty of the past, there is no going back to it. Not even with the use of arbitrary power, coercion or violence. The continued development of modern communication plays a pivotal role in this. In the next chapter I shall elaborate in detail the rise and subsequent development of the internet and raise some serious questions we need to confront.

2

The rise of the internet

Modern organizations and individuals increasingly exist in the same information environments. Such a major development is inseparable from the rise of new communication networks such as the internet. Almost all these technologies have started off as significant matters of actual or potential military power and have later spread to other areas of society. The advent of the internet also displays this typical push and pull of military, scientific, commercial and countercultural innovation.[1] My aim in this second chapter is to trace the rise and subsequent development of the internet and make a start at linking up the emergence of the internet with the developments that have transformed modern societies.

Unlike media such as newspapers, radio and television, the history of the internet is only just beginning to be written. Most accounts of its development hardly progress beyond the construction of time-lines setting out important events. The rapidly changing developments are evidence of the kind of social transformations the internet itself facilitates. In this brief history I shall emphasize thematic and analytical issues that are relevant to the dynamism of reflexive modernization. It is not my intention to provide an up-to-date overview of aspects that will obviously change very rapidly. The developments in the history of the internet that I shall describe here will continue to be consequential in the future.

I shall first construct an account of the origin and subsequent development of the internet, a period that corresponds with the acceleration in the manufacture of risk in late modernity. Katie Hafner and Mathew Lyon's work *Where Wizards Stay Up Late* and Peter Salus's *Casting the Net* serve as valuable sources of evidence here.[2] Second I shall explain some of the different ways in which individuals, groups and organizations have come to terms with the emerging options and burdens of the internet. In doing so, I shall highlight some of the complex issues we might encounter when studying the impact of the internet on modern culture. I shall demonstrate that such issues are part of much broader transformations and opportunities associated with the arrival of new intelligent technology in a period that Shoshana Zuboff has called 'the age of the smart machine'.[3] In discussing these issues, I shall lay the foundations for the next step in the book and set out the need for a systematic theoretical reflection on the impact of the internet on modern culture, one which takes more account of the internet as a contextualized social phenomenon.

The emergence of the internet as a global constellation of computer networks

The origin of the internet is firmly rooted in the circumstances of the Cold War, a period during which nuclear conflict featured as potentially the most immediate and catastrophic of all global dangers. The launch of Sputnik 1 on 4 October 1957 by the Soviet Union spawned a very specific fear: if nations were capable of launching space satellites, they might also be capable of launching long-distance nuclear attacks. Although state security was never seriously threatened by this event, it did contribute to the setting up of the Advanced Research Projects Agency (ARPA) within the United States Department of Defense.

ARPA: the Advanced Research Projects Agency

The agency's task was to establish and maintain a worldwide lead in science and technology. Its first director, however, defined the agency's role almost completely in military terms, and failed to recognize the importance of cutting-edge research taking place in the nation's universities at that time. This misjudgement was to threaten the continuation of the agency during its early years, and in 1958, ARPA saw many of the projects and programmes it had initiated transferred to the National Aeronautics and Space Administration (NASA). Consequently, the agency was forced to rethink its mission or face being abolished.

The Advanced Research Projects Agency's reputation as an innovative research institution only really began in 1961 when Jack Ruina was appointed as its director. He decentralized the structure of the agency and redefined its role as a body supporting and funding the work carried out by teams of researchers on special projects. One of the most important research programmes supported by the agency involved the investigation of techniques and technologies for interlinking computer networks of various kinds. The objective was twofold: first, to develop a communication network which would facilitate the exchange of information between various research centres involved in ARPA projects, and second, to allow participants in the network to share scarce computer resources. The creation of this so-called ARPANET in 1969 has become widely recognized as the origin and advent of the internet.

A number of developments in the history of computer-mediated communication were fundamental to the success of the ARPANET project. The first was the idea of communicating with computers at a distance. In September 1940, George Stibitz had decided to demonstrate a calculator to a meeting of the American Mathematical Society. The complex machine took up lots of space, so rather than transporting it to the meeting with the risk of it getting damaged, Stibitz set up a teletype terminal so that the calculator could be used remotely via a telegraph connection.

A second development was that computers had to be seen as more than just devices for solving mathematical problems. In 1945, Vannevar Bush published an article, 'As we may think', in which he described the 'Memex', a communication system for storing and retrieving information.[4]

A third, and crucial, development for setting up the ARPANET was the invention of packet-switching communication technology. Packet-switching involves the breaking down of digitized information into packets or blocks that are labelled to indicate both their origin and their destination, and the sending of these from one computer to another. The advantages of packet-switching are twofold. First, network resources are used more efficiently because a single channel can carry more than one transmission simultaneously. Second, communication is more robust because information can still reach its destination even if a large portion of the network is not functioning. The packets bypass the problem by taking a different route to their destination. The number of possible routes is referred to as the network's level of redundancy. The higher the level of redundancy, the greater the safety margin and thus the more robust a network is.

The technology necessary for packet-switching was developed independently at a number of research centres around the world, for example, at the National Physical Laboratory in Great Britain, and the Massachusetts Institute of Technology and the RAND Corporation in the United States.[5] Of these, the research done by Paul Baran at the RAND Corporation deserves particular attention. Baran had been commissioned by the United States Air Force to do a study on how the military could maintain control over its missiles and bombers in the aftermath of a nuclear attack. In 1964 he proposed a communication network with no central command or control point. In the event of an attack on any one point, all surviving points would be able to re-establish contact with each other.[6] He called this kind of network a distributed network. It was from this RAND Corporation study that the false rumour started that the ARPANET was somehow directly and primarily related to the building of a communication network which would be resistant to nuclear attack.[7]

While Baran had been conducting his study into packet-switching, Joseph Licklider had been appointed to head the computer research programme at ARPA. As a psychologist with a background in hearing and speech research at MIT, he was mainly interested in computers as communication devices. Licklider saw networking not so much as a way of connecting computers, but as a way of connecting people. In his paper 'Man–computer Symbiosis'[8] he had already explored the idea of interconnected networks of information storage and retrieval centres supporting the team effort of groups and individuals. These ideas were reflected in his work for ARPA as he continued to decentralize the activities of the agency, setting up research contracts and bringing together computer scientists from MIT, Stanford, the University of California at Los Angeles, Berkeley and a number of companies. He nicknamed his dispersed team of scientists the 'intergalactic network'. Licklider later extended this concept to mean a globally interconnected network which would allow all participants to access and use information and programs from any site.[9] When Licklider left ARPA in 1964 the name of the research programme he had led changed from 'Command and Control Research' to the 'Information Processing Techniques Office'. This change symbolizes and reflects both the changes that had taken place in ARPA as an organization and the changing role of computers in human activity.

In 1968, ARPA awarded the contract to build the ARPANET to Bolt, Beranek and Newman, a consulting firm in Cambridge, Massachusetts, specializing in information systems. Licklider, who had returned to work at MIT, claimed that in a few years individuals would be able to communicate more effectively through the digital computer than face to face. He wrote:

> we are entering a technological age in which we will be able to interact with the richness of living information . . . We want to emphasize something beyond its one-way transfer: the increasing significance of the jointly constructive, the mutually reinforcing aspect of communication – the part that transcends 'now we both know a fact that only one of us knew before.' When minds interact, new ideas emerge.[10]

Although there were clearly definite conceptions as to the use of computer-mediated communication, this is not to say that all those involved were fully aware of the possibilities. Within ARPA opinions diverged as to the necessity of a decentralized computer network to promote new opportunities for horizontal communications between the various research centres. This is well documented by Hafner and Lyon, who explain that few of ARPA's researchers wanted to participate in such a project. 'This attitude was especially pronounced among researchers from the East Coast universities, who saw no reason to link up with campuses in the West.' Individual researchers located in the various centres could not understand that others had information relevant to their work or that they themselves had material others wanted to see. In any case, they argued, researchers could always read each other's reports.[11] A very different perspective, however, emerges from the account given by Hafner and Lyon, describing the terminal room attached to the suite of Bob Taylor, director of the Information Processing Techniques Office at ARPA headquarters:

> There, side by side, sat three computer terminals, each a different make, each connected to a separate mainframe computer running at three separate sites . . . Each of the terminals in Taylor's suite was an extension of a different computing environment – different programming languages, operating systems. . . . Each had a different log-in procedure; Taylor knew them all. But he found it irksome to have to remember which log-in procedure to use for which computer. And it was still more irksome . . . to remember which commands belonged to which computing environment.[12]

From the ARPANET to the internet

The ARPANET was launched at the end of 1969, creating the first long-haul computer network and connecting four sites: the University of California at Los Angeles, the Stanford Research Institute in Menlo Park, California, the University of California at Santa Barbara, and the University of Utah. These sites did not remain alone for long. Within sixteen months there were more than ten sites with an estimated 2,000 users and at least two routes between any two sites for the transmission of information packets.[13]

A public demonstration of the ARPANET was held during the first International Conference on Computer Communications in Washington DC in October 1972. Representatives from projects in countries such as Great Britain, Sweden, Norway, Japan, France, Canada and the United States were present. The gathering highlighted the beginnings of networking elsewhere in the world and resulted in the setting up of the InterNetwork Working Group which was to begin to discuss global interconnectivity. The first international connections were soon to be set up with Norway and Great Britain. At a conference held in Brighton in 1973, data was sent by satellite to Goonhilly Downs in Cornwall and from there by cable via the University of London, so that delegates could use the ARPANET as if they were themselves in the United States.

An important part of the ARPANET was the Network Control Protocol which governed how packets of data were to be transmitted from one computer to another. Because the ARPANET was the only network being used, a very high level of reliability could be achieved. With the advent of global information infrastructures, however, involving the connecting up of a variety of computer networks, the same sender-to-receiver reliability could not be provided. Weak connections were the cause of transmission errors and different networks often used incompatible protocols.[14] A new protocol was therefore needed, one which would allow individual networks to be designed separately in order to meet local requirements while still allowing distant users to communicate with each other. On a global scale this would have to be achieved without the need for any kind of direct control or intervention.

The answer was first introduced by Bob Kahn in 1972, the same year in which ARPA was renamed DARPA, the Defense Advanced Research Projects Agency. It involved the idea of so-called open architecture networking. Kahn and Vint Cerf, who had been involved in the original Network Control Protocol development, set to work on what would become the Transmission Control Protocol/Internet Protocol (TCP/IP). The TCP organized the data into packages, put them into the right order on arrival at their destination, and checked them for errors. The IP was responsible for the routing of packages through the network. By 1983 all networks connected to the ARPANET had to make use of TCP/IP and the old Network Control Protocol was replaced entirely. From then on, the collection of interconnected and publicly accessible networks using the TCP/IP protocols came to be called the 'internet'.

The emergence of the internet, however, is not only the outcome of military and scientific endeavour, and the activities of big business. The invention of the modem and the development of the Xmodem protocol in the late 1970s by two Chicago students allowed for the transfer of information between computers over the regular telephone system. Using such technology, computer networks which had so far been excluded from connecting to ARPANET, or other backbone systems, were now also able to communicate with each other. In its restricted way it pointed to the existence of a wider potential demand for computer-mediated communication and to the wide range of situations in which it could be successfully used. The modem, together with the advent of the personal computer, particularly contributed to the development and worldwide proliferation of electronic notice boards such as bulletin board systems (BBSs) and electronic discussion forums such as USENET. The internet, however, with its global reach and local call accessibility, soon surpassed the opportunities offered by such networks, whereupon many of them became connected to the internet themselves.

The internet constellation

By 1983 the open nature of the ARPANET was causing a concern for security. It was therefore split into the MILNET, which would serve military operational requirements, and the ARPANET, which continued to support research needs. However, during the 1980s the ARPANET's role as a long-haul network or backbone providing an important link between networks was gradually taken over by the network of supercomputing centres (NSFNET) set up by the National Science Foundation. In 1990 the ARPANET was decommissioned and taken out of service altogether.

Like the Joint Academic Network in Great Britain, NSFNET prohibited the use of its backbone for purposes other than research and education. However, the 'acceptable use policy' which governed the use of NSFNET did allow its commercial use on a local and regional level.[15] This generated revenue which was then used to lower the subscription fees and make the network more accessible to smaller academic institutions. This exclusion of long-distance commercial traffic stimulated and speeded up the growth of competitive private backbone networks.

The growing importance of commercial traffic and commercial networks was discussed at a series of conferences initiated by the National Science Foundation on the commercialization and privatization of the internet in 1988. However, by this time the National Science Foundation had already decided to privatize key parts of its network operation and had awarded a contract to Merit Network, Inc., in partnership with IBM and MCI Communications Corp., to manage and modernize the internet backbone. Later the National Science Foundation awarded a further three contracts. One was awarded to Network Solutions, allowing them to assign internet addresses. Another was awarded to AT&T to maintain internet directory and database services. A third was awarded to General Atomics, which was contracted to maintain the provision of information services to internet users. In 1995 the NSFNET was shut down completely. Most internet traffic is now carried over networks and backbones provided by commercial enterprise. This has a significant impact on the nature of the networks which make up the internet constellation. In most industrialized countries of the world, by the end of the millennium the digital economy was growing at double the rate of the overall economy.

Most individuals and small businesses access the internet by connecting to the host computer of an internet service provider (ISP) where they hold an account. Such connections can be made from homes or places of work via a telephone line or other cable facilities. Access is also possible via terminals placed in public spaces, such as airport and hotel lounges, internet cafés and on street corners. Large and medium-sized organizations often have direct access to the internet.

From the mid-1990s the development of the internet took a new turn as a growing number of large and medium-sized organizations started running the TCP/IP protocols on their intra-organizational communication networks. These private internets are called 'intranets'. Smaller intranets may be confined to connecting up computers in a single building; larger ones may connect up computers into a system which spans the globe. For security purposes, intranets are shielded from the outside world by so-called firewalls. These protection systems often allow for the exchange of information with the internet via so-called 'gateways'. A group of organizations can also use the TCP/IP protocols on their interorganizational networks. These private networks are called 'extranets' and allow organizations to exchange data with each other. By 1997 the market for intranets and extranets was growing annually at a rate of 40 per cent worldwide and 60 per cent in the United States. This rate of increase prompted the view that the intranet market would exceed the size of the internet market by a ratio of two to one.[16] In this book I shall be examining all three of these kinds of network.

Many internet service providers have extended their services to include intranets and extranets, supplying them with a full range of value-added services such as network backbones and network security. Internet service providers thus vary greatly in size and in the services they offer. Some are major global online services, such as Microsoft Network, America On-line, and CompuServe. Others have fewer than a thousand subscribers and act only as intermediaries – leasing line capacity from larger providers and telecommunication companies who own the long-haul network facilities. This situation, however, is changing rapidly as many of the small and medium-sized ISPs are taken over by a small number of big corporations seeking to become one-stop suppliers of telecommunication and internet services.

Probably one of the most globally consequential events in this field at the end of the millennium, with repercussions stretching well beyond the top end of the market, involved the acquisitional activities of WorldCom. Its dealings meant that it was set to carry more than half of all internet backbone traffic, control more than half of all direct connections to the internet, and lease line capacity to two-thirds of all internet service providers. All major telecommunication players, and indeed governments, are having to respond strategically to these kinds of developments. It is feared that a few powerful organizations will be able to charge internet service providers prohibitive fares for leasing lines, exclude certain users and interfere with content and also with the speed at which information is transmitted over sections of the networks, giving some users an unfair advantage over others.

Applications across the internet

A baffling variety of applications have been developed and implemented to meet both the general and specific needs of internet users. I shall not attempt to provide an all-inclusive description of applications, but instead give a chronological account of some of the main kinds of development. The various kinds of applications I consider here are also used on intranets and extranets. I shall begin to explore and reflect on the ends to which users deploy some of these kinds of applications in the final section of this chapter, although this is a concern which continues throughout the book.

E-mail, newsgroups, MUDS and IRC

Telnet, FTP and TALK were the first applications to become available on ARPANET and are still used in some form on the internet today. Created in 1969, Telnet applications allow users to log on and to operate remote computers. Such applications can, for example, be used to search and consult remote databases such as library catalogues. FTP is a file transfer application; it was released three years later and facilitates the uploading and downloading of files from one computer to another. TALK was the first programme that allowed users to engage in a real-time conversation over the network. It involved users typing messages on to one half of a split screen and reading replies from the other.

It was, however, yet another application for disseminating messages which proved to be an immediate success at this early stage. Although programs like MAILBOX had been available in the early 1960s, these had been used for exchanging messages locally, often on a single computer which was being shared by a number of individuals. The first network mail program was created by Ray Tomlinson of Bolt, Beranek and Newman in 1972.[17] Electronic mail or 'e-mail' allows users to send each other messages and to attach other information, such as files containing text or computer programs. Messages can be exchanged between two users or between one user and several others, and e-mail can therefore be used for private discussion groups where messages are sent to a number of users who have subscribed to a list. For many people today, e-mail has become synonymous with the internet.

The development of public discussion groups was made possible by so-called newsgroups, a phenomenon first associated with USENET. The groups are organized hierarchically into different forums. Within each subject area a range of newsgroups debate different topics. In the newsgroup 'talk.politics.mideast', for example, users debate the political situation in the Middle East. Users participate in these public discussions by posting their messages to the group and reading the reactions given by others.

Real-time interaction has also been extended in many ways. One example of this was the creation of so-called multi-user dungeons (MUDs). Initially, these were developed as a multiplayer adventure game by Roy Trubshaw and Richard Bartle at Essex University in 1979. The first external players logged on via the ARPANET in 1980. MUDs allow users to move around text-based virtual environments and to chat to other users. Soon, more sophisticated versions of MUDs were developed. These enabled users to construct their own text-based personalities, and build and furnish their own text-based virtual spaces, inviting other participants to enter into them. Although MUDs started life within the realm of entertainment, they have also been used for other objectives such as group decision-making.

Another example of how real-time interaction has been extended is the creation of applications such as internet relay chat or IRC. This was designed as a multi-user variation on TALK by Jarkko Oikarinen at the University of Oulu, Finland in 1988. IRC allows participants to gather in 'channels' and talk about specific subjects by typing in text. Participants can create their own channels or join channels created by others. IRC also allows users to engage in private conversations. Participants can become channel operators which gives them the power to change the channel settings. Operators may decide on the channel topic, limit the number of participants in a channel, remove and ban troublemakers and invite others to join. All IRC applications allow users to transfer data files to each other. IRC systems accessible via the internet can be local or global or created specifically for a particular group of users.

Early use of the internet required specialized training and experience, and users were generally limited to using Telnet or FTP in order to use all of the applications described above. From 1990 onwards, however, a whole range of 'user-friendly' internet interfaces was developed. Users no longer had to type in obscure commands and transcribe complicated network addresses. From then on they could navigate the various opportunities offered to them by pointing and clicking on graphic devices consisting of buttons, choosing from pull-down menus and using an array of 'windows' to enter and display information. Further developments, such as Cuseeme and Internet Phone, augmented the possibilities for text-based conversation by incorporating video and audio technology, allowing participants to see and hear each other. Some of these applications gave users the digital equivalent of a whiteboard so that they could use drawings to support their discussions. All these enhancements required ever faster network connections and computers.

WWW: the world wide web

One of the most innovative and comprehensive devices for the exchange of information via the internet today is undoubtedly the world wide web (WWW). It developed from an application first introduced by Tim Berners-Lee and Robert Cailliau. It was demonstrated at the headquarters of the European Laboratory for Particle Physics (CERN) in Switzerland in December 1990. CERN is one of the world's largest scientific laboratories and involves many thousands of people working on different projects in various locations around the world. During the late 1980s, Berners-Lee became worried about the efficiency and effectiveness of the management of information from projects carried out at CERN. There were three main causes for his concern. First, the high turnover of people meant that information was often lost. Second, the introduction of new people demanded a lot of effort before they could be given any idea of what went on in the organization. Third, stored information about research projects often could not be retrieved. Berners-Lee argued that the reason for these problems was that research projects and their participants were 'nominally organized into a hierarchical management structure', while 'the actual observed working structure of the organization is a multiply connected "web" whose interconnections evolve with time.'[18]

It was Berners-Lee's view that although hierarchical information systems have the practical advantage of systematically ordering information, they do not allow a communication system to model and properly slot into what goes on in the real world. Berners-Lee argued that the newsgroup system, for example, 'is a very useful method of pooling expertise, but suffers from the inflexibility of its tree-structure. Typically, a discussion under one newsgroup will develop into a different topic, at which point it ought to be in a different part of a tree.'[19] Such a system is also cumbersome because information can only be found by tracing it down hierarchically from one subclass to another. Unless it is duplicated, it can only be found in one place and people have to know which path to follow in order to locate it.

Berners-Lee and Cailliau proposed and subsequently developed a system within CERN for storing, retrieving and communicating information based on a web of hyperlinks and hypertext. It was run on a multi-user system so that many people could access the same information at the same time. It satisfied the information management needs of CERN because it allowed 'a pool of information to develop which could grow and evolve with the organization and the projects it describes'.[20] The new tool was soon picked up by the users of the internet.

Today, the world wide web – often called an enterprise wide web when it is installed on an intranet – can be used both to receive information and to make it available to others. Using hyperlinks embedded in hypertext, users acting as producers of information link up files containing text, sound and graphics to create so-called webpages. Information displayed on webpages is viewed by means of an interface known as a browser. The sources of information linked in this way can be located on any computer that is also part of the web. Each information source may itself be linked to an indefinite number of other webpages. Hypertext and hyperlinks allow users acting as receivers of information to wander from one source of information to another seamlessly, deciding for themselves which information they wish to have transferred to their browser and which links they want to skip. There are now many millions of so-called 'homepages' or webpages owned by organizations and private individuals. The addresses of webpages can found by using the many hundreds of general and specialized search engines which provide access to databases which hold information on them. Once a webpage has been found, hyperlinks may point to other places of interest on the web. Addresses of webpages also appear in other more conventional media, such as magazines, newspapers and television programmes, and on posters. Webpages, in their turn, facilitate access to information made available by other forms of media, for example, collections held in libraries or programmes broadcast on television.

Most webpages offer interactive opportunities which go beyond merely allowing visitors freedom as to when and how they visit a page and where they might choose to go next. Feedback can be kept formal via a questionnaire which can be filled out, or informal by providing an address for e-mail or even by installing a digital guest book for comments left for other users to read. Although all webpages are protected so that unauthorized visitors cannot make unsolicited changes to them, it is also possible to limit access to pages on the internet to those holding a password.

Ongoing developments

Many new internet applications now combine several applications into one facility. WWW browsers have become particularly multifunctional in this way, allowing users to send electronic mail, chat, transmit files, and automatically load other helper applications when these are needed.

Various kinds of media are increasingly being integrated. There are now thousands of radio stations distributing information on the web and a growing number of television channels are also engaged in distributing programming.[21] One interesting development regarding web TV has been the creation of websites which allow users to meet up and discuss and watch television programmes broadcast over the internet together. Applications such as web TV and radio do not replace more conventional means of communication, but it is becoming ever more difficult to distinguish between them. Moreover, a variety of systems allow viewers to access the world wide web and read and write e-mail on their television sets without the use of a computer.[22]

Providers of information via the internet and intranets have also been making extensive use of so-called push technologies in order to get the attention of their audiences. Browsers can be fitted out with buttons giving their users access to information channels which they can view much as they would conventional television channels.

The ongoing development of applications for the internet has also involved the extension of facilities to allow individuals to share applications and to collaborate on tasks in their work. Two or more individuals may, for example, team up and share in the use of a word-processing programme and jointly craft a document. Applications such as ICQ have built their rapid success around the need for users to announce and coordinate their online presence availability so that other users know they are there. As well as becoming more integrated, applications have increasingly become tailor-made and customized to be used for specific tasks and by particular users.

As happened with the computer networks themselves, the implementation and further development of internet applications has rapidly become the domain of big business. One of the most protracted struggles for this market so far has involved Microsoft and Netscape Corp., each trying to expand and consolidate its position as a supplier of internet software. Microsoft held only 20 per cent of the browser market in 1996: continually criticized for its aggressive marketing, it had gained over half the market by 1999.[23] While some of the broad patterns of the political economy of this section of the communication industry have been studied over the years, the research remains fragmentary. Existing patterns of ownership, much like the technologies involved, are in a constant state of flux. Given the complexity of global networks and of the international information and communication conglomerates, it is unlikely that our understanding of these developments will ever be more than partial. But continued research effort is necessary to establish the significant trends and their characteristics.

The increasing influence of big business on the internet brings with it at least two fears for regulators and internet users. First, there is concern that if builders of network applications hold a monopoly, they may be in a position to determine licence fees for the use of their products. Second, there is the worry that those who build applications and control the interfaces may gain a considerable say over the content of the information communicated and accessed by way of the net. The Microsoft WWW browser was often pre-installed on newly purchased computers, which gave it a head start in competing for users. It also pre-selected a number of favourite websites for the user to visit. It came as little surprise in 1998 when the United States government began legal action against Microsoft as an illegal monopoly.[24]

Yet other, less obvious examples of interfaces interfering with content also exist. Users of some applications are exposed to continuous advertising. Others find that when they type certain words which have been programmed into the applications as taboo, these are replaced automatically with '#' signs. For example the word 'gay' becomes '###'. This has resulted in users resorting to innovative ways of spelling the word 'gay' in order to avoid censorship, like 'g@y', which consists of signs that are not barred by the interface.

Information-filtering systems designed to block access to certain information on the world wide web have also been created.[25] The main thrust behind this development was the problem of young people accessing potentially harmful material on the net. I want to discuss the development of rating and filtering systems in detail in chapter 9 where I shall examine issues concerning the regulation of the internet.

A brief analysis of internet users

While the internet is global in extent, it is by no means a general medium of communication in the way that radio or television already are. Nevertheless, the number of internet users has expanded at such a phenomenal rate that estimating their number with any accuracy is quite impractical. Common sense, together with a few simple calculations, soon reveals the problematic nature of available statistical evidence. Moreover, information about internet users is often presented in general numerical terms. Interesting patterns emerge, however, when overall user statistics are unpacked and variations are examined over time and space.

The number of internet users

The total number of internet users worldwide by 1999 was estimated to be between 150 and 180 million. A report on the economic impact of the internet published by the United States Department of Commerce expected the numbers to rise to one billion by 2005.[26] Such claims were made despite an overall slowdown in internet growth towards the end of the millennium.

By the late 1990s the internet was still very much a communication medium for the industrialized world. Almost 99 per cent of all internet connections were in North America, Western Europe and Japan, with 1 per cent being shared among the 4 billion people who made up the rest of the world's population. Although estimates still put the highest number of users in the United States, the number of users in other areas is growing fast. Most of the recent growth outside the United States has, however, taken place in Europe.

Comparisons of internet use data between countries are made easier where the number of internet users has been related to the total size of the population. By 1999 Finland was the most 'wired' country in the world, with over 35 per cent of its population online. The United States had just over 30 per cent of its population accessing the internet in 1999. Other countries with large online populations include Australia with 23 per cent, Sweden with over 30 per cent, Switzerland with over 16 per cent, the United Kingdom with over 15 per cent, the Netherlands with over 12 per cent and Japan with over 7 per cent of their populations online by 1999.[27]

The characteristics of internet users

In the late 1990s the internet began to shed its one-time image of being predominantly a medium of communication for highly educated and affluent white males living in the metropolitan areas of the industrialized world. Yet it will take a major influx of users from other areas of the globe to change significantly the worldwide number of users at that time, estimated at 4.3 per cent of people worldwide. In South America, for example, internet growth remained severely hampered by the poor telephone infrastructure. In Rio de Janeiro, internet users could wait up to twenty minutes or more simply to get a dialling tone. Moreover, being a competent user of the English language is still a prerequisite to be able to navigate the web.[28] Surveys have suggested, however, that the online population in Brazil may grow to well over 7 million by 2010.[29]

The conditions for growth have varied by country. In India, the government has held a monopoly over internet access. In Vietnam the cost of internet access was calculated to be a third of the average yearly salary, which served to deter any substantial growth. In China and Singapore, internet users had to register with the police. Despite the many restrictions, China's state news agency, Xinhua, estimated that there were over 4 million people online by the end of the millennium.[30] Yet the number of China's internet users is expected to swell due to the redevelopment of its telecommunications network with AT&T.[31] The total number of internet users in Africa in the late 1990s was estimated to be 1.14 million.[32] However, when South Africa was excluded from the count, there was only one user for every 5,000 people. Africa had the lowest number of telephone lines per capita in the world, and most of these were in urban centres where less than 20 per cent of the population lived. There were actually more telephone lines in Tokyo or New York than in the whole of Africa. The high cost of personal computers (PCs) and the lack of skilled labour, including the absence of a basic level of literacy, particularly among women, has made it very difficult for African countries to even begin to take advantage of opportunities offered by internet technology.

The high price of information technology (IT) equipment and PCs also hindered growth in the numbers of internet users in Russia. According to the Russian Non-profit Centre for Internet Technologies, there were more than 600,000 users online by 1997, continuing an annual growth rate of 100 per cent.[33] By 1999 Russia had over 1 million internet users.

Within the constraints of reported evidence it is also possible to get a glimpse of other key features of internet users in early years. According to many surveys carried out at the end of the millennium, the proportion of women using the internet in industrialized countries was approaching 40 per cent of all users. The number of women online in Japan was, however, considerably less, at 17.2 per cent of all users.[34] In Brazil, the proportion of women was about 25 per cent at this time.[35] In a different survey regarding gender and sexuality, 92 per cent of users interviewed stated that they were heterosexual,[36] a percentage which corresponds roughly to the probable extent of homosexuality in Western cultures. The fact that in a relatively short timespan such an oppressed group in society has managed to have its numbers so well reflected and represented is rather extraordinary. This has not been so with such groups in other communication media. It demonstrates how the internet favours relatively uninhibited communication and stimulates the participation of individuals whose interests are both geographically and culturally dispersed. Although the gender gap in internet use seemed to be gradually closing, this has not been the case for the differences that exist between other minority groups, for example, between African-Americans and white Americans.[37]

By the century's end the average age of internet users worldwide was thirty-five and was rising slowly. In the United States the average age was thirty-eight, with the largest proportion of users aged between eighteen and thirty-four.[38] One study found that there were 9.8 million people under the age of eighteen online in the United States.[39] Combining the statistics for age and gender, some studies have shown that the percentage of female users decreased with age.[40] However, there were major differences between countries.

By the end of the millennium, research still indicated that over 65 per cent of internet users in the United States lived in households with incomes of 50,000 dollars or more, as opposed to 35 per cent of the population as a whole. More than 75 per cent of them had attended college as compared with 46 per cent of the total population.[41] Over 30 per cent of internet users worldwide were estimated to be in computer-related work; 24 per cent had occupations in education, including being a student, and 24 per cent were in management and other professional positions.[42] An overwhelming proportion of users used the internet in work-related situations.

Organizational and educational users

A study of United States households by the century's end stated that 30 per cent of workers who did part or all of their jobs from home used the internet, compared to only 8 per cent of non-homeworkers.[43] In a different study, the number of internet users at work in the United States was estimated at 19 million.[44] Internet access at work in Europe was reported to be higher than in the United States.[45] A survey conducted of 4,810 workers in various industries in the United Kingdom indicated that e-mail was used by 5 million people at work.[46] In Spain, 39 per cent of those who accessed the internet did it from home, 37 per cent from work and 19 per cent from universities and other centres of study.[47] In Japan, the internet had mostly been accessed from work, although home use was estimated at 54 per cent.[48] By 1999, a survey carried out by International Research Institutes found that the high usage at work had been overturned in Denmark, Sweden, Australia, Canada and the Netherlands, in favour of the home.[49]

The International Data Corporation (IDC) calculated that by 1997, 50 per cent of all United States companies had set up sites on the internet.[50] The percentage of small to medium-sized enterprises having websites was put at 40 per cent. This figure corresponded with similar findings in the United Kingdom.[51] An international benchmarking study published by the Department of Trade and Industry in the UK in 1998 claimed that 49 per cent of UK companies had access to the internet, as compared to 44 per cent in Germany and 24 per cent in France.[52] The same study claimed that 37 per cent of UK companies owned websites, as compared to 30 per cent in Germany and 14 per cent in France. By 1999, a survey claimed that 89 per cent of the largest companies around the world had a website.[53] Whereas private internets had been almost non-existent in 1994, the IDC estimated that 59 per cent of United States companies and 38 per cent of European companies had implemented intranets by 1997. According to the IDC, US companies spent 10.9 billion dollars on intranet development in 1998, and the total number of intranet users was likely to reach 133 million in 2001.[54]

Internet use was not confined to individual users and commercial organizations. A wide variety of organizations began to use the internet for their external and internal communications. Governments and state agencies were particularly eager to explore and develop its possibilities and this was demonstrated nowhere more than in the G7 Government On-line Project. This ongoing project was launched in 1995, its primary objective being 'to investigate the scope for a significant increase in the use of online technology to transform government so that, by the turn of the century, most administrative business will be conducted electronically'.[55] Participation rapidly extended to twenty governments, including the European Commission, all the G7 countries, Brazil, Egypt, Czech Republic, Finland, Hungary, Ireland, Republic of Korea, Malta, Russia, South Africa, Sweden and Switzerland. Three themes are being examined in particular. First, the replacement of paper-based mail by e-mail, not only within government itself but also with the public. Second, the provision of interactive online services allowing the public to both obtain and provide information from a variety of locations. Third, the development of online transaction processing for the support and delivery of routine services. According to the General Accounting Office in the US, there were over 4,300 WWW sites maintained by the United States government by the end of 1997.[56]

Although some institutes of higher education have been in the forefront of internet use, this is not to say that internet use has been widespread in all centres of learning from the start. Towards the end of the millennium, more that 75 per cent of publicly funded schools in the United States were connected to the internet, as opposed to 35 per cent four years earlier. However, only 27 per cent of classrooms had access.[57] In Britain, the central government was hoping to connect the 32,000 publicly funded schools to what it has called a 'national grid for learning' by 2002. The UK government committed £100 million in 1998–9 for schools to acquire computers and software, but for a long time it failed to make any significant progress and availability of computers in schools remained low.[58]

The impact of the internet on the mediazation of modern culture

Although the internet is being actively adopted into the day-to-day lives of many millions of people, there is a growing unease that this is happening without full cognizance of the consequences of its use. The opportunities created by the internet mean many different things to different people. It is useful first to consider some ideas that Zuboff discusses in her work *In the Age of the Smart Machine*.[59] Zuboff argues that many of the choices we face regarding new intelligent technologies concern different ways of conceptualizing and distributing knowledge, and this has led her to recognize a number of alternative futures arising from the 'smart machine'. Second, I shall carry Zuboff's arguments through to the internet, where we also see two alternative perspectives developing. I shall argue, however, that overly positive or dismal accounts of the impact of the internet on modern life are not conducive to the development of an active engagement with the unpredictable environment in which we live today.

Alternative futures in the age of the smart machine

Zuboff's study analyses the introduction of new intelligent technologies such as the computer into the workplace during the 1980s. It provides us with an excellent starting point for relating the rise of the internet to the conditions of reflexive modernization. She describes how people fear 'that today's working assumptions could not be relied upon to carry them through, that the future would not resemble the past or the present' (pp. 4–5). She goes on to ask:

> Should the advent of the smart machine be taken as an invitation to relax the demands upon human comprehension and critical judgement? Does the massive diffusion of computer technology throughout our workplaces necessarily entail an equally dramatic loss of meaningful employment opportunities? Must the new electronic milieu engender a world in which individuals have lost control over their daily work lives? (p. 5)

These are all questions which we might ask about the internet today.

In examining these questions Zuboff refers to the two faces of intelligent technology. On the one hand, such technology can be used to *automate* organizational processes and procedures such that it provides 'substitutes for the human body that reach an even greater degree of certainty and precision' (p. 8). On the other, such technology can be used to '*informate*' organizational processes and procedures such that it introduces

> an additional dimension of reflexivity: it makes its contribution to the product, but it also reflects back on its activities and on the system of activities to which it is related. Information technology not only produces action but also produces a voice that symbolically renders events, objects, and processes so that they become visible, knowable, and shareable in a new way. (p. 9)

Zuboff claims that a succession of dilemmas results from the introduction of intelligent technologies into the workplace. These slot directly into the conditions that describe reflexive modernization. First, there are the dilemmas associated with the changing grounds of knowledge. These involve the emergence of intellective skills that often surplant the body as a primary source of knowledge. Individuals have to develop skills, for example, that allow them to confidently monitor other people or processes relevant to their tasks without necessarily being physically present themselves. Second, there are the dilemmas associated with the blurring of the traditional opposition between those in authority and those in positions of subordination. As the demand for new intellective skills increases, the dismantling of traditional hierarchies progresses. Third, there are the dilemmas related to attempts to bolster threatened authority hierarchies with new techniques of control that draw on the intelligent technology's tendency to extend the visibility of organizational processes. However, as Zuboff explains, such efforts 'engage a series of organizational responses that, ironically, weaken managerial authority even more profoundly' (p. 16).

She argues that we are in danger of failing to meet the challenges of 'informating' technology by polarizing two approaches. If intelligent technology is used

> only to intensify the automaticity of work, it can reduce skill levels and dampen the urge toward more participatory and decentralized forms of management . . . In contrast, an approach to technology deployment that emphasizes its informating capacity uses technology to do far more than routinize, fragment, or eliminate jobs. It uses the new technology to increase the intellectual content of work at every organizational level, as the ability to decipher explicit information and make decisions informed by that understanding becomes broadly distributed among organizational members. (p. 243)

She warns that 'a redistribution of authority is both the basis upon which intellective skill development can proceed and the necessary implication of its success. Unless informating is taken up as a conscious strategy, rather than simply allowed to unfold without any anticipation of its consequences, it is unlikely to yield up its full value' (pp. 309–10).

The internet: towards a positive or a negative pole?

As the contours of intensified globalization, decentred authority and intensified reflexivity continue to interlace with both modern institutions and with individual life, it is possible to recognize Zuboff's dilemmas within the development and deployment of the internet. While aware of the complexities this conceals, I would suggest that the perspectives on the impact of the internet on society tend towards two poles of optimism and pessimism. I shall deal with each of these in turn.

An unclouded celebration of the internet's opportunities

In circumstances of late modernity it is not difficult to be somewhat naively optimistic about the opportunities the internet offers. Those tending toward this positive pole are by no means confined to groups seeking to sell new computers or internet accounts. They can also be found among a wide range of technological crusaders convinced that the internet is about to change the world. Indeed, most internet users would admit to having been somewhat inspired by awe when they first launched a homepage or heard the distant voice of a stranger coming from their computer. In a world in which interaction has become increasingly stretched across time and space, the internet is acting as a catalyst, releasing a pent-up demand for more reciprocal and sophisticated control over the exchange and use of information.

Clearly, the internet seems to go some way in fulfilling this demand for positive forms of control and is helping nation-states, economic organizations and individuals to cope with the consequences of intensifying globalization, the emergence of post-traditional forms of organization and the expansion and intensification of social reflexivity. On an unprecedented level, the internet is presenting individuals and organizations with new opportunities for responsive action by allowing them to display their integrity and maintain and build up the trust of others in their actions. It also offers new ways of accessing such information anywhere and at any time. As such, the internet is radically altering the degree to which individuals and organizations can enter freely into discourses across extended time-space. It opens up new opportunities for dialogue and deliberation, empowers people to make things happen rather than have things happen to them, and facilitates new forms of solidarity and cooperation.

Let me describe some features of internet use which have contributed to certain accounts of the internet tending toward this positive pole. First, confronted by accelerated risk and uncertainty, with citizens critically questioning many of their actions and policies, governments have been making clear their intent to use the internet in order to be more open and responsive towards their citizenry. In November 1996 the Conservative government in Great Britain published 'Government Direct', a green paper in which it set out its ideas for using information technology to empower people in their dealings with government; and this vision was taken further by the Labour government which came into power in 1997. The green paper was published on the government information service website.[60] Here, visitors were invited to participate in the debate on how government should use IT to serve people better and were able to submit their contributions via e-mail. Additional webpages provided access to a virtual library of responses which had already been submitted by various officials, citizens and organizations.

A similar initiative was unveiled by the Dutch Ministry of Transport in the Netherlands in 1996. The ministry set up an interactive forum called the 'Digital Roundabout',[61] a website where ministry officials, citizens and interested organizations could meet and discuss various policy issues. Discussions focused on projects which were posted on the website, which also enabled participants to enter into real-time debate via a chat system and to contribute to newsgroup discussions. What all these public sector initiatives have in common is that they are not aimed merely at providing one-way channels for funnelling official information about national, regional and local government projects, but rather at two-way interfaces for facilitating dialogue, sharing knowledge and giving participants an opportunity to make a difference.

A second feature of internet use which has given cause for optimism for some is that, like governments, commercial organizations are also displaying their intention to use internet technology to revitalize their external and internal communications. The Boeing Company,[62] for example, has designed and implemented an intranet to facilitate and support the dissemination of information within the organization. Like many modern organizations, the company is assessing and rethinking its managerial information flows and decentralizing its operations. Intranets have become key tools in many such projects. Like the examples discussed earlier, this intranet offers its users a wide range of webpages and interactive forums. Employees can access information without having to wait for it to filter down through traditional lines of communication. The interactive forums create a sphere in which employees can discuss their ideas, share knowledge and engage in collaborative work across organizational boundaries.[63]

A similar initiative has been undertaken by the Ford Motor Company,[64] connecting up some 120,000 computers at offices and production units around the world. Webpages provide users with marketing information, analyses of competitors' components and information on suppliers. A product development system houses information on the assembling and testing of vehicles, and lets designers, engineers and suppliers collaborate using the same data. Teams working on one kind of vehicle have their own website where they can publish progress reports, ask questions, warn about problems and actively build quality into their work processes. Knowledge sharing is helping the organization to reduce the time it takes to get new vehicles to market from thirty-six to twenty-four months. The company is also considering linking its 15,000 dealers to its intranet as this will open up possibilities for custom ordering and cars 'made on demand'.[65] As such, intranets and extranets are radically changing the nature of supply chains of commercial organizations, offering new opportunities for partnering and alliances, cutting out some 'infomediaries' and introducing new ones.

A third feature of internet use which contributes to the feeling of optimism is the way individuals using the internet are experiencing matching transformations in their day-to-day lives. Let us focus a while on the internet relay chat channel '#Gay.nl'.[66] It first took shape as a permanent channel with a small group of regular users in 1993, although it existed intermittently well before that. Today, it frequently has over a hundred users online at a time, sometimes reaching over 130 at weekends. Channel users vary in age and social background, and come from all over the Netherlands, and also from other countries. By no means all users are gay; some are just interested or genuinely curious. Although much of the discourse includes having a bit of fun and a laugh, #Gay.nl is indicative of how the internet is helping individuals cope with modern everyday life. The channel creates a forum in which they can negotiate the standardized influences of sexual values, acquire knowledge and skills, and forge new commitments and mutuality. The channel operators, consisting of a group of regular users, run a #Gay.nl webpage[67] which provides information about the channel, invitations to meetings and hyperlinks to various other webpages, including those belonging to channel users. Users frequently meet up face to face, and a number of organized channel meetings are held every year where on some occasions over fifty people have been known to turn up.

The #Gay.nl webpage also lists channel rules which prohibit harassment and abusive language. However, transgressors typing gay abuse are rarely 'kicked off' the channel immediately. Experienced channel users often first ignore them and then enter into discussion with them, challenging their views, and after a good deal of amusement and banter the incident is soon over. Despite various security systems, more aggressive attacks sometimes result in the channel being taken over completely. While they attempt to sort the problem out, the operators simply create a temporary channel with a different name. Sometimes the discourse in the main channel is logged by the operators so that they can later analyse incidents in order to deal with them more effectively in the future.

The internet and the fear that chaos
might overwhelm the world

Balanced against these positive images of the consequences of internet use is, however, an opposite set of complex attitudes which, taken together, tend towards a rather more cynical and sometimes even pessimistic pole. Here the centrifugal tendencies and the dislocating character of internet use are brought into the forefront. The internet, more than any other medium, is seen by some as eroding 'community' and 'emptying' day-to-day life by allowing individuals and organizations to enter into a virtual time-space which is seen as competing with reality and which clouds whatever they do with a sense of inauthenticity. Accompanying this are worries that individuals and organizations using the internet are in danger of becoming dispersed and rendered powerless by the fragmenting of experience, resulting in conditions which preclude, rather than facilitate, collaborative action.

One of the most dismal and disturbing visions of the future of social interaction is suggested by Castells in the general conclusion to his three-volume work *The Information Age: Economy, Society and Culture.* In *End of Millennium*, the final volume,[68] Castells concludes that a 'network logic', which he describes as 'a dynamic, self-expanding form of organization of human activity', is transforming all domains of social and economic life (pp. 336–7). He believes that a new world is beginning to emerge, a network society, consisting of network enterprises, network states and networks of people, a world 'dominated by a network geometry' and connected by way of global financial networks which he sees as 'the nerve center of informational capitalism' (p. 343).

Castells observes that this new system of production is sharply differentiated according to people's characteristics. On the one hand, there are those whom he defines as 'self-programmable labor'. He explains, 'whoever is educated, in the proper organizational environment, can reprogram him/herself toward the endlessly changing task of the production process.' On the other hand, there are those whom he defines as 'generic labor' or as 'human terminals'. Generic labor, according to Castells, is 'assigned a given task, with no reprogramming capability, and it does not presuppose the embodiment of information and knowledge beyond the ability to receive and execute signals' (p. 341). He explains that the network geometry is 'incarnated by different subjects, even though these subjects often work with historical materials provided by the values and organizations inherited from industrial capitalism and statism' (pp. 350–1).

Under this new system, Castells warns, 'a considerable number of humans . . . are irrelevant, both as producers and consumers, from the perspective of the system's logic' (p. 344). The 'social exclusion and economic irrelevance of segments of societies, of areas of cities, of regions, and of entire countries' constitute what he calls the 'Fourth World' (p. 337). Under the informational paradigm, he writes,

> the space of flows dominates the space of places of people's cultures
> . . . dominant functions and values in society are organized in simultaneity
> without contiguity; that is, in flows of information that escape from experi-
> ence embodied in any locale . . . dominant values and interests are con-
> structed without reference to either past or future, in the timeless landscape
> of computer networks and electronic media, where all expressions are

either instantaneous, or without predictable sequencing. All expressions, from all times and from all spaces, are mixed in the same hypertext, constantly rearranged, and communicated at any time, anywhere, depending on the interests of senders and the moods of receivers' (pp. 349–50).

Yet despite his warning, Castells also claims that 'societies of the Information Age cannot be reduced to the structure and dynamics of the network society' (p. 352). However, desperate attempts by some groups and areas to link up with the global networks and to escape marginality have led to what Castells calls the 'perverse connection', a concept he uses to analyse criminal activity (p. 337). He is rather sceptical and not very hopeful regarding new avenues of social change. On the one hand, he observes the 'retrenchment of dominant global elites in immaterial palaces made out of communication networks and information flows'. On the other, he describes proactive identity-based social movements where people's experience remains 'confined to multiple, segregated locales, subdued in their existence and fragmented in their consciousness. With no Winter Palace to be seized, outbursts of revolt may implode, transformed into everyday senseless violence.' This is truly a frightening prospect. In the Information Age, Castells claims, instead of social classes, we are witnessing the rise of 'tribes' and 'cultural communes' (p. 352). And, as a reaction against social exclusion, marginalization and economic irrelevance, he sees the beginnings of 'the exclusion of the excluders by the excluded' (p. 354).

A way ahead

In his thoughtful and wide-ranging argument, I think Castells like Zuboff is right to point out that while new communication networks are opening up new opportunities for human intervention, they also create new uncertainties. Moreover, these new technologies are spreading the consciousness that the world we live in today is a highly risky and unpredictable environment. However, while being on our guard against euphoric interpretations and the excesses of futurology, we must be careful not to present an overly dismal account of the transformations taking place. I want to argue in this vein that Castells's conclusions are, in many respects, one-sided and too negative. I shall elaborate this argument by briefly considering six important aspects of his work: (1) his notion of 'network logic'; (2) his distinction between 'self-programmable labor' and 'generic labor'; (3) his conception of people as 'human terminals'; (4) his notion of the 'Fourth World'; (5) his conception of senders with 'interests' and receivers with 'moods'; and (6) his account of the 'rise of tribes'.

The notion of 'network logic'　Castells uses the notion of 'network logic' to explain why particular social processes are as they are. He even portrays 'network logic' as some kind of self-expanding form of organization, which is somehow similar to a nerve centre. This portrayal invites a view that network enterprises, network states and networks of people are all governed by the teleology of a system which supplants that of actors themselves. I take the view, however, that not even the most worrying features of modern societies come about, persist or disappear because a network's geometry forces them to do so. All networks of social interaction consist of 'social practices, situated in time-space, and organized in a skilled and knowledgeable fashion by human agents'.[69] Of course, human knowledgeability, as Giddens argues, is always bounded by unacknowledged conditions and by unintended consequences of human activity.[70] But even this is a very complex process and it cannot so easily be referred to as involving the characteristics of network society being simply 'incarnated by different subjects'. Moreover, our world today is connected by a dazzling variety of networks, as Castells himself admits, so it would seem all too simplistic to suggest that networks create unitary conditions. Consequently, I do not believe that the notion of 'network logic' explains very much at all.

The distinction between 'self-programmable labor' and 'generic labor'　Castells's distinction between 'self-programmable labor' and 'generic labor' suggests that there are those who are bestowed with a good deal of fortune and those who are bestowed with a good deal of bad luck. Yet many questions cloud such a distinction, not least that of how to go about establishing to which group one might belong. While all networks promote horizontal relationships, they by no means do away with hierarchical authority altogether. Participants in networks may thus have at their disposal varying degrees of authority: their options are not restricted to being either connected or unconnected. We might also wonder how we became 'self-programmable labor' or 'generic labor'. Is this feature pre-set by the system too? And is there any chance, or danger, that we might at some point in time change positions?

The designation of people as 'human terminals'　According to Castells, the designation of people as 'human terminals' describes a considerable proportion of humans, probably growing in number. However, I think it conjures up a quite inadequate vision of people as cultural dopes. Moreover, Castells seems also to suggest something far worse: the idea that if people do not perform according to the 'network logic', they will simply be switched off. While there may indeed exist significant differentials of power in network society, I do not think that any individual can be satisfactorily interpreted in this way. It renounces once again the idea that all individuals are skilled and knowledgeable human agents, as Giddens so rightly emphasizes, and fails to recognize that 'all forms of dependence offer some resources whereby those who are subordinate can influence the activities of their superiors.'[71] Moreover, capitalist ventures would not make much profit if they switched nearly everybody off.

The notion of the 'Fourth World'   Castells's notion of the 'Fourth World', I think, fails to recognize the extent to which in many ways we now all live in *one* world, a world in which there are no others. Our world today may have become increasingly decentred, but it has also become all-enveloping. As Giddens writes, the day-to-day actions of an individual today are globally consequential. The notion of the 'Fourth World' distracts us from this accelerating connectedness, and from the fact that it is more and more unlikely that those retrenched in 'immaterial palaces' will find a world from which the mass of the population is excluded even remotely an acceptable place to live in.

The conception of senders with 'interests' and receivers with 'moods'   Castells's conception of senders with 'interests' and receivers with 'moods' does not do justice to a new agenda for mediated communication, one in which individuals are potentially both senders and receivers. Even when individuals are excluded from one channel of communication, they can find others to make themselves heard.

The 'rise of tribes'   Castells's account of the rise of modern-day tribes is superficial and not at all useful. Premodern tribal culture was very confined in terms of its time-space span. Equipped with access to modern communication networks, social groups in the late modern age have access to unprecedented opportunities for cultivating images and controlling their diffusion. This, I think, precludes any serious comparison with tribalism of the past.

In the light of Castells's warnings we need urgently to follow Zuboff's advice that it is necessary to take up a conscious strategy, rather than to simply allow new forms of human interaction to unfold without any anticipation of their consequences. The unpredictable environment we live in today demands our active engagement. Yet while Castells elaborates on some trends that may configure society in the early twenty-first century, he makes no attempt to sketch a way out of the problems they may create. And, as I already stated in the introduction, isn't an alternative path of development the surest way to avert some of the perverse and unintended consequences of networked social interaction?

   If we are to develop positive ways of using the internet, we need to develop a more informed understanding and a firmer grasp of what it amounts to and what its consequences are for modern culture, and use such knowledge to cope more effectively with the current crisis in the management of risk. Contributing to the further polarization of the different perspectives tending towards either the pole of optimism or the pole of pessimism would serve only to continue a rather fruitless debate; instead I want to take both of these perspectives seriously. Taken together, they reveal that it is no accident that the internet has originated in an environment bequeathed to us by the developments that have transformed modern societies. These are developments for which the internet is also an essential tool. As a consequence, there is much to be said in support of arguments which sensitize us to the dual potentialities of information technology, referring as they do to the capability of the same technology to produce one set of effects or their opposite.[72]

Any benefit from such an insight cannot, however, be satisfactorily pursued from the premises of the internet understood simply as a *new medium*. Instead we must first attempt to develop a framework which may help us to properly understand how the internet is resulting in new ways of relating to others and to ourselves. It must be a framework which does not treat the 'uncertainization' of modern life merely as a backdrop, but one in which the internet is treated comprehensively as a contextualized social phenomenon. Such a framework must enable us to break away from lists of arbitrary strengths which are offered in praise or in defence of this new medium: moreover, its weaknesses may become challenges which we might be able to do something about.

3

Cultural transmission
and the internet

The impact of the internet on modern life cannot properly be assessed in terms of online experience and content. In a fundamental way, the use of the internet is creating new forms of action and interaction, and reordering the way in which individuals interpret and respond to the social world. While simply calling attention to examples of this is relatively easy, systematically analysing the often contradictory implications is more difficult. How then might we go about understanding the impact of the internet on modern culture? What conceptions might usefully be placed in the service of this endeavour?

In some respects, the answer to these questions can be put quite bluntly. When we address the way in which the internet is making possible new ways of using and articulating information – in the sense that it is facilitating the reorganization of social relations – then we are studying how the internet is involved in *cultural transmission*. Consequently, it is a theory of cultural transmission which must provide us with a framework for understanding the internet's interactional impact.

While some recent studies rightly emphasize the importance of 'internet culture', their accounts leave the development of a cultural approach as urgent as ever. In *Internet Culture*, for example, David Porter observes that the culture that the internet embodies is 'a product of the peculiar conditions of virtual acquaintance that prevail online, a collective adaptation to the high frequency of anonymous, experimental, and even fleeting encounters. . . . The majority of one's correspondents in cyberspace, after all, have no bodies, no faces, no histories beyond what they may choose to reveal.'[1] Such accounts focus almost entirely on '*online culture*'. A major rethinking is called for, because accounts like the one given by Porter largely ignore the social contexts within which, and by virtue of which, information and other symbolic content are produced and received. A new focus is needed on how the use of the internet is contributing to the rise of new forms of human association and the way the internet is affecting all forms of organization and the daily lives of individuals. We need to open up its implications for a new concept of publicness and how this relates to the globalization of communication. The internet is challenging the ways we seek to manage openness and visibility in modern culture; it has consequences as a new modality of cultural transmission, increasing the mediazation of culture in late modern society. I shall discuss all of these themes in subsequent chapters.

In this third chapter, though, I want to prepare the way for a more constructive approach to understanding the impact of the internet on modern life and to refute any suggestion that the internet is merely 'a medium of disembodied voices and decontextualized points of view' resulting in some form of virtual society.[2] I want to begin to understand virtuality, in Bruno Latour's terms, 'not as something which is disembodied, but something which is more material than real'.[3] The approach which I develop here will allow us to begin to think more rigorously about the issues set out above and allow us to start to ask more revealing questions. In doing so, I shall draw on the work of John Thompson, who has paid particular attention to explicating a basic conception of culture and a theory of cultural production.[4] I shall examine the relevant aspects of his work and attempt to extend his ideas to the study of the internet. I shall want to explore in detail the way in which the internet is changing the modes in which social relations are constituted across time-space. Most social analysts unthinkingly treat time and space as mere environments of interaction,[5] and with the coming of virtual reality, time and space seem to have become dimensions which can be conveniently folded away altogether. I shall argue that a more constructive approach to understanding the interactional impact of the internet will involve not the cancelling out of time-space, but rather the reiterating of the significance of time-space and the 'situatedness' of human interaction.

The concept of culture

'Culture' is an exceptionally complex term. In 1952, Alfred Kroeber and Clyde Kluckhorn developed a taxonomy of the concept of culture, bringing out the convergences and divergences in no less than fourteen definitions.[6] The concept of culture has since become one of the key notions in contemporary social thought. However, even today, to put it in Raymond Williams's words, 'both the problem and the interest of the sociology of culture can be seen at once in the difficulty of its apparently defining term.'[7] In this section, I shall examine critically Thompson's account of the main episodes in the development of the concept of culture. In doing so, I shall follow his account closely and only examine some of the dominant trajectories. Even Kroeber and Kluckhorn argue that there is an excellent case for grouping together mixed and borderline definitions,[8] and Thompson has taken the bold step of recognizing three basic strands: the *classical* conception of culture; the *descriptive* anthropological conception of culture; and the *symbolic* anthropological conception of culture.[9] Let me deal with each of these in turn and set out against them his alternative approach: the *structural* conception of culture. At the same time, I shall reconsider some of the major sources Thompson draws on and add fresh material to the debate which may assist us further in relating his theory of cultural transmission to the impact of the internet.

The classical conception of culture

The first interpretation of the concept of culture that Thompson considers is one which is particularly evident in debates that took place between German philosophers and historians during the eighteenth and nineteenth centuries. The earliest appearance of the term 'culture history' is believed to be in Johann Christoph Adelung's *Geschichte der Cultur* published in 1782.[10] Johann Gottfried Herder's *Reflections on the Philosophy of the History of Mankind*, a four-volume work published between 1784 and 1791, is the best known early example of such histories.[11] For Thompson, these studies view culture as: 'the process of developing and ennobling the human faculties, a process facilitated by the assimilation of works of scholarship and art and linked to the progressive character of the modern era'.[12]

Although most writings of this kind were historical, they privileged the values of the German intelligentsia. During the second half of the nineteenth century, however, this ethnocentric notion of culture began to drop out of fashion. This was particularly so among anthropologists, many of whom were strongly influenced by 'cultural relativism'. Thompson distinguishes two basic uses of the concept of culture in ethnographic anthropological studies: the descriptive anthropological conception and the symbolic anthropological conception.

The descriptive anthropological conception of culture

Thompson traces the descriptive conception of culture back to Gustav Klemm, who in 1843 published the first of ten volumes of his *Allgemeine Cultur-Geschichte der Menschheit*.[13] In setting out 'to investigate and determine the gradual development of mankind from its rudest . . . first beginnings', Klemm's work continues to demonstrate the evolutionary character of the classical notion of culture: the idea that culture progresses in stages. Yet Klemm's writings also display a new concern for generating descriptions of mostly non-European cultures, such as those of the 'South American Indians' and the 'savage hunting and fishing tribes of South and North America'.[14] According to Kroeber and Kluckhorn, however, it was Edward Tylor, Professor of Anthropology at Oxford University, who in 1871 first formalized this approach. In his book *Primitive Culture*, Tylor writes that culture, 'taken in its wide ethnographic sense, is that complex whole which includes knowledge, belief, art, morals, law, custom, and any other capabilities and habits acquired by man as a member of society'.[15] Thompson summarizes this descriptive conception of culture as follows: 'the culture of a group or society is the array of beliefs, customs, ideas and values, as well as the material artefacts, objects and instruments, which are acquired by individuals as members of the group or society.'[16]

The main difficulties with this approach have more to do with the grand evolutionary schemes and the functionalist arguments of, for example, Alfred Radcliffe-Brown and Bronislaw Malinowski, which have been called upon to play an explanatory role, than with the descriptions themselves.[17] However, this approach has also been criticized, Thompson asserts, for the very breadth of studies it allows, reducing the discriminatory power of the notion of culture and rendering it rather vague.[18]

The symbolic anthropological conception of culture

According to Thompson, a very different approach to culture began to emerge from anthropological studies during the 1940s. The symbolic conception of culture, as Thompson names it, reoriented the analysis of culture 'towards the study of meaning and symbolism'.[19] Leslie White was the first anthropologist to emphasize symbolism in this way.[20] He writes,

> culture is the name of a distinct order, or class, of phenomena, namely, those things and events that are dependent upon the exercise of a mental ability, peculiar to the human species, that we have termed 'symbolling'. To be more specific, culture consists of material objects – tools, utensils, ornaments, amulets, etc. – acts, beliefs, and attitudes that function in contexts characterized by symbolling. It is an elaborate mechanism, an organization of exosomatic ways and means employed by a particular animal species, man, in the struggle for existence or survival.[21]

Evidence of this reorientation can, however, also be found in work by Read Bain who writes that 'culture is all behavior mediated by symbols',[22] and in Kingsley Davis's work, *Human Society*, where culture is understood to embrace 'all modes of thought and behavior that are handed down by communicative interaction'.[23] Thompson characterizes this distinctive conception of culture as follows: 'culture is the pattern of meanings embodied in symbolic forms, including actions, utterances and meaningful objects of various kinds, by virtue of which individuals communicate with one another and share their experiences, conceptions and beliefs.'[24]

The writings of Clifford Geertz, Thompson argues, in particular his essays collected in *The Interpretation of Cultures*, are an invigorating attempt to work out the implications of such an approach for anthropological investigation.[25] As he explains in this book, Geertz believes (like Max Weber) that 'man is an animal suspended in webs of significance he himself has spun', and understands culture 'to be those webs, and the analysis of it to be therefore not an experimental science in search of law but an interpretative one in search of meaning' (p. 5). Geertz compares culture to a text, an 'acted document', and the work of the anthropologist with that of a 'literary critic' (pp. 9–10). As such, the anthropologist, as an 'ethnographer "inscribes" social discourse' (p. 19), that is, writes it down. This is by no means an easy task, Geertz warns, for 'what we inscribe (or try to) is not raw social discourse, to which, because, save very marginally or very specially, we are not actors, we do not have direct access, but only that small part of it which our informants can lead us into understanding' (p. 20). Yet,

> undirected by culture patterns – organized systems of significant symbols – man's behavior would be virtually ungovernable, a mere chaos of pointless acts and exploding emotions, his experience virtually shapeless. Culture, the accumulated totality of such patterns, is not just an ornament of human existence but – the principal basis of its specificity – an essential condition for it. (p. 46)

Although Geertz's writings are admirable in that he attempts to distance himself from some of the more peculiar assumptions of earlier conceptions, Thompson argues that his interpretive theory of culture is not without its own set of limitations, each of which demand further emendation.[26] Let me for a moment dwell and expand on three of these limitations recognized by Thompson which are particularly relevant to our present concerns.

The first difficulty with Geertz's approach in *The Interpretation of Cultures* is that 'culture patterns' feature only as a backdrop against which social interaction becomes intelligible. Although he describes them as 'historically transmitted', they appear as given, and not as a negotiated product of human action. The origins of the patterns are left shrouded in mystery. The problem is particularly evident in the following passages in Geertz's essays. He writes:

> Beavers build dams, birds build nests, bees locate food, baboons organize
> social groups, and mice mate on the basis of forms of learning that rest
> predominantly on the instructions encoded into their genes. . . . But men
> build dams or shelters, locate food, organize their social groups, or find
> sexual partners under the instructions encoded in flow charts and blue-
> prints, hunting lore, moral systems and aesthetic judgments molding form-
> less talents. (pp. 49–50)

And elsewhere: culture is 'best seen not as complexes of concrete behavior
patterns – customs, usages, traditions, habit clusters – as has, by and large,
been the case up to now, but as a set of control mechanisms – plans,
recipes, rules, instructions (what computer engineers call "programs") –
for the governing of behavior' (p. 44). Geertz, however, does not attempt
to explain to us how instructions are encoded and how programs are
written into our culture patterns. Moreover, the idea that social interaction is somehow moulded, controlled and governed brings his approach
very close to the kinds of conception of culture which he believes he has
succeeded in avoiding.

The second difficulty in Geertz's work concerns the notion of culture
as an 'acted document'. While he recognizes that 'acted documents' are
not 'raw social discourse', he gives insufficient attention to the problems
that differential interpretation might pose. Documents and texts, and for
that matter culture patterns, do not explain themselves. In his 'Notes on
the Balinese Cockfight', one of the selected essays in the book, Geertz
writes: 'The culture of a people is an ensemble of texts, themselves en-
sembles, which the anthropologist strains to read over the shoulders of
those to whom they properly belong' (p. 452). Yet Geertz manages to
acquire what he calls an 'inside-view' (p. 416). He refers to the cockfights as an 'art form' (p. 443). However, he does not support the claim
that such a privileged understanding is indeed 'a story they tell themselves about themselves' (p. 448). In fact, throughout the essay a number
of vying interpretations of cockfights come into view. Geertz writes of
the elite in Balinese society and how 'it sees cockfighting as "primitive",
"backward", "unprogressive", and generally unbecoming an ambitious
nation. And, as with those other embarrassments – opium smoking,
begging, or uncovered breasts – it seeks, rather unsystematically, to put
a stop to it' (p. 414). Different interpretations of 'acted documents',
however, lie at the heart of struggles based on divisions of interest, and
cannot be ignored in this way.

The third difficulty with Geertz's approach is also generated by the
notion of culture as an 'acted document'. While considerable illumina-
tion of problems of cultural analysis can be derived from this analogy, it
offers only a very limited understanding of the structural properties of
culture in general. And it obstructs any understanding of the relationship

between cultural phenomena, institutional transformation, and history. In reading the 'Balinese way of life' as an 'acted document', for example, Geertz does not adequately recognize the centrality of power in social life. He does not explain why for some people cockfights are an embarrassment and why, in the event that the police turn up, others scuttle up coconut trees or claim to have spent all afternoon drinking tea (pp. 414–15). Cultural phenomena always express asymmetries of power and cannot be regarded simply as the collaborative work carried out by peers. The text analogy cannot sufficiently deal with the involvement of individuals with the practical realization of the interests they may have.

Thompson argues that the importance of Geertz's conception of culture consists primarily in bringing to prominence the study of cultural phenomena as meaningful symbolic forms. The further development of his contribution, however, demands that we take an alternative approach. This other approach, Thompson insists, must also pay attention to the structured social relations and contexts within which information and other symbolic content are produced and received.

The structural conception of culture

Thompson qualifies his own preferred concept of culture as not so much an alternative to the symbolic conception as a modification of it. It allows us to take up the problems of the symbolic conception of culture and to attempt to provide an answer to them. Thompson describes the structural conception of culture as: 'the study of symbolic forms – that is, meaningful actions, objects and expressions of various kinds – in relation to the historically specific and socially structured contexts and processes within which, and by means of which, these symbolic forms are produced, transmitted and received'. The exchange of information and other symbolic content between individuals and organizations located within specific contexts always presupposes the mobilization of specific means of transmission. Thompson calls the conditions and apparatuses which facilitate this process the 'modalities of cultural transmission'.[27]

What I think makes Thompson's structural perspective so interesting is that it represents a radical departure from existing cultural approaches to the study of the internet. Rather than just calling our attention to what is happening on the internet, it allows us to focus on the socially structured contexts and processes of production, transmission and reception as well as on the information and other symbolic content. In other words, it offers an opportunity for us to reinstate and reclaim Porter's 'disembodied voices' as articulated 'voices' produced and received by real people embedded in specific socially and historically structured contexts and processes.

In the rest of this chapter, and indeed throughout the rest of this book, I shall try to show what the study of the internet as a modality of cultural transmission might involve and work out the benefits we might expect from this approach.

Aspects of cultural transmission

The circulation of information and other symbolic content in socially structured contexts involves what Thompson calls *aspects of cultural transmission*.[28] There are three such aspects, he argues:

1 A *technical medium* of transmission.
2 An *institutional apparatus* of transmission.
3 A certain kind of *space-time distanciation* involved in transmission.

As a modality of cultural transmission, the internet combines these three aspects in a unique way. Let me now discuss each of these aspects in detail and also begin to explore their particular importance for the understanding of the role of the internet in the mediazation of modern culture.

The technical medium of transmission

The technical medium of transmission, Thompson argues, consists of the material components by virtue of which information and other symbolic content are produced, transmitted and received. It is important to take these into account when examining the cultural impact of a medium because, as Harold Innis and Marshall McLuhan claim, the nature of social interaction may be affected by the very form of this material substratum.[29] Thompson recognizes three related *attributes of technical media* which are of particular importance here. These are:

1 *Fixation.*
2 *Reproduction.*
3 *Participation.*

In order to highlight features relevant to the internet, I shall begin from the elaboration of the development of this medium in the second chapter of this book and relate each of the attributes Thompson recognizes to internet examples. It must be remembered, however, that the internet cannot be approached as a single communication entity in this respect. It consists of an array of different technical applications. A more detailed study would involve the examination of various internet applications, for example WWW, e-mail, IRC, etc., and the unique way in which they combine Thompson's 'attributes of technical media'. This reservation also holds true for my discussion of the two other aspects of cultural transmission. Moreover, it will also become apparent that while there are significant differences, there are also many similarities between *new media* and the mass media which were the original subject of Thompson's study.

Fixation   The *degree of fixation*, Thompson argues, is the capacity of a technical medium to store information. Stored information can be considered as a resource for the exercise of power because it can be used by individuals and organizations in the pursuit of certain ends. In this way, a technical medium can be approached as a power container or as a generator of power. The manner in which information can be stored is indicative of both a technical medium's potential as a tool for surveillance, the transmission of information, and the nature of the control which may be exercised over it. The mode of information storage affects the way in which we might approach questions such as who may store information, what kind of information may be stored, who may access the information and to what ends it may be used.

All communication media, Thompson claims, allow for some degree of fixation. The degree of fixation conferred by the internet is, however, to some extent more complicated by comparison with single media such as paper, film or television. This is because the codification of information and its transmission in a digital form create a new technical scenario, one in which the internet can integrate various modes of communication – text, sound, images, etc. – into a vast interactive network. This does not mean, however, that we now have a 'supermedium', capable of 'fixing' anything, and that we can now discard the claims made by Innis and McLuhan concerning the role of technical media in communication. On the contrary, there are several reasons why the degree of fixation allowed by the internet is still of central importance in understanding its interactional impact. First, the exploitation of digital technology has vastly increased the capacity for information storage. Second, the internet provides us with a greater choice of forms in which to do so. Third, without wishing to downplay the threats posed by 'hackers' and other individuals who ingeniously expose the vulnerability of computer systems, the internet has extended the scope for surveillance. It has greatly expanded the ways in which we can generate control over the processes of storing, accessing and mobilizing information in the pursuit of particular aims.

Let me illustrate this using the website of the Ford Motor Company discussed earlier.[30] The website allows the organization to store vast amounts of corporate information about itself, its products and services

– far more than it would be feasible to store and make available on a billboard or in a television commercial. The webpages allow the company to control precisely which information is stored and made available, channelling information to specific audience groups ranging from family car owners to shareholders. It provides the company with a unique forum for generating a display of trustworthiness and integrity.

While the website of the Ford Motor Company offers new opportunities, it might also bring new problems. Stored information can become outdated, be factually incorrect or contain little of interest to the user. Users may feel powerless, being given only a limited ability to 'store' information themselves by writing an e-mail or by filling out a form. The Ford Motor Company website is thus a locale of empowerment and disempowerment. Users, for example, may link their own webpages to the company's site, yet guidelines explicitly forbid the use of Ford's 'icons' on webpages which disparage the company's products or services.

Reproduction   The second attribute of a technical medium of transmission Thompson recognizes concerns the *degree of reproduction* of the information and other symbolic content it affords. The storing of information in digital form, coupled with the emergence of a vast interactive network and universal interfaces such as browsers and other programs – not forgetting the hardware in the form of computers, monitors and printers – have made the reproduction of information transmitted over the internet almost limitless.

The website of the British Broadcasting Corporation, for example, potentially allows the BBC to make information available to interested internet users anywhere in the world and at any time.[31] Moreover, any changes made to the pages are immediately available to all those who visit the website. However, popular webpages, for example those that were run by the BBC covering the report of Independent Counsel Kenneth Starr on his investigation of the US President Bill Clinton and the Lewinsky affair, still come to a grinding halt when many millions of people attempt to access them at once. But despite technical hitches, these websites do at least display in principle that such information is capable of being reproduced infinitely on a global scale.

The way in which information and other symbolic content can be reproduced by using the internet is heightening what some theorists call the *collage effect*. This term is used by Giddens to describe the ways in which 'media presentation takes the form of the juxtaposition of stories and items which share nothing in common other than that they are "timely" and consequential.'[32] The way in which I use the term does not coincide entirely with Giddens's use. I wish to describe 'collage effect' as a consequence of the intensity with which and the scale at which the internet acts as a disembedding mechanism, prizing information and other symbolic content free from the hold of specific locales and allowing for its recombination across wide time-space distances. These collages of assembled and reassembled information are brought about by internet users themselves. Let me illustrate the complexity of this mode of reproducing information at three different levels of internet use.

First, a visit to the website of the Ford Motor Company, for example, starts off with information located on a computer in the United States. In a matter of seconds, a hyperlink can take users from here to information held about the company on a computer in Portugal. Other links take users to information about local car dealers, credit facilities, and stocks and shares involving multiple locations all over the world. In using the internet, the Ford Motor Company suspends itself in a web of significance which it itself has spun. As such, it succeeds in bringing together a 'collage' of information and other symbolic content from widely dispersed sources, produced in a variety of different contexts. It allows for the recombination and reproduction of this content in a variety of other contexts, thereby radicalizing and globalizing pre-established institutional traits and creating a vast range of opportunities for new ones.

Second, the collage effect extends to individual webpages themselves. A webpage appears on the screen as a unity, yet it is in fact made up of various elements such as text and images, and possibly sound and video. These elements may be physically stored in files on one site and may be drawn on to constitute one webpage. Equally, these separate elements may also be stored at various different sites around the world and be called on to slot into the collage of a variety of webpages. No matter where the information is stored, once the information has been retrieved by a user's browser it will be reproduced and appear as a seamless whole with its own internal referentiality.

Lastly, the collage effect also extends to the computer screen itself, where, as explained in the previous chapter, the user may have a wide range of applications running at the same time. The screen is thus a patchwork of various information flows, a negotiated dynamic narrative made up of the juxtaposition of what otherwise might be heterogeneous items of knowledge and information.

Participation   The final attribute Thompson recognizes with respect to the technical medium of transmission refers to the nature and *degree of participation* it grants to and requires from those who use the medium. All media require skills in this way. Using the internet is thus a skilled performance and its successful use is an accomplishment demanding particular capabilities, resources and attentiveness. The BBC website, for example, displays the skills of the internet specialists who constructed it. Those visiting the website have of course to be literate and need a basic understanding of how to use a computer. However, without wishing to deny their importance, I want to shift attention away from these more obvious skills to others which are intensely required of users of the internet – probably more so than is the case with any other medium. These are the skills needed to negotiate what Giddens calls *place as phantasmagoric*. This notion describes a situation in which the externalities of place within which users are situated become

> thoroughly penetrated by disembedding mechanisms, which recombine the local activities into time-space relations of ever-widening scope . . . Familiarity (with social events and with people as well as with places) no longer depends solely, or perhaps even primarily, upon local milieux . . . Place thus becomes much less significant than it used to be as an external referent.[33]

The internet has accelerated and intensified this process.

The lack of skills users have in this respect can be easily demonstrated by studying the typical exchanges of newcomers on internet relay chat who join a channel greeting others with 'good morning', unconscious of the fact that for many others on the channel it might be late evening. However, even experienced users refer to 'channels' as being 'American' or 'South African', unable to grasp the fact that channels are mostly open to anyone, anywhere. At first sight, these may seem rather innocuous slip-ups, yet they display the complexity of developing skills needed to gear regular internet practices to specifics of time and place. The use of analogies such as 'digital cities', 'virtual shopping malls', 'cybercafés', etc., are all creative attempts to organize and re-embed information and interaction into familiar settings. Of course, this process also involves attempts to create dialectical forms of counterskills in order to actively re-embed otherwise vague mediated experience. Organizations with intranets, for example, where large numbers of staff no longer have traditional office space and lead a 'nomadic' existence, often create café-like settings or office-gardens where employees can meet and entertain clients face to face.

The institutional apparatus of transmission

Besides a technical medium of transmission, Thompson argues, the exchange of information and other symbolic content also involves an *institutional apparatus of transmission*. This is the second of the three aspects of cultural transmission. Thompson defines the institutional apparatus as being 'a determinate set of institutional arrangements within which the technical medium is deployed and the individuals involved in encoding and decoding symbolic forms are embedded'.[34]

Most accounts of the internet tend to focus on its economic aspects at the expense of the political, or focus on the normative aspects at the expense of analysing power. I believe, however, that a better understanding of the internet can only be reached if we approach the institutional arrangements comprehensively as 'rules and resources, organized as properties of social systems'.[35] Within such systems, the exchange of information does not take place separately from the operation of political and economic power, or outside the operation of normative sanctions. Internet use is always situated within intersecting sets of rules and resources and reflects features of the social system as a whole. The institutional arrangements within which internet use is situated are thus always socially stratified, involving hierarchical relations of power between individuals and organizations. Examining the website of the Universidade de São Paulo,[36] for example, we can see that a number of institutional arrangements are relevant to the exchange of information taking place here. Among these are, of course, the arrangements governing the publication and transmission of material by the university, but also those involving the activities of individuals who access the website to obtain information about the university and its departments, and even to communicate with them. Communication by all parties involves the use of power and the application of norms.

The institutional apparatus of transmission of symbolic forms always involve what Thompson calls:

1 *Channels of selective diffusion.*
2 *Mechanisms for restricted implementation.*[37]

Both these aspects are institutionally involved in the enabling and the constraining of certain forms of media use, and encompass users in asymmetric relations of autonomy and dependence. Let us now look at each of these aspects of the institutional apparatus of transmission.

Channels of selective diffusion The channels of selective diffusion, Thompson explains, constitute the institutional framework controlling access to a technical medium and the opportunities for using it to circulate and exchange information and other symbolic forms. As such, they lock into the characteristics of its storage capacity as explained earlier. If we are to understand the impact of the internet on modern culture, we need to identify sources of constraint and the opportunities which follow from the 'situatedness' of its use in time-space.

The website of DDS, the Digital City Amsterdam,[38] offers a good example. The site is run by a foundation and is supported by Amsterdam City Council, the Dutch Ministry for Economic Affairs and Ministry for Internal Affairs, and various other sponsors. It started in 1994 as an experiment to promote private and public awareness of the internet and is now one of the largest online communities in the world. The circulation and exchange of information on this website is structured around the metaphor of a 'city square'. There are a number of squares, for example the café square, the computer square, the film square, the art square, the music square, the multicultural square and the health square, each acting as a meeting place for all those interested in the particular theme connected with it. One of the foundation's major achievements has been to offer selective, but free of charge, access to the internet. This means that DDS allows users to avoid the normal channels of selective diffusion which mostly involve users having to pay for a commercial account with an internet service provider. However, users who phone in cannot access the internet fully in this way. Access may be free of charge, yet they still have to pay their phone bills and wait for long periods while the telephone lines are busy. In addition to the phone-in access, the Digital City website is also accessible by those who are already on the internet. Users accessing the website in this way are able to avoid the busy phone lines.

As the DDS example shows, patterns of internet access are typically tied to the properties of the internet as a technical medium and to the ways in which these properties interact with the constraints and capabilities afforded by the institutional arrangements within which its use is embedded. Moreover, these conditions can vary when individuals, going about their activities, move in time-space. Although it is technically feasible to use the internet at any time and any place, only a few individuals so far have continual access to it. Individuals connected to an intranet may check their e-mail regularly throughout their working day, yet when they are in transit or removed from their normal opportunities for access, new patterns of capabilities and constraints emerge.

Mechanisms for restricted implementation   The diffusion of information is a process which can itself be controlled and regulated in various ways. The *mechanisms for restricted implementation*, writes Thompson, 'assume a major role and may serve to limit or deflect the diffusion of symbolic forms'.[39] Returning to the example just given, all those 'entering' the Digital City can choose to do so either as a 'resident' or as a 'tourist'. In order to become a resident, individuals have to register by filling in a form at the central square in the city. Residents of the Digital City have more opportunities open to them than tourists. They are able to build their own homepages on one of the many squares, chat in cafés, take part in discussion forums, use a free worldwide e-mail facility and take part in elections. Tourists, on the other hand, are only able to have a look around.

There are also other rules governing the activities of residents of the Digital City and their ability to exchange information. Residents are, for example, given a fixed amount of computer memory in which to store their incoming e-mail and the files which make up their homepage. If they exceed this amount, mail sent to them is returned to the sender. The foundation charges special rates for webpages containing commercial information. Homepages belonging to residents are not permitted to contain pornographic material. The reason for this, the Digital City claims, is not so much a moralistic one, but rather an economic one: pornographic material would generate too much traffic over the network and would drain the foundation's funds. Residents are not allowed to protect their homepages with passwords and hide pornographic or commercial information in this way. The foundation can ultimately 'banish' transgressors, particularly for harassing other residents or if they have been caught vandalizing information stored by others.

The DDS example shows that internet use, like the deployment of any other form of mediated communication, expresses both the material axes of the technology and the ways in which users accommodate these material axes in the contexts of institutional arrangements which are thereby produced and reproduced across time-space.

The time-space distanciation in transmission

The third of Thompson's aspects of cultural transmission refers to the *degree of temporal and spatial distancing* involved in the circulation of information and other symbolic content.[40] This time-space distanciation, Thompson argues, is dependent both on the technical medium and on the institutional apparatus discussed above. Whereas face-to-face exchanges take place in what Giddens refers to as 'contexts of co-presence', technical media facilitate the 'extension of availability' of symbolic forms in time-space.[41] The pressures and opportunities for mobilizing time-space during the exchange of information constitute the 'grounding' for the way in which such exchanges are organized and sustained.

In discussing time-space distanciation, Thompson argues that we need to return to Innis's work *The Bias of Communication*.[42] In this book, Innis not only stresses the importance of the form of the technical medium, he also calls our attention to the centrality of time and space in the analysis of systems of communication. Writing in the 1940s and early 1950s, Innis was one of the first to study the complex relationship between media of communication and the spatial and temporal organization of power. Indeed, much of his work focuses on the examining of the conditions that have to be maintained if a particular form of social organization is to persist in a relatively stable form in time-space. He draws on the notion of 'empire' to denote the institutionalization of power implicated in the production and reproduction of such conditions. Innis writes that a medium of communication has an important influence on the dissemination of knowledge over space and over time and it becomes necessary to study its characteristics in order to appraise its influence in its cultural setting. According to its characteristics it may be better suited to the dissemination of knowledge over time than over space, particularly if the medium is heavy and durable and not suited to transportation, or to the dissemination of knowledge over space than over time, particularly if the medium is light and easily transported. The relative emphasis on time or space will imply a bias of significance to the culture in which it is embedded.[43]

According to this view, forms of social organization in which individuals have access to spatially biased communication media may stretch across wide spans of space. On the other hand, control over time may be generated through other types of media, enabling the reproduction of social systems over long periods of time. It is also possible to combine time-biased with space-biased media in order to achieve more stable organizational cultures.

Although Innis's ideas about time-space distanciation in transmission are still rather sketchy, they do highlight in an elemental way that individuals and organizations do not just use media 'in' time-space, they use it to organize time-space. By examining the internet in this light, we can begin to make an effort at grasping its impact on the volume of time-space available to individuals and organizations in the pursuance of their projects. We can study, for example, how the internet is affecting individuals and organizations in their ability to mobilize space and, by using the internet to facilitate the routinized specification and allocation of tasks, to coordinate the time-space trajectories of their projects.[44] As such, internet use always involves asymmetries of power and each communicative act has to be successfully 'brought off' by those using it. The transformative capacity of internet use, that is the way it can be deployed to 'make a difference', is thus, among other things, dependent on the characteristics of the individuals and organizations involved, their location in time-space, the institutional arrangements within which they act, and the means which they have at their disposal.

Let me illustrate these points with an example taken from internet relay chat. It can happen that a user receives a message telling them that they are banned from using a channel they wish to join, even though they are unaware of any legitimate reason for this to be the case. This usually means that all users accessing the channel from a particular host have been banned. Channel operators take this drastic measure because an individual who is banned for causing a nuisance can simply rejoin the channel under a different name but cannot so easily change their host. An individual unfairly banned because of the 'bad' behaviour of someone else will often send messages to the channel operators pleading to have the ban lifted. If the user is known to the operators, or can somehow display their good intentions by rallying others to their defence, then the ban may be lifted. It also helps if there are operators present who know the circumstances behind the ban and why it was placed.

This example of a routine occurrence on internet relay chat shows how users can have a differing volume of time-space available to them and that their ability to use the internet to organize time-space is always a matter of potential contestation. So far, however, those studying the internet have tended to confuse expectations concerning the temporal and spatial consequences of internet use with uncritical ideas concerning the time-space organization of so-called 'virtual reality'. In the latter, the consequences of internet use, as some would have us believe, are to produce a flat, immaterial and malleable surface of time-space patterning, one in which individuals and organizations seem to become endowed with the ability to play God. Such a point of view is suggested by Barrie Sherman and Phil Judkins, who describe virtual reality as a place where

> we can make water solid, and solids fluid; we can imbue inanimate objects (chairs, lamps, engines) with an intelligent life of their own. We can invent animals, singing textures, clever colours or fairies . . . We cannot make our real world whatever we wish to make of it. Virtual Reality may turn out to be a great deal more comfortable than our own imperfect reality.[45]

This is also the point of view which is prevalent in work of Sadie Plant, who treats virtual reality as a zone of unfettered freedom, describing it as 'a grid reference for free experimentation, an atmosphere in which there are no barriers, no restrictions on how far it is possible to go'.[46]

We need to take a critical approach to the claim that with the coming of virtual reality, time and space have become dimensions that can be folded away. We have to acknowledge that the time-space patterning of information and other symbolic content made available over the internet is always in some way the expression of the activities of real individuals and real organizations. All of them are engaged in projects involving the negotiation of constraints and opportunities of the varied environments and regions of internet use. Deirdre Boden and Harvey Molotch also argue that modern communication systems

> inevitably rest on micro-orders; modernity is achieved not just through computer circuit boards and devices such as voice mail, video conferencing, and fax reproduction but through the intensely social daily routines of humans thinking, cooperating, and talking face-to-face. Rather than being antithetical to advanced modernity, intimacy is the basis for it.[47]

Of course, some electronically mediated environments explicitly motivate users into entering into fantasy worlds where they might adopt 'floating identities' and 'let's pretend' attitudes. This is often the case with MUDs where it is made pretty obvious to users that they are expected to behave in this way. Even so, their communications must still be examined, and understood not just as mere 'hallucinations' but as the meaningful expressions of real individuals who are using this medium in very complex ways to bind time-space and communicate with others.

The points I make here have a direct bearing on the debate concerning the *authenticity of virtual reality*. The 'authenticity' of individuals and the contributions they make to a 'community' traditionally refers to an embedded affinity to a particular place. Technologies such as the internet pose a serious threat to this kind of 'grounding' of authenticity. Robert Sack writes:

> To be an agent, one must be somewhere. This basic and integrative sense of place has come to be fragmented into complex, contradictory and disorienting parts. Space is becoming far more integrated and yet territorially fragmented. Places are specific or unique, yet in many senses they appear generic and alike. Places seem to be 'out there', and yet they are humanly constructed. . . . Our society stores information about places, and yet we have little sense of place. And the landscapes that result from modern processes appear to be pastiches, disorienting and juxtaposed.[48]

By stressing the 'situatedness' of those using the internet, the 'places' in virtual reality – the webpages, the IRC channels, the newsgroups, etc. – are no longer just 'out there'. They become articulated with reality.

Towards a social theory of the internet

In setting out a framework for the analysis of the forms of action and interaction created by the internet, I shall first draw out some of the implications of conceptualizing the internet as a modality of cultural transmission. It will be helpful to begin this process by comparing the internet with some of the general characteristics of mass communication, a comparison which will alert us to some of the transformations taking place. Second, I shall follow through Alvin Gouldner's claim that the emergence of mass communication and of the 'public' are mutually constructive developments, and begin to explore the way in which the internet is transforming the public sphere. Third, I shall examine various kinds of interactional situations created by the use of the internet. Finally, in setting out the analytical framework itself, I shall attempt to create a heuristic device which will prove useful for examining how the interactional features established by means of the internet are affecting the social organization of day-to-day life.

Mass communication and the internet

McLuhan writes that 'the advent of a new medium often reveals the lineaments and assumptions, as it were, of an old medium.'[49] Accordingly, Merrill Morris and Christine Ogan point out that scholars in the field of mass communication have much to gain from studying the internet.[50] However, while there are important similarities between new media and mass media, Morris and Ogan fail to explore the complexities involved in defining the internet as a mass medium. Their interest seems to be first and foremost to celebrate the applicability of established theories and methodologies of mass communication to this new medium. Let us now try to develop a more critical account by comparing the internet with Thompson's definition of *mass communication*. In his definition, Thompson clearly builds on his approach to the way in which such media are involved in cultural transmission.

The term 'mass communication', which refers to a wide range of media institutions and services, Thompson argues, is misleading in many respects. The first part of the term suggests that the information transmitted is potentially available to large audiences. In practice, however, audiences are often small and specialized. They by no means constitute a 'mass' in the sense of an uncritical crowd, involved only in the passive consumption of media messages. The second half of the term is misleading because the 'communication' involved is very different from face-to-face communication. In situations of co-presence, the producer of information is normally also a potential recipient, thus permitting a high degree of dialogical participation. Mass communication, however, Thompson writes, 'institutes a fundamental break between the producer and receiver, in such a way that recipients have relatively little capacity to contribute to the course and content of the communicative process'.[51] Thompson goes on to conceptualize mass communication as 'the institutionalized production and generalized diffusion of symbolic goods via the transmission and storage of information/communication'.[52]

By giving this definition Thompson focuses on four characteristics of mass communication which I shall employ here to reflect on the nature of the internet:

1 The *institutionalized production and diffusion* of symbolic goods.
2 The *instituted break* between production and reception.
3 The *extension of availability* in time-space.
4 The *public circulation* of symbolic forms.

Institutionalized production and diffusion of symbolic goods Mass communication generally involves large-scale institutions concerned with the production and diffusion of symbolic goods. In this respect, we may think of large broadcasting institutions, such as the BBC, CNN and MTV, and perhaps also some smaller production units. Television requires expensive equipment, studios and expertise, and amateur video is still easily distinguishable from regular professional television. By contrast, the internet is a relatively open communication system. It does not require large-scale expert systems for the production of content, and the large-scale institutions are mainly involved in the design and sale of software, the provision of access, and the storage and transmission of information. There are, of course, organizations that specialize in the building of websites and intranets, and there are sophisticated private networks which require investments only large organizations can afford. Yet homepages built by some schoolchildren are in many respects barely distinguishable in quality from webpages belonging to most of the multinational companies.

Instituted break between production and reception The second of Thompson's characteristics of mass communication has to do with the dichotomy that exists between sender and receiver. While all mediated communication institutes some kind of break between production and reception, mass communication generally involves the one-way flow of information. Recipients have only a very low capacity to intervene. This paradox of isolation and visibility means that producers of information must treat their audiences on peculiar terms of equality. After all, those deciding what may be communicated and by whom can never be completely certain that their decisions will meet with the agreement of the recipients – if those recipients' opinions could be heard.

The internet, on the other hand, blurs the conventional producer/receiver dichotomy. Information flows two ways, and internet users can equally well be producers of information as receivers of it. The interactive capacity of the internet thus offers them a higher capacity to make their opinions heard, and provides them with a greater degree of control over the transmission process.

While in potential at least, the internet goes a long way towards overcoming the conventional break between production and reception, in practice the degree of interactivity may vary from encounter to encounter and from application to application. A few examples will suffice to illustrate these points. First, an organization may have a website, yet have no control over the transmission process. Internet users only become recipients if they actively choose to visit the website and 'fetch' the information. Second, an organization may adopt some form of push technology in the distribution process, thereby regaining some control by actively sending the information to the receiver. Third, an organization may set up an intranet which allows only a specific group of users to publish information and act as producers, and thus re-establish the conventional producer/receiver dichotomy associated with mass communication. Fourth, if we take a narrow view, webpages often permit only a low level of clarifying feedback and questioning. After all, recipients often have only an e-mail address to respond to.

However, if we take a broader view, then the potential for deliberative participation, or at least the potential for making an opinion publicly available, is far more evident with the internet than in mass communication. One example of this is chat systems such as IRC. Here users become potential producers or receivers, and can join a variety of forums for real-time debate on a global scale. Another example is e-mail. When a personal e-mail is sent to a single receiver, the producer of the message is more on a par with the receiver who might potentially send an e-mail in reply. When e-mail is used to distribute information to a long list of subscribers, however, the break between producers and receivers of information becomes greater.

On balance, these examples show that while specific levels of interactivity and control may vary, in comparison with mass communication the internet does in general seem to challenge the old dichotomy of sender and receiver, shifting the balance of power in favour of the receiver.

Extension of availability in time-space   The third of Thompson's characteristics of mass communication has to do with achieving availability in time-space. While mass communication generally involves a high degree of space-time distanciation in transmission, the extension of the availability of information in time-space also depends on the institutional arrangements involved. For example, in order for information to be disseminated using television, the information has to concern an event which is either entertaining or newsworthy, and above all which is televisable. In the case of advertisements, the producer of the information has to be prepared to pay for airtime. Even so, the degree of visibility achieved will at best be patchy in both time and space, as it depends on whether the moment of broadcasting coincides with the everyday activities of potential receivers. The internet is upsetting established patterns of availability in this respect. Organizations can now store masses of information on their websites and achieve around-the-clock availability, establishing communicative relationships with interested users on a global scale even before they set foot outside their homes. Moreover, even small and medium-sized companies and individual users can potentially accomplish a degree of availability which vastly exceeds that of even the most privileged users of mass communication.

Public circulation of symbolic forms   The final aspect of Thompson's characteristics of mass communication concerns the public circulation of symbolic forms. The products of mass communication are, as I described earlier, generalized forms of communication produced for an indefinite, or at least a large range of potential recipients. However, with new kinds of satellite and cable technology, television for example is steadily shifting away from traditional forms of public service broadcasting produced for a plurality of recipients and moving towards the establishment of channels which are increasingly oriented towards restricted ranges of specialized audiences.

Despite the increasing numbers of channels, however, it is still difficult to deny the continuing significance of large-scale broadcasting institutions and their role in the formation of public opinion. Indeed some public service channels have attempted to create a new niche for themselves by exploiting the fact that they bring together the fragmented 'publics' of some of the more specialized channels. Without wishing to underplay these examples of changes taking place in modern television, one can say that the internet is radically transforming the nature of the public circulation of symbolic forms. I want to explore this transformation by starting up a discussion, to be continued in chapter 7, concerning the notion of 'publicness' and the internet. In this discussion, I shall relate the internet to the theory of the public sphere.

The internet and the public sphere

When Jürgen Habermas's early work *The Structural Transformation of the Public Sphere* was translated into English by Thomas Burger in 1991, it sparked off an ongoing debate among social theorists and communication scholars regarding the possibility of reconstituting the idea of a critical public sphere on a different basis today.[53] Given that all forms of mediated communication, including the internet, contribute to a sphere in which knowledge is shared and opinion is formed, examining this issue becomes a task of central importance.

On the basis of his research into the development of media institutions from the seventeenth century to the present day, Habermas accounts for the emergence and subsequent disintegration of what he calls the *public sphere*. He claims that the emergence of the public sphere as a forum of communication and debate was stimulated by the emergence of mass communication in the form of a small and independent press. By the end of the seventeenth century a new realm of communication had come about which, while guaranteeing the sphere of private autonomy, restricted the excesses of public authority. For Habermas, this critical public sphere embodies the idea of a forum, constituted by a community of individuals, coming together as equals, capable of producing and reproducing a public opinion through critical discussion, argument and reasoned debate. However, this ideal was never fully realized. Both the commercialization of the mass media and the expansion of state intervention led to what Habermas refers to as a kind of 'refeudalization' of the public sphere. The public sphere collapsed into a fantasy world of image and opinion management.

Although there is a great deal of sympathy for the notion of a critical public sphere as a kind of ideal-type, many critics tend to side with Habermas's opinion that the reconstitution of a critical public sphere is today being hampered by mass media such as television. Habermas writes, 'insofar as mass media one-sidedly channel communication flows in a centralized network – from the center to the periphery or from above to below – they considerably strengthen the efficacy of social controls.'[54] Thompson on the other hand remains very sceptical about such a stance and has put forward a mixture of historical, conceptual and practical difficulties concerning Habermas's work in this respect.[55] However, neither Habermas's account of the public sphere nor Thompson's critique of his early work refers to the possible consequences of internet use. Let us now look closely at three of Thompson's criticisms and examine what impact they have on opportunities and constraints associated with internet use.

The public sphere was not open to all   There is considerable historical evidence, Thompson claims, that the public sphere Habermas describes was never open to all, but was very much restricted to the educated and propertied elites. It was also a male preserve. Moreover, Habermas neglects the role of popular social movements, which were often at odds with the public sphere, and ignores the commercial character of the early press.

Although this may be a very forceful line of criticism, it would in any case make little sense to model a modern public sphere on one of a bygone age. New communication technologies such as the internet, together with some of the developments that have transformed modern societies, make it almost impossible to establish a specific historical interpretation of a public sphere as a collective goal.

However, while it is significant, Thompson's critique does not necessarily refute Habermas's conceptual understanding of a public sphere entirely. Habermas's concept can still serve as a theoretical pointer towards what it might mean to affirm and implement a critical principle within mediated publicness. Moreover, given that the internet creates new opportunities for 'dialogic spaces', we might need to consider how to implement such a critical principle which, as Ronald Dworkin explains, gives direction to human activity but does not necessitate a particular outcome.[56]

The recipients of media products are not passive consumers   Thompson criticizes Habermas's idea of the 'refeudalization' of the public sphere in that it treats the recipients of media products as passive consumers. Thompson writes: 'Assumptions of this kind have to be replaced by a more contextualized and hermeneutically sensitive account of the ways in which individuals receive media products, use them and incorporate them into their lives.'[57]

Such criticism must not, however, detract from Habermas's more general point that we must be aware of certain important issues. One is the commercialization of the media, which can distort mediated publicness. Another is the fragmentation of mediated experience, which might hamper the formation of effective oppositional movements. The internet opens up unprecedented opportunities for participatory opinion formation, making it even more urgent for us to explore how individuals and collectivities might actively participate in critical discussion and debate, and how this participation may be liable to be thwarted.

The traditional model of publicness is no longer adequate The last of Thompson's criticisms which I shall discuss here is directed at the traditional model of publicness employed in Habermas's account. Thompson asserts that it no longer provides an adequate way of thinking about public life today because new forms of mediated publicness, facilitated by the mass media, are mostly non-dialogical in character.[58] This means that information is predominantly channelled one way, from the producer of information to the receiver.

The interactive qualities of the internet, however, create new possibilities for participatory opinion formation. Unlike the mass media, the internet cannot so easily be dismissed as being non-dialogical. I shall now pursue this matter further by exploring the various types of interactional situations which the internet gives rise to. A full discussion of the distinctive type of publicness created by the internet must wait until chapter 7 where I shall also examine the critical literature dealing with Habermas's conception of discourse ethics.

Types of interactional situation

In order to draw out some of the implications of conceptualizing the internet as a modality of cultural transmission we need to study the various kinds of interactional situation the internet gives rise to. What are the various options that exist for social interaction? Thompson distinguishes three *types of interaction* and I shall relate all three of these to the internet. I shall also use the concept of *arenas of circulation* in order to grasp the regionalization which occurs in what Thompson calls the circulation and mediation of information and other symbolic content. Drawing on Pierre Bourdieu's work, I shall also introduce the concept of *repertoires of possibilities.*[59] This describes the extent to which individuals and collectivities can draw on various kinds of rules and resources to organize and sustain the circulation of information.

Types of interaction   The three types of interaction distinguished by Thompson are (1) 'face-to-face interaction', (2) 'mediated interaction', and (3) 'mediated quasi-interaction'.[60] The internet gives rise to all three of these interactional situations and changes their interactional and organizational characteristics.

Face-to-face interaction, Thompson argues, involves individuals who are co-present and who thus share a time-space reference system. Participants have a multiplicity of symbolic cues available to them and communication is mostly oriented towards specific others. Participants can be both receivers and producers of information, and encounters are dialogical in character. However, if, like Sherry Turkle, we focus our attention on 'living in the MUD' or 'life on the screen', then we miss out on the intricate ways in which internet use interlaces with face-to-face discourse. For example, two individuals may be having a discussion in a room while at the same time taking turns to type messages to a distant friend on IRC. Similarly, members of a project team responsible for building a website might e-mail each other and arrange to meet face to face to discuss the project's progress.

Mediated interaction, Thompson argues, involves the separation of the contexts of the production and the reception of symbolic goods. Conventional mediated interaction, such as writing letters and using the telephone, has predominantly involved individuals orienting themselves towards specific others. The actions and utterances of participants are essentially dialogical in that they give rise to forms of responsive action. Mediated interaction deprives participants of a range of symbolic cues normally available to them when they meet face to face. The narrowing of symbolic cues gives rise to all sorts of problems involving, for example, the opening and closing of encounters, the taking of turns to communicate, etc. The successful accomplishment of mediated interaction often depends on the degree of knowledge participants already have of each other.

The internet clearly contributes to the repertoire of possibilities for the two-way flow of actions and utterances in the form of e-mail, internet phone calls and chat options between individuals privately. However, besides one-to-one encounters, the internet creates a range of public, many-to-many dialogical domains – for example, IRC channels – where individuals can orientate their actions towards many others and enter into reciprocal relationships with them. Such forums constitute structured situations in which large numbers of individuals can produce symbolic forms for others who are not physically present, while, at the same time, no individual is receiving symbolic forms produced by others to whom they cannot respond. Although telephone chat systems have already demonstrated the need for such forums in modern societies, the scale and the possibilities opened by the internet are unprecedented.

Mediated quasi-interaction differs from mediated interaction, as Thompson explains, in that it involves communication oriented towards an indefinite range of potential recipients and is generally monological. It refers, for example, to the social relations established by the media of mass communication, such as books, newspapers, radio and television. Webpages probably create the nearest match to this kind of communication, yet even here, individuals and collectivities can respond by creating their own pages. Moreover the internet, more than any other medium, opens up opportunities to mix different forms of interaction. Webpages may take on a hybrid character involving both mediated interaction and mediated quasi-interaction. The combining of sound, video and text also opens opportunities for producing and receiving a wider range of symbolic cues. Web TV and radio also involve mediated quasi-interaction, although, as I explained earlier, some webpages allow users to watch web TV communally and so to engage in mediated interaction with one another.

Arenas of circulation   On a logical level, the concept of arenas of circulation enables us spatially and temporally to separate out the different areas of interaction which are involved in internet use. An arena of circulation of information and other symbolic content can be mapped out in space as an arena of 'position-takings' and in time as a 'set of trajectories' which individuals follow during the course of their day-to-day lives.[61] Although it is important to separate them out conceptually, arenas of circulation will always intersect with an actual constitution of social practices which cannot be reduced to such clear cut time-space patterns.

In many respects, this approach to the 'spacing' of encounters echoes the ideas present in the work of Torsten Hägerstrand.[62] A simple example can be given. Two individuals living in different parts of the city agree to meet in a coffee shop downtown. Their time-space paths meet while they chat and drink coffee, after which they part and diverge again. In this way we can construct a narrative of their biographies through time-space and even collate bundles of paths of many individuals to compose a map of human association. Hägerstrand's time-space geography, however, is mainly concerned with the physical movement of individuals through time-space and their association in conditions of co-presence. The trajectories of individuals, Hägerstrand writes, 'have to accommodate themselves under the pressures and the opportunities which follow from their common existence in terrestrial space and time'.[63] However, his framework can also be used to consider the paths which individuals take through extended time-space.

The use of internet technology gives rise to a series of articulated arenas of circulation in Thompson's orginal analysis of mass communication and we need to relate these now to internet use.[64] First, there are the arenas of circulation involving primary regions of internet use, for instance the structured contexts of mediated interaction and mediated quasi-interaction between internet users situated in separate locales. This primary arena of circulation concerns all the action and interaction online. Second, there are the arenas of circulation involving the secondary region of internet use, such as the structured contexts of face-to-face interaction between internet users sharing the same locale. Third, there are the arenas of circulation involving the peripheral regions of internet use, for example the structured contexts of face-to-face interaction between internet users and non-internet users. All of these regions can be further differentiated along the lines of internet, intranet or extranet use.

Distinguishing arenas of circulation allows us to study the state of their boundaries as time-space edges.[65] It is helpful here to follow Thompson again in recognizing three sets of interlocking time-space coordinates. First, there are the time-space coordinates of the context within which individuals act as producers of information. Second, there are the time-space coordinates involved in the transmission of information and other symbolic products. Third, there are the time-space coordinates of the context within which individuals act as recipients of information. Time-space edges of arenas of circulation cross these coordinates and are often disputed frontiers. Each of these frontiers is a stake of long-lasting or temporary struggle and concerns issues of inclusion and exclusion.[66] Firewalls erected to shield intranets from the outside world are clear-cut examples of time-space edges in internet use. The configuration of arenas of circulation is a manifestation of the institutional arrangements involving the 'channels of selective diffusion' and 'mechanisms for the restricted implementation', both concepts which I elaborated earlier in this chapter.

Repertoires of possibilities   Pierre Bourdieu's concept of 'repertoires' describes the plane of possible strategic position-takings within arenas of circulation. This is dependent on the rules that individuals and collectivities are able to rely on and the resources they are able to muster in respect of their communicative interests. Intranets often involve users endowed with varying degrees of authority. Some users, for example, may view only enterprise-wide webpages while others may establish external connections with the world wide web. There are also intranets which allow users to send e-mail to others individually but not to entire groups. Individuals can also take up different positions in several arenas of circulation. In some households, for example, parents only allow their children to access the internet from home a couple of hours a week, whereas at school other rules may prevail. Parents may also install filtering and information blocking systems which prevent certain websites from being accessed, drastically reducing the repertoires of those affected.

Social organization and the internet

In this chapter I have attempted to explore what it means to use arguments, concepts and ideas developed by Thompson to approach the internet as a modality of cultural transmission. In conclusion, I would like to recapitulate some of the basic ideas contained in the preceding sections by illustrating them in a series of figures based on those Thompson created for the analysis of mass communication. These figures map out the social organization of various forms of interaction and expose how the interactional features established by means of the internet are making a difference. It is not my intention, however, to suggest that the operation of the various arenas of circulation can be reduced to such diagrams, but rather to draw attention to the situatedness of internet use and to demonstrate that the consequences of internet use cannot be gleaned primarily from what goes on online. All of these figures are relatively abstract and do not attempt to capture the detail of exposition set out in this chapter. An analysis of the internet may, for example, call for the unpacking of the primary arena of circulation in recognition of a more detailed regionalization of the time-space coordinates involved in the transmission of information and other symbolic products. Moreover, in the third step towards the central aim of this book I shall elaborate in depth the operation of the various arenas of circulation attended to here.

Figures 3.1, 3.2 and 3.3 summarize and illustrate the social organization of face-to-face interaction, mediated interaction and mediated quasi-interaction and are based on Thompson's work *The Media and Modernity*.[67] Figure 3.4 is my extension of Thompson's work in order to visualize the social organization of interaction facilitated by the internet.

Let me explain how these figures can be read. Figure 3.1 shows that face-to-face interaction takes place between individuals who share a common communication arena. Figure 3.2 sketches the situation which occurs when individuals in distant locations communicate using, for example, a telephone or some form of written communication. Figure 3.3 maps out the situation involving mass communication. The fundamental break between producers and receivers is clearly visible and information travels predominantly one way. Information here is not directed at specific others but rather towards an indefinite range of recipients.

Figure 3.4 describes the social organization of mediated symbolic exchanges using the internet. The internet involves users in both interactive frameworks of production and in interactive frameworks of reception.

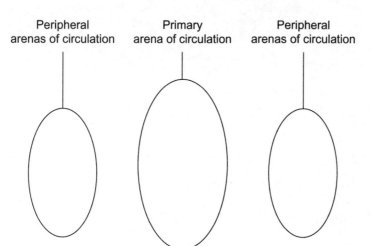

Figure 3.1   The social organization of face-to-face interaction

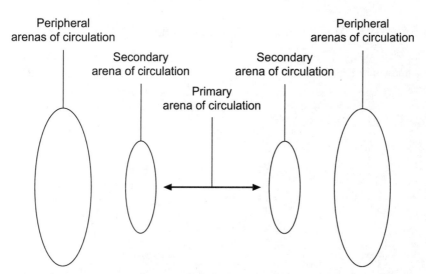

Figure 3.2   The social organization of technically mediated interaction

When they produce information they can make it available for specific others, or make it generally available for an indefinite range of recipients. An example of information made available for specific others is an e-mail message sent to a friend or colleague. An example of information made generally available for an indefinite range of recipients is a homepage published on the world wide web. The transmission of information is

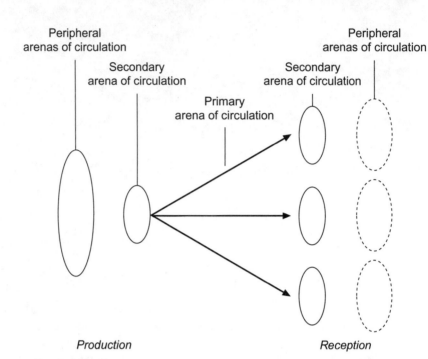

Peripheral
arenas of circulation

Secondary
arena of circulation

Primary
arena of circulation

Secondary
arena of circulation

Peripheral
arenas of circulation

Production

Reception

Figure 3.3   The social organization of mediated quasi-interaction

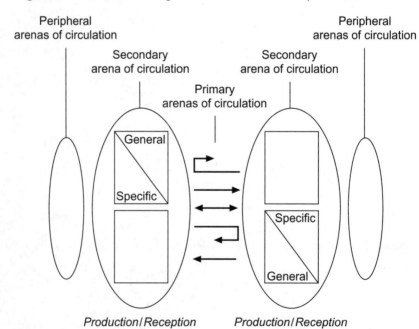

Peripheral
arenas of circulation

Secondary
arena of circulation

Primary
arenas of circulation

Secondary
arena of circulation

Peripheral
arenas of circulation

General

Specific

Specific

General

Production/Reception

Production/Reception

Figure 3.4   The social organization of mediated symbolic
exchanges using the internet

represented by a series of arrows. The process of information transmission may be a direct result of an initiative undertaken by the producer, for example, when they send an e-mail message. This is represented by the straight arrow. However, the process of information transmission may also be a direct result of an initiative undertaken by the recipient themselves, for example when a user downloads and retrieves information from a website. This form of transmission is represented by the 'return' arrow. Moreover, participants can be both producers and recipients at once. This is represented by the straight arrow pointing in both directions. This occurs, for example when participants are engaged in chat using IRC. The characteristics of the internet facilitate a disembedded arena of circulation which makes possible new forms of human association and social organization. It also opens up new opportunities for individuals to participate in social life. However, as I have demonstrated in this chapter, this disembedded arena of circulation can best be understood as a result of the tensionful pushing and pulling of real people often situated in very different technical and social conditions.

The internet: transforming the way we create and communicate

Social theory has no rationale if it does not somehow generate concepts which can be placed in the service of empirical work. In the final section of this chapter my aim is to begin to demonstrate some of the practical consequences of the theoretical framework I propose. I shall do so by considering Johnson's analysis of what he calls *interface culture*. As I explained in chapter 2, interfaces play a pivotal role in internet use.

Interface culture

The central theme of Johnson's book *Interface Culture* is 'the fusion of art and technology' within what he refers to as interface design.[68] An interface, he claims, is the 'software that shapes the interaction between user and computer' (p. 14). It is the way in which the computer 'represents itself to the user; in a language that the user understands'. The digital language of zeros and ones, he writes, 'unintelligible to most humans – is replaced by a metaphor' (p. 15). He gives an example of a virtual folder residing on a virtual desktop. In his definition of interfaces he includes both software such as web browsers and e-mail programmes, but also digital environments such as town squares, shopping malls, offices and living rooms which we connect to by using such software (p. 18). For Johnson, interfaces are 'laboring away in that strange new zone between medium and message' (p. 41).

Johnson regards the interfaces we use on computers as fundamental to the way in which we make sense of our modern information environments. Interfaces do not just frame online interaction – they are, he argues, central components of it (p. 73). He explains:

> The Victorians had writers like Dickens to ease them through the technological revolutions of the industrial age, writers who built novelistic maps of the threatening new territory and the social relations it produced. Our guides to the virtual cities of the twenty-first century will perform a comparable service, only this time the interface – and not the novel – will be their medium. (pp. 19–20)

In *Interface Culture*, Johnson elects to focus on five interrelated components of modern interfaces: (1) 'the desktop', (2) 'windows', (3) 'links', (4) 'text', and (5) 'agents'. Let us briefly consider his treatment of each of these components in turn.

The desktop When interface designers first started work, Johnson claims, they were confronted by a 'tabula rasa, an empty space waiting to be filled . . . You could build anything you wanted in that new information space . . . Our own lives now revolve around a more prosaic text: the computer desktop. Understanding the implications of that metaphor – its genius and its limitations – is the key to understanding the contemporary interface' (pp. 44–5).

Windows Johnson describes the 'window' as the shorthand for a range of innovations that constitute the modern interface. In essence, he claims, the layout of window-driven interfaces is fluid. He writes: 'You can drag them across your screen, resize them with a single mouse click. They're designed to be malleable, open-ended' (p. 77).

Links Whereas the window in Johnson's terms allowed us to flexibly frame information, 'the hyperlink lets us stitch that world together into a more coherent shape' (p. 105). He continues: 'the link should usually be understood as a synthetic device' (p. 111). Yet, he goes on to warn, 'until users can create their own threads of association, there will be few genuine trailblazers on the net' (p. 123).

Text The desktop, the window and the link have not, Johnson argues, undermined the significance of text in the future of interface design. He celebrates a possible paradigm shift: instead of desktops being organized around virtual spaces they would be organized around meaning and language (p. 169). For example, information would not simply be contained in a virtual folder and in one particular location on a desktop. It would be organized according to semantic relationships based on attributes such as the key words contained in it.

Agents The last component of modern interface culture that Johnson discusses are what he calls 'intelligent-agents'. These are automated devices that help interface users to complete tasks and achieve goals. A wide variety of such 'agents' are now built into interfaces. 'Agents', for example, may be built into web browsers to assist parents in blocking access to websites they do not want their children to visit. Other examples of agents include devices embedded in e-mail software to assist users in sorting out wanted from unwanted messages they receive.

Problems and a new way forward

Johnson's contribution to the analysis of interface culture provides some valuable insights. First, he attempts to fuse the world of technology and culture. Second, he attempts to recognize the interface medium as a means of cultural transmission. Third, he attempts to relate interface design to risk and uncertainty in our modern information environments. Yet his work also reflects and shares some of the major weaknesses in the current understanding of the interactional impact of the internet. Let us now look constructively at some of these weaknesses.

Writing about the creation of computers as if they might somehow, with the right kind of attention, become *machines worth living in* is not a good basis for contemplating the criteria by which interfaces should be judged.[69] While Johnson recognizes risks and uncertainty in modern information environments, he defines them almost solely in terms which are internal to interface design itself. He is concerned more about how the design of an interface might allow us to misplace our virtual 'trash can' than about how an interface might help us to relate mediated experiences to the practical contexts of our day-to-day lives.[70] By holding out the possibility of *machines we might live in*, Johnson largely ignores the social contexts within which, and by virtue of which, interfaces are designed, made and used. In any case, given further thought, such a stance is rather odd. No matter how realistic and engaging a film or a television programme might appear to be, we would not easily want to admit that we wish to 'live' in them. The mouse, as Johnson claims, may well allow 'the user to enter that world and truly manipulate things inside it', but surely that does not support a case for denying the situatedness of the user's actions.

Those designing interfaces or building webpages are never, as Johnson suggests, confronted by a 'tabula rasa' or 'an empty space waiting to be filled'. Their activities are both enabled and constrained by the social structures on which their creativity rests and by the social processes of which their creativity is the outcome. They never have a free hand. I would argue, for example, that when individuals create a website they bring to the situation a legacy of deeply ingrained assumptions about the proper use of communication media which they are usually very reluctant to abandon. This would explain the large number of websites that have the appearance of 'printed' brochures, their creators as yet unaware of the new options and burdens this new technology brings.

Those using interfaces are also by no means always able to do so at their own leisure, making windows 'bigger or smaller, pushing them off to the peripheries of the desktop or bringing them into focus'.[71] Their use of interfaces links together with their repertoires of possibilities. This means that unequal resources, differential interpretations and particular normative expectations are relevant to the processes of interchange between individuals and interfaces. Access to many interfaces used on the internet, for example, is often only possible if the user has acquired a serial number which is only obtainable legitimately after the payment of a fee. The use of some interfaces is free of charge yet they display windows containing commercial messages which the user cannot close. Other interfaces may be used for a trial period after which a window opens with a message nagging individuals to register as a legitimate user if they are to enjoy the continued use of the product. The scope for interface use is very much dependent on the status and authority of the user and the kind of power they can bring to bear.

Moreover, Johnson describes the links on commercial websites that point to the websites of other companies as 'a particularly mindless use of hypertext'.[72] Of course we may resent particular uses of the internet, but commercial activity constitutes a major part of interface culture. When such websites are understood as embedded in the structured social relations and contexts within which they are created, the links they display may no longer seem so mindless after all. They may, for example, be traces of real economic and political relationships on which the future of the organizations they link depends.

Understanding the semantic organization of an interface is of great significance. Yet the creation of interface culture cannot be reduced to linguistic practices in which most people, give or take minor variations, are deemed to share the same rules and resources. Given the structural inequalities of the contexts within which interfaces are created and deployed, it is rather offensive to suggest that the management of information may simply evolve around textual associations that can be made at will. The involvement of individuals with interfaces brings in not just linguistic practices but the practical realization of interests. The management of information in interface culture expresses particular asymmetries of power.

The trappings of intelligent agents, for example those designed to block young individuals accessing potentially harmful material, also cannot be understood in a vacuum. They must be related to the normative properties of the contexts within which their design and their use is embedded.

All these examples demonstrate how Johnson's analysis of interface culture neglects crucial aspects of the social contexts within which, and by virtue of which, information and other symbolic content is produced and received. Such an analysis of interface culture hampers hopes of developing an active engagment with the new options and new burdens created by networked interaction. His analysis does not allow him to attend to many of the matters that concern real people and real organizations in late modernity. Even if we could agree with Johnson that it is a desirable aim that individuals should be able to 'create their own threads of association' – we are left asking how such an aim might be achieved given the premises of his analysis.

My aim in this chapter has been to deal with some of the major weaknesses in the current understanding of the interactional impact of the internet. I have drawn heavily on Thompson's major effort to construct arguments, concepts and ideas in order to help us understand the changes taking place in our mediated world. I believe that such an approach will allow us to understand better the new options and new burdens the internet creates but also how we might use the internet in an active way to deal with some of the profound social challenges we face. However, although internet use had already gained considerable momentum by 1995, Thompson's *Media and Modernity* makes no mention of the internet or of the developments I described in chapter 2. Moreover, as Thompson writes: 'Some readers may find it surprising that in a book concerned with social theory and the media I draw so little on the literature generally referred to . . . with the labels "post-structuralism" and "postmodernism".'[73] Thompson's dissatisfaction with this body of ideas, however, is not sufficient reason to largely ignore this literature in studying the media. In particular, understanding of the interactional impact of the internet urgently calls for a direct confrontation with the ideas and arguments of postmodernism.

4

The internet and forms
of human association

The internet is enabling the emergence of new mechanisms of human association which are shaped by – yet also shape – the development of this new medium of communication. My starting point in this chapter is the view that, in late modernity, we are increasingly engaged in forms of social interaction which are becoming intensely reflexive and open-ended. In this respect, technologies such as the internet are serving to increase the capacity for both reciprocal and non-reciprocal communication. These new conditions challenge individuals and organizations to seek out new possibilities for reciprocal bonding and collaboration, and to create opportunities which were previously only associated with the sharing of a common locale. Taking up these challenges, however, raises issues of a complicated kind which are part and parcel of our attempts to generate active trust and integrity in social relationships in which knowledge is increasingly uncertain, and in which clear-cut answers to problems are increasingly absent. A proper understanding of these processes will afford us with an essential grounding in our attempts at developing new ways of coping with risk and uncertainty.

Although I shall be arguing in favour of a very different interpretation of the issue, the use of the internet to facilitate gatherings in virtual meeting places has already generated a considerable amount of interest. Howard Rheingold's work, for example, is often mentioned in this context. He argues that when 'enough people' carry on these relationships in virtual reality with 'sufficient feeling', and for a 'long enough' period of time, 'virtual communities' emerge which are only accessible via a computer screen.[1] He describes these communities, in a somewhat traditional fashion, as self-defined networks of interactive communication organized around particular interests or purposes.

> People in virtual communities use words on screens to exchange pleasantries and argue, engage in intellectual discourse, conduct commerce, exchange knowledge, share emotional support, make plans, brainstorm, gossip, feud, fall in love, find friends and lose them, play games, flirt, create a little high art and a lot of idle talk.

People in virtual communities, Rheingold writes, 'do just about everything people do in real life'.[2]

Available studies of online community often have lofty goals and a sense of urgency about them. Rheingold, for example, hopes to 'inform a wider population about the potential importance of cyberspace to political liberties and the ways virtual communities are likely to change our experience of the real world as individuals and communities'.[3] The problem, however, with most of these studies is that they elaborate the impact of the internet on forms of human association and conduct within strictly limited terms. They do not develop a critical approach to the concept of 'community' in late modernity. As such, they fail to grasp the broader implications of the internet for human association and conduct, beyond that of narrowly conceived online interaction. They often think of participants in these online communities as 'leaving their bodies behind' and 'migrating to virtual communities' where they are deemed to spin 'webs of personal relationships in cyberspace'.[4]

By contrast, we need to start working out the implications of Mark Poster's claim that

> the internet and virtual reality open the possibility of new kinds of interactivity such that the idea of an opposition of real and unreal community is not adequate to specify the differences between modes of bonding, serving instead to obscure the manner of the historical construction of forms of community.[5]

In this respect, Rheingold's own observations concerning his personal experiences of virtual communities are very much at odds with the way he himself approaches them. He explains, for example, that his 'invisible friends sometimes show up in the flesh, materializing from the next block or other side of the planet'.[6] From this vantage point, he cannot get close enough to the significance of such face-to-face confrontations and the situated character of everyday life. He writes:

> I remember the first time I walked into a room full of people IRL ('in real life') who knew many intimate details of my history and whose stories I knew very well. . . . I looked around the room full of strangers when I walked in. It was one of the strangest sensations of my life. . . . There wasn't a recognizable face in the house. I had never seen them before.[7]

We must resist any temptation to follow Rheingold in laughing off such situations as merely involving the clumsiness of a first acquaintance. We must instead take a more positive approach and examine how the internet is contributing to the construction of forms of solidarity and association in which the most intimate and the most distant have become directly connected. We must ask why we are increasingly prepared to subject ourselves to these mixed feelings of intimacy and estrangement in our day-to-day lives. What is it about our modern condition that motivates so many millions of individuals and organizations to participate in forming new forms of social relationship via the internet or intranets? Will the rise of 'virtual' communities mean that 'real' communities are on their way out, or will 'real' communities be transformed and endowed with a new lease of life? How can we relate the reported mediated experiences within online communities to the practical contexts of our day-to-day lives? If we do not begin to sort out issues like these, then we cannot hope to understand how nation-states might, for example, use the internet to tackle problems of governability by fostering new forms of solidarity and identity. Nor will we be able to understand how organizations might use intranets or extranets to promote team work, intrafirm networking and knowledge sharing. Nor will we be in a position to properly comprehend the ways in which individuals might use the internet or intranets in their day-to-day communication to forge new kinds of commitment and mutuality. Moreover, we may not be fully aware of the dangers these new situations might hold and the unintended consequences which might flow from them.

Towards a new sense of community?

The concept of 'community' is a particularly elusive one. It might be used to refer to the communal life of a sixteenth-century village – or to a team of individuals within a modern organization who rarely meet face to face but who are successfully engaged in online collaborative work. In this section, I shall start by examining two usages of the concept of 'community' in the light of the complexity of both the reality and the idea. Both usages still occupy a central place in social and political thought today. Second, I shall discuss in what sense these usages are being eclipsed by new forms of human association, and consider critically the appropriateness of the concept of 'community' as a way of describing them. I shall end this section by highlighting some of the key difficulties that those wishing to establish new forms of communal solidarity might encounter.

Real and imagined communities

The importance of the idea of community in modern social life is often demonstrated by referring to the idea of 'nation-ness'. It is often perceived of as a phenomenon which has achieved the most profound emotional legitimacy in our time.[8] The nation, Mark Poster explains, is 'generally regarded as the strongest group identification in the modern period and thus perhaps the most "real" community of this era'.[9] Consequently, the modern nightmare, in Manning Nash's words, 'is to be deracinated, to be without papers, alone, alienated, and adrift in a world of organized others'.[10] Yet although a nation may be a 'real' community, territorially or by way of its symbols – and most certainly so for those who are excluded from it – it differs greatly from the *Gemeinschaft* of Ferdinand Tönnies. Tönnies formulated this ideal-type to describe cosy realities, where social relationships are based on locality and neighbourliness, fellowship, a sharing of responsibilities, and a furtherance of mutual good through understanding and the exercise of natural sentiment.[11] Viewed from this end of the continuum of social organizations, nations are best defined as what Benedict Anderson calls 'imagined communities'.[12]

Now, we might argue that there is a fundamental sense in which all communities are imagined, given that their very production and reproduction always presumes the employment of a range of symbolic devices. But in modernity, for nation-states and other forms of modern organization, this is brought to a more intense pitch by the mobilization of power through the storage and control of information and other symbolic content. Tönnies-type communities linger 'effortlessly, as if merely by dint of physical proximity and absence of movement'. As for communities that are imagined, 'belief in their presence is their only brick and mortar.'[13] Anderson sets out four senses in which modern communities can be described as being 'imagined'. First, members of an imagined community will never know most of their fellow members and will never meet, 'yet in the minds of each lives the image of their communion.' Second, they are imagined as limited in that even the largest of communities is finite and has boundaries beyond which lie other communities. Third, these communities are imagined to be sovereign and their members dream of being free from the interference of outsiders. Finally, these communities are imagined because, regardless of the inequality and exploitation that might prevail among their members, they are always conceived of as exhibiting 'a deep, horizontal comradeship'.[14]

Communication media facilitate the representation of this constructed 'reality' by making possible the transmission of shared histories of common 'hows' and shared landscapes of common 'essences'. But also by the sequestration and symbolic expulsion from the imagined community of anything which might intrude.[15] This whole process has, of course, important ideological implications, as Jean-Luc Nancy argues: 'the thinking of community as essence . . . is in effect the closure of the political.'[16] In this respect, there are a number of strategies that have gone a long way towards pacifying conflict over the outcome of political and economic decisions. These have greatly contributed to stability in the production and reproduction of imagined communities over time-space. One way in which modern communities have generated a cloak of permanence is by reflexively organizing the horizons of possible activity, for example by inventing a variety of traditions and modern rituals, or by drawing up rules of conduct. A second way involves the defining of issues that may count as being political and, therefore, open to intervention and critique. A third way involves the process of defining generally accepted standards and practices which, if pursued, will make the community better off as a whole.[17] Mostly these strategies went undiscussed, or were pushed through by ritual assertion, or by the enactment of centralized control. They result in forms of human association constituted by *modes of relationship* which Michael Oakeshott characterizes as 'organic, evolutionary, teleological, functional or syndromic'.[18] Under such circumstances, when individuals are confronted with forms of association with two or more discrepant purposes, they have a limited range of options open to them. Either discrepant purposes have to be suppressed, or they have to be 'related to one another systematically or in terms of means to end'.[19] Although these kinds of association do not exist in these strict terms, they are what Oakeshott refers to as 'compulsory associations', 'because the relationships they constitute are those recognized by the authority of common purposes and in terms of the authority of managerial decisions which specify how the common purpose should contingently be pursued'.[20]

These pacifying strategies are quite successful where, as Giddens writes, 'people have relatively stable preferences and where their level of reflexive involvement with wider social and economic processes is relatively low'.[21] Today, however, the success of these strategies is severely hampered by the conditions of late modernity. In culturally cosmopolitan societies, for example, the representations of 'nation-ness' are no longer taken as given and acted upon as a matter of course. We only need to think of the various crises which have confronted the Balkan states. But in modern commercial enterprises as well, such conditions are both demanding, and leading to, greater autonomy of action. This is a process which increasingly involves companies having to reinvent themselves in an attempt to gain competitive advantage by allowing their employees to team up non-hierarchically as 'clever people', empowered to take decisions themselves on the basis of their knowledge and skills.[22] Organic, evolutionary, teleological, functional modes of relationship would stifle much of the cutting-edge creativity needed for such a process.

The revival of community in late modernity

In late modernity, the fear of social disintegration as an unintended consequence of the levelling of hierarchies and the demise of 'official approving agencies' is resulting in a renewed interest in community. It is in this context that Habermas draws our attention to the resurgence of communities which he sees as 'the revaluation of the particular, the natural, the provincial, of social spaces that are small enough to be familiar'.[23] Bauman also writes that 'community is now expected to bring the succour previously sought in . . . the legislative acts of the national state.'[24] He points to the new kind of togetherness brought about by so-called 'neo-tribes' that are 'conjured up with the intention of giving those choices that solidity the choosers sorely miss'.[25]

There is, however, a good deal of scepticism concerning the possibility of restoring the certainties traditionally associated with community in present-day social conditions. Giddens, for example, describes it as being an 'impractical dream',[26] and Bauman argues that the modern-day tribes 'share in the *inconsequentiality* of choices, and change little in the episodicity of the chooser's life'.[27] The communities of late modernity are, therefore, anything but cosy and natural. They are

> hard work and uphill struggle, a constantly receding horizon of the never-ending road . . . The foremost paradox of the frantic search for communal grounds of consensus is that it results in more dissipation and fragmentation, more heterogeneity . . . The only consensus likely to stand a chance of success is the acceptance of heterogeneity of dissensions.[28]

Community today, Bauman asserts, is

> thought of as the uncanny (and in the end incongruous and unviable) mixture of difference and company: as uniqueness that is not paid for with loneliness, as contingency with roots, as freedom with certainty; its image, its allurement are as incongruous as that world of universal ambivalence from which – one hopes – it would provide a shelter.[29]

This process of 'uncertainization' is one which is only bound to continue and intensify in late modernity.[30]

Given these observations we might begin to doubt the appropriateness of the concept of 'community' to describe the rise of new forms of human association in late modernity. There is an obvious tension arising from a general longing for community together with a gradual realization that we cannot go back to the certainties of social arrangements which no longer exist. Let us dwell on this problem for a while, for it would seem that there is a need to seek to understand the opportunities for new forms of association in somewhat different terms, and to rethink what we should expect from them.

At a first glance, it is not difficult to see why, as Castells sometimes suggests, new forms of human association seem to resemble the kind of fragmented 'tribal' societies of days gone by.[31] Yet such a similarity is more apparent than real. Premodern tribal culture may well have been highly fragmented and segmented, but it also displayed a high level of presence availability and it was confined in respect of its configuration across time and space.[32] Modern developments in communication media are creating new networks of information diffusion which are profoundly altering the way in which we can construct shared 'realities'. Any comparison between tribalism of the past and the practices of groups of individuals in the late modern age is at best only superficial and not really very useful.

Neither should we equate new forms of communal life like those described by Claude Fischer in our modern cities with those available in premodern settings.[33] Fischer demonstrates that the infrastructure of modern cities and modern communications provides the means for generating new forms of human association which were unavailable to individuals in premodern settings.[34]

Applying the concept of community to the creation of new forms of human association tends to narrow down the spatial and temporal coordinates of their creation in a way which is mostly irrelevant to modern social life. Instead, we ought to emphasize and examine the ubiquitous nature of the thrust towards new kinds of human association, occurring as it does at all levels of our organizational culture: from national and paranational communities to regional and local ones, from communities in economic organizations engaged in collaborative work to communities created by social movements and other groups. No matter how fragmented human experience has become, under reflexive modernization most of us live in the same 'discursive space'. Giddens writes that 'there has never been a time when information about current events and problems has been more publicly debated, in a chronic fashion, than in the present day.'[35] In this respect, the idea of a twenty-four-hour economy refers to the fact that those who can afford to participate in it now also live in the same 'discursive time'.

What we are coming to terms with today is that modern communication technologies such as the internet are opening up opportunities for new forms of human association. Today, the production and reproduction of social reality is becoming re-embedded in local communal life in ways which were largely unavailable in previous modern settings. The possibilities of virtual reality are boosting to the extreme the dynamism of modern everyday life by heightening the process which Giddens describes as tearing 'space away from place by fostering relations between "absent" others'; 'the severing of time from space', he continues, 'provides a basis for their recombination in relation to social activity . . . This phenomenon serves to open up manifold possibilities of change by breaking free from the restraints of local habits and practices.'[36] In late modernity, the settings for human association come and go at an unprecedented rate, and more often than not individuals participate in a multitude of them.

Such a view radically opposes Rheingold's interpretation of 'community', which he still regards as necessarily deeply sedimented in time. These new forms of human association demand the spontaneous coordination constituted by modes of relationship characterized by Oakeshott not as the 'organic, evolutionary, teleological, functional or syndromic relationship' associated with traditional communities, but as 'an understood relationship of intelligent agents'.[37] Being in an *intelligent relationship*, Giddens writes, 'means living along with others in a way that respects their autonomy'.[38] Consequently, individuals who are thus associated 'are not partners or colleagues in an enterprise with a common purpose to pursue or a common interest to promote or protect . . . They are related in terms of a practice.'[39] The efficiency of these new ways of teaming up can no longer be measured in terms of goals alone, but needs to be evaluated in terms of 'their capacity to share in a give and take experience'.[40]

Unlike traditional communities, these new forms of association embrace in Giddens's view 'cosmopolitanism, as an attitude of mind and as an institutionalized phenomenon'.[41] The cosmopolitan, Giddens argues, often misunderstood as an individualist and as an enemy of old-style communities, is 'someone who is able to articulate the nature of those commitments, and assess their implications for those whose values are different'. As such, a cosmopolitan attitude is not one in which anything goes, and thus is not a threat to communality and commitment. Nor is it an attitude which insists that all values are equivalent. It is an attitude which, according to Giddens, emphasizes 'the responsibility that individuals and groups have for the ideas they hold and the practices in which they engage'.[42]

There are those who claim that the beginnings of the new kinds of human association we are witnessing today signal our entry into a new age which they label as 'postmodernity'. However, as Thompson writes,

> if the debates sparked off by postmodernism have taught us anything, it is not that the developmental processes characteristic of modern societies have propelled us beyond modernity to some new and as yet undefined age, but rather that our traditional theoretical frameworks for understanding these processes are, in many respects, woefully inadequate.[43]

As we shall see later in this chapter, the discussion concerning 'virtual communities' is deeply steeped in postmodern rhetoric, thus making this a matter to which we shall need to return.

The problems of solidarity in late modernity

Group identity, Fredrik Barth writes, is always exclusionary in that the way forms of human association are perceived depends on the way their participants view outsiders.[44] Any attempt to create new forms of human association on more spontaneous and 'inclusive' grounds is therefore beset by a range of problems. Bauman rightly observes that 'in the world of imagined communities, the struggle for survival is a struggle for access to the human imagination.'[45] Besides a great many practical problems, mobilizing the opportunities offered by new technologies of communication will always involve interests which may be contested by others. Let us therefore look at some of the problems which Giddens claims might be encountered in a quest for establishing new forms of human conduct and solidarity in late modernity.[46]

First, the idea and reality of community has long been bound up with forms of centralized authority and claims to universal truths defended within hierarchically organized social settings. Now, in an era of intensified detraditionalization, neither states nor economic organizations have clear-cut ideas about how dynamic, high-paced, ephemeral forms of human association ought to be run, or about how the direction of their progress ought to be judged. For Jean-François Lyotard,

> the community required as a support for the validity of such judgement must always be in the process of doing and undoing itself. The kind of consensus implied by such a process, if there is any consensus at all, is in no way argumentative but is rather allusive and elusive, endowed with a spiral way of being alive, combining both life and death, always remaining *in statu nascendi* or *moriendi*, always keeping open the issue of whether or not it actually exists. This kind of consensus is definitely nothing but a cloud of community.'[47]

Thus in an age of detraditionalization we urgently need to address the renewal of tradition guided by tolerance and dialogue.

A second problem to be encountered in establishing new forms of human conduct, Giddens claims, is that the levelling up of hierarchies and of 'official approving agencies' could quite easily prove dangerous and result in 'tyranny' rather than in new forms of solidarity.[48] The prospects hailed by Rheingold and other writers of the anarchic characteristics of the internet might not turn out to be so exciting after all.[49] In most industrialized societies, the nation-state has achieved a very high level of consolidation and internal pacification, and hierarchical organizations have equally achieved high levels of administrative unity and control.[50] The opening up of all forms of authority to critical questioning results in yet more conflict and struggle. Giddens, in this respect, warns of the possible upsurge of fundamentalisms.[51] We might also fear the return of oppressive parochiality and other communal pressures as organizations increasingly involve the work of autonomous teams, empowered by new information technologies, striving to deliver projects and benefits at the expense of those preferred by others. Frustrations may run high as we begin to realize, as Bauman explains, that

> even with absolute truth defunct and universality dead and buried – some people at least can still have what their past (legislatively predisposed) benefactors, now decried as deceitful, promised to give: the joy of being 'in the right' – though now perhaps not at all times, not in all places at the same time, and only for certain people.[52]

The third problem in establishing new forms of human conduct, Giddens argues, is that the idea of democratization, and thereby the revitalization of community, is a problematic one.[53] Guaranteeing the rights of members of a community to free speech and free association, for example, has never led to the successful creation of community. Without some kind of balance between individual freedoms on the one hand and responsibilities for issues that go beyond individual needs on the other, any sense of community may soon evaporate, like Lyotard's cloud, in the heat of the moment.

The fourth problem recognized by Giddens is that while new technologies of communication may provide the means for creating new forms of action and interaction, they do not automatically result in understood relationships of intelligent agents.[54] We need, I think, to be strongly reminded of Thompson's critique of the notion of *participatory opinion formation*, a possibility that he believes to be far removed from the political reality and possibility of our time. He writes that 'at the level of national and international politics, and at the upper levels in which power is exercised in large-scale civil and commercial organizations, it is difficult to see how the idea of participatory opinion formation could be implemented in any significant way.'[55]

Despite these problems, new forms of human association remain of central importance because they constitute the spaces in which the processes of meaning generation and truth validation are set. As Bauman writes:

> Privatized existence has its many joys: freedom of choice, the opportunity to try many ways of life, the chance to make oneself to the measure of one's self-image. But it also has its sorrows as well: loneliness and incurable uncertainty as to the choices made and still to be made . . . This is why we all feel time and again an overwhelming 'need of belonging' – a need to identify ourselves not just as individual human beings, but as members of a larger entity.[56]

However sceptical we might be about the nature of and need for new forms of human association in late modernity, we need to develop an understanding of the kinds of threats and chances they may bring.

The virtualization of community

Over the past decade a large number of studies have attempted to illuminate the way in which the renewed quest for community interlaces with internet use. My discussion of these attempts will, necessarily, be selective, and will neglect many contributions that would warrant discussion in a more comprehensive survey. But I shall aim to identify some of the main lines of debate in order to engage with them critically and attempt to rebut some of the more extreme claims that they make. This will involve relating the insights gained in the first half of this chapter to the internet and drawing on the theoretical framework developed in chapter 3.

In this context, I shall focus particularly on the work of Elizabeth Reid, Howard Rheingold and Sherry Turkle. Their writings are often cited, giving them a considerable prominence in this area, and will suffice to give an idea of the main contours of the debate.

'Appearing to be whoever you wish'

In *Electropolis: Communication and Community on Internet Relay Chat*, Elizabeth Reid sets out to study the ways in which users of internet relay chat (IRC) utilize the medium to create and sustain online communities.[57] She argues that this process results in the emergence of new kinds of culture which, she says, must be understood in Geertz's sense as 'a set of control mechanisms'. She addresses this claim from two related perspectives, which she refers to as the *deconstruction of social boundaries* and the *construction of communities*. Her arguments are buttressed with extracts of dialogue taken from IRC log files. Let us take a look at each of these perspectives in turn.

The deconstruction of social boundaries   The deconstruction of social boundaries occurs on two levels in Reid's account. First, she claims, 'interaction on IRC is . . . carried out in the knowledge that users are on a rough equality – according to conventional economic measures – and members of similarly privileged social groups. This 'equality' is not intrinsic to IRC, but is a by-product of the social structures surrounding computer technology.' Second, she claims, 'the structure of IRC causes its users to deconstruct the conventional boundaries defining social interaction.'

It is this second level of deconstruction which commands most of Reid's attention. She argues that individuals using IRC are denied 'the more traditional methods of sustaining a community' on two counts. First, on IRC 'it is possible to appear to be, quite literally, whoever you wish.' Users, she explains, can experiment with crossing the boundaries of gender-specific social roles. They can also provide overly attractive descriptions of themselves to others online. According to Reid, the attitudes individual users take regarding these problems of anonymity range from full-blown hostility to viewing it as 'part of the game', and she illustrates this by the following extract:[58]

```
<saro> KAREN IS A BOY
<saro> KAREN IS A BOY
<saro> KAREN IS A BOY
<SmilyFace> aros: so?????????
<Karen> yes aros I heard you
<FuzzyB> Takes a relaxed place beside Karen offering her her favourite
    drink
```

Second, Reid claims, not only does IRC allow boundaries to be crossed, it 'encourages disinhibition', because it 'obscures the boundaries that would generally separate acceptable and unacceptable forms of behaviour ... Disinhibition and the lack of sanctions encouraging self-regulation lead to extremes of behaviour on IRC.' According to Reid, this can result in deep and highly emotional relationships between participants in virtual communities. She illustrates this phenomenon with the following extract:

```
<Lori> After just a few chats on irc, it became obvious to me that this was
    someone I could easily become good friends with him ...
<Lori> The more we talked, the more we discovered we had in common ...
<Lori> By this time, I knew I was starting to have 'more than just a friend'
    feelings about Daniel ...
<Lori> I told him that I was starting to get a crush on him ...
<Lori> Anyway, it's grown and grown over the months.
<Daniel> A few mishaps, but we've overcome them, to bounce back stronger
    than ever.
<Lori> And, as you know, we'll be getting together for 3 weeks at the end of
    November, to see if we're as wonderful as we think we are.
```

These obscured boundaries also encourage 'people to use IRC as a forum for airing their resentment of individuals or groups of individuals in a blatantly uninhibited manner'. Here, Reid provides an example of a channel takeover incident involving #GBLF, an IRC channel for 'gays, bi-sexuals, lesbians and friends', an incident which vividly displays a high level of intolerance on the part of one individual IRC user towards these groups.

The construction of communities   Having been forced by IRC to deconstruct the more traditional methods for sustaining community, Reid argues, 'users of IRC must develop alternative or parallel methods.' She refers to these measures collectively as their 'common culture' of 'shared significances' and 'social sanctions'. Examples of 'shared significances' include 'textual substitution for traditionally non-verbal information' which Reid illustrates by the following extract:

<Prince> Lioness: please don't eat him . . .
<storm> *shivers from the looks of lioness*

Reid claims that groups of people who fail to develop such measures fail to communicate and fail to compose a common culture.

According to Reid, 'social sanctions' on IRC are related to the 'expectation of personal integrity and sincerity . . . upheld by convention and enforced by structure'. She refers, for example, to the 'taboo' of using another user's nickname to interact with others and the power of operators to sanction unacceptable behaviour. She writes: 'the ideas of authority and freedom are often in opposition on IRC, as the newly invented social conventions of the IRC community attempt to deal with emotions and actions in ways that emulate the often violent social sanctions of the "real world".'

Reid concludes that the emergent culture of IRC is essentially heterogeneous given that it is 'not uncommon for IRC channels to contain no two people from the same country'. She juxtaposes two possible societal effects from the kinds of phenomena that she has described as happening on IRC. 'IRC users can share a sense of community and commonality, but they can also exhibit alienation and hostility. It is impossible to say which, if either, will prevail.' Nonetheless, she writes, 'players of the IRC game are involved in turning upside down the taken-for-granted norms of the external culture . . . it is this style of playful rebellion, irreverent subversion and juxtaposition of fantasy with high-tech reality that impels me to interpret IRC as a postmodernist culture.'

'Communities as microorganisms'

In *The Virtual Community: Homesteading on the Electronic Frontier*, Howard Rheingold sets out to support a 'human-centered vision' of the 'democratizing potential of virtual communities', which he sees as places 'to talk, gossip, argue, size up each other, find the weak spots in political ideas by debating them'.[59] He describes his work as 'a tour of widening circles of virtual communities', claiming that 'some knowledge of how people in a small virtual community behave will help prevent vertigo and

give you tools for comparison when we zoom out to the larger metropolitan areas of cyberspace' (p. 16).

Rheingold claims that studying virtual communities is like studying
the physiology and reproductive characteristics of an organism. He writes:

> in terms of the way the whole system is propagating and evolving, think of
> cyberspace as a social petri dish, the Net the agar medium, and virtual
> communities, in all their diversity, as colonies of microorganisms that grow
> in petri dishes. Each of the small colonies of microorganisms – the commun-
> ities on the Net – is a social experiment that nobody planned but that is
> happening nevertheless . . . Whenever CMC [computer mediated commun-
> ication] technology becomes available to people anywhere, they inevitably
> build virtual communities with it, just as microorganisms inevitably create
> colonies. (p. 6)

Individuals participating in such communities pursue 'collective goods'
which 'bind isolated individuals into a community' (p. 13). He writes of
'the need for rebuilding community in the face of America's loss of a
sense of a social commons' (p. 12).

Against this backdrop, Rheingold goes on to examine a variety of
different virtual communities as they exist today, for example Usenet,
MUDs, BBSs, mailing lists, e-journals and IRC, all as part of his endeavour to steer the internet towards some form of 'electronic agora'. Let us,
however, concentrate on his analysis of IRC in order later to be able to
tease out some similarities and differences compared to Reid's work.

Rheingold stresses the importance of analysing IRC used not just for
play but also for 'real work' by 'far-flung business groups, task forces of
technical experts, and scholars' (p. 177). Like Reid, he argues that

> IRC is what you get when you strip everything that normally allows people
> to understand the unspoken shared assumptions that surround and support
> their communications, and thus render invisible most of the web of socially
> mediated definitions that tells us what words and behaviors are supposed
> to mean in our societies . . . Words, and the elegance of expression and
> timing that accompany their use, exist in a purely disembodied state in
> IRC. (pp. 178–80)

The mastery of IRC, in Rheingold's words, 'requires creativity, quick
thinking, imagination, and either a literary sensibility or the style of a
stand-up comedian'. You know, he writes, when 'you've arrived in the
social hierarchy of an IRC channel when the regulars begin to greet
you heartily when you arrive . . . Personal attention is a currency in IRC:
everyone is on stage who wants to be, everyone is the audience, and
everyone is a critic' (p. 182).

Rheingold also points to the possibility of IRC fostering cross-cultural
understanding when, for example, people from various national and

political backgrounds meet online (p. 185). His interest here is in keeping with his wish that the internet be used to 'build stronger, more humane communities' (p. 300). He asks: 'Which scenario seems more conducive to democracy, which to totalitarian rule: a world in which a few people control communications technology that can be used to manipulate the beliefs of billions, or a world in which every citizen can broadcast to every other citizen?' (p. 14).

'Real life as just one more window'

In *Life on the Screen*, Sherry Turkle searches for community in cyberspace, echoing the type of interpretation offered in the other two accounts.[60] She argues that 'in the recent past, we left our communities to commute to . . . distant entertainments; increasingly, we want entertainment . . . that commutes right into our homes. In both cases, the neighborhood is bypassed' (p. 235).

Like Reid, Turkle argues that the internet and the way in which computers are used today embodies postmodern theory (p. 18). As such, Turkle explains, 'the meaning of the computer presence in people's lives is very different from what most expected in the late 1970s.' She continues, 'one way to describe what has happened . . . is to say that we are moving from a modernist culture of calculation toward a postmodernist culture of simulation' (p. 20). Consequently, 'there has been a shift away from the traditional modernist desire to see beneath the surface into the mechanics of the operating system. We are increasingly accustomed to navigating screen simulations' (pp. 41–2). Interaction, for example, takes place in 'boxed-off areas on the screen, commonly called windows. Windows provide a way for a computer to place you in several contexts at the same time . . . your identity on the computer is the sum of your distributed presence' (p. 13). Citing Doug, a MUD user whom she encountered during her research, she explains that 'experiences on the internet extend the metaphor of windows – now RL (Real Life) itself, as Doug said, can be "just one more window".' For Turkle, 'life on the screen' and life in 'reality' consists of parallel lives in which the self becomes 'a decentered self that exists in many worlds and plays many roles at the same time' (p. 14). Her interpretation of this fragmented experience explicitly suggests that 'the search for depth and mechanism is futile, and that it is more realistic to explore the world of shifting surfaces than to embark on a search for origins and structure' (p. 36).

It is against this general background that Turkle proposes that rather than viewing virtuality and real life as two competing areas of interaction, we should try and get the best of both. She argues that 'if the politics of virtuality means democracy online and apathy off-line, there is reason for concern' (p. 244). In making the virtual and the real more permeable to each other, she argues, 'we don't have to reject life on the screen, but we don't have to treat it as an alternative life either . . . Having literally written our online worlds into existence, we can use the communities we build inside our machines to improve the ones outside of them.'[61] The culture of simulation, she explains, 'may help us achieve a vision of a multiple but integrated identity whose flexibility, resilience, and capacity for joy comes from having access to our many selves'.[62]

For Turkle, virtuality is to be understood as a transitional space that can be put in the service of the embodied self. Ludwig Wittgenstein, she argues, 'takes up a similar idea in the *Tractatus*, when he compares his work to a ladder that has to be discarded after the reader has used it to reach a new level of understanding'.[63]

The problems of virtual community: an alternative view

The three accounts that I have just sketched have the considerable merit of highlighting the significance of the impact of the internet on forms of human association today. They have also helped to illuminate some of the internal structural features of online communication. Yet there are many difficulties with these accounts. Some of these have to do with socio-historical processes that have taken place over the past decade. First, the number of IRC users has greatly increased since Reid carried out her study in 1991, and so too has their social and economic diversity. Second, technological change is leading to anonymity becoming much less automatic and much more of a conscious choice on the part of the internet user. It is, therefore, regarded with more suspicion when users of IRC conceal their identity. Many individuals will now go to great lengths to display accountability as real people by exchanging e-mail and homepage addresses, and digitally scanned photographs of themselves. Third, users have also developed new social skills, for example, cross-referencing information before others are trusted. Moreover, as the number and diversity of virtual 'meeting places' increases, they acquire a greater degree of focus. Users are now more likely to know what kinds of individuals they will encounter when they visit them.

Rather than dwell on these socio-historical processes, however, in concluding this chapter I will seek to develop a constructive and systematic critique of these accounts of 'virtual community'. I shall try to show how, by approaching the internet as a modality of cultural transmission, we might open up the debate on this issue. Finally, I shall question the inevitability of our world moving towards a condition of postmodernity.

Limitations of accounts of 'virtual communities'

While the concept of 'community' is a central feature in each of the accounts of Reid, Rheingold and Turkle, none of them discusses it critically. As such, they do not attend to the dilemma which Bauman describes as being, 'as old as modernity itself': 'either "community" is a *result* of individual choices . . . or . . . "community" precedes all choice.'[64] In effect, each of the three accounts goes its own way in glossing over this problem.

Reid's approach tries to have it both ways. On the one hand, she claims that the individual can appear to be whoever they wish, while on the other, she draws on Geertz's idea that there exist plans, recipes, rules, instructions for the governing of behaviour. Rheingold makes a similar attempt. He starts off by claiming to develop a 'human-centered vision', yet then takes a rather different route, one tending to accord primacy to the social object which, like colonies of microorganisms growing in petri dishes, nobody has planned but happens nevertheless.

In stressing that virtuality and real life do not compete as areas of interaction, Turkle seems at first to take a very different stance. However, by conceptualizing these domains as parallel lives in which real life is just another window, she effectively joins Reid and Rheingold in extricating human interaction in 'virtual communities' from the contextuality of time-space. It is difficult to see how she might recover the permeability of these two separated domains. She moves even closer to according primacy to the social object when she claims that internet use allows for the decentring of the self that can exist in many worlds and play many roles at the same time. People appear to be able to do whatever they fancy and need not take anything anyone else does too seriously.

All three of these positions, in respect of Bauman's dilemma, are worrying. Although Reid discusses IRC use in the context of 'play', she sketches users as individuals who are permanently engaged in experiments with trust, as people named 'George' who go about calling themselves 'Alice'. If internet use really were like this, it would offer only a very limited range of opportunities for human association.

Rheingold's account evokes a spectre of individuals being propelled by uncontrollable needs comparable with those of biological organisms. He argues that America has lost a sense of a social commons and that, in the face of such a loss, 'virtual communities' just happen to come about to fulfil this need. In this fashion, internet users tend to appear as what Giddens describes 'as "cultural dopes", not as actors who are highly knowledgeable (discursively and tacitly) about the institutions they produce and reproduce in and through their actions'.[65] There is thus not much room for viewing their relationships as intelligent ones.

Turkle's account invokes the decentring of the subject. In doing so, she overexaggerates the hold which the internet has over the conduct of individual users. Like Rheingold, Turkle tends to treat life on the screen as determined by forces that operate exclusively behind the backs of those individuals involved. We may indeed experience our 'identity as a set of roles that can be mixed and matched, whose diverse demands need to be negotiated'.[66] But what powers of negotiation might a decentred subject have? All three of these accounts add, in their own way, to 'a state of mind marked above all by its all-deriding, all-eroding, all-dissolving destructiveness'.[67]

An important mainstay for all three of these approaches to 'virtual communities' is the way in which their authors consistently cordon off these forms of association from the real world. Rheingold refers to them as self-defined electronic networks. Reid regards them as an alternative virtual world where social boundaries have become deconstructed. Turkle sees them as occupying a space that we can only reach by a ladder which we must later discard. This, conveniently, leaves what goes on in 'virtual communities' open to a variety of different readings and interpretations.

There are, however, a number of instances in their writings which intrude on this 'land of lost content'. Take Reid's example of the incident involving the channel takeover of #GBLF. Why should we not take this example to show that individuals using the internet do not simply appear to be whoever they wish, but produce or enact particular social and historical ideas concerning what they have come to consider to be acceptable sexual norms? The fact that IRC might offer participants in #GBLF new ways of contesting such ideas, and that these ideas may change in the process, is another matter which remains ignored.

Rheingold writes: 'every cooperative group of people exists in the face of a competitive world because that group of people recognizes there is something valuable that they can gain only by banding together.' He speaks of following eyewitness reports from Moscow during the coup attempt against Gorbachev, and from China during the Tiananmen Square incident, and from Israel and Kuwait during the Gulf War.[68] Why should we not take this example to show that individuals using the internet do not band together because of some mysterious biological attraction but for reasons which pertain to their active involvement, the interlocking of different purposes or projects in the specific social and historical circumstances in which they find themselves?

Maybe Turkle is right when she applauds Fredric Jameson's characterization of the "depthlessness" of postmodern life, and in referring to a new nonchalance in social life such that 'the search for depth and mechanism is futile.' But then, how will we ever know whether we have attained what she calls 'the best of both virtuality and real life' and 'a vision of a multiple but integrated identity'?

Finally I want to dispute the notion of the internet as the embodiment of postmodern theory, the claim that so-called 'virtual communities' are the result of processes which are propelling us beyond modernity into what both Reid and Turkle refer to as *postmodernity*. Reid offers no further arguments as to why this should be so, other than suggesting that it is to do with what she refers to as the individual's 'style of playful rebellion, irreverent subversion and juxtaposition of fantasy with high-tech reality'. It is not clear why the development of an oppositional culture can be uniquely assigned to an era of postmodernism in this way. It would be more plausible to infer that the formation of oppositional cultures is a generic feature of modern everyday life, and then go on to examine how the internet is contributing to the intensification of opposition to relations of authority. In this way, 'playful rebellion' may, for example, be seen to result in only a partial penetration of the opportunities offered by the internet and, as a consequence, as unintendedly limiting the 'deconstruction of boundaries' which Reid is so eager to demonstrate.

Turkle is also vague in this respect. Her arguments as to why we are moving beyond modernity and into a different era are illustrated only by the changes she claims are taking place in the way we approach computers. In the 1970s, she argues, we approached computers as 'bare machines' which could be understood by discovering their constituent elements, for example, by removing their plastic covers. Today, she claims, we have moved from this modernist approach to a postmodernist approach where users stay at the surface level of representation, where all hint of the inner mechanisms of these machines is banished from view.

It might be helpful here to recall the characteristics of industrial design. Early designs of products often exhibited details which were later covered up. The first automobiles, for example, had exposed engines, levers, and spare wheels, but from the 1930s onwards they became increasingly hidden from view. The complexity of such aesthetics today is apparent in that it can become fashionable to reveal hidden features once again. The Beaubourg building in Paris, with services such as piping stuck to the outside, is an example of this.

It would be more plausible to relate this discussion to issues of deskilling and reskilling in our modern age. In 1979, Turkle was one of the happy few to have a computer. Today, many millions of people do so. I would argue that rather than being less aware of how these machines work, their owners now know, and have the potential to know, a great deal about them. People are more inclined to take their computers to bits than ever before, and they are often even encouraged to do so. As ready-assembled computers in shops or at home become rapidly outdated, these machines are increasingly put together on demand or upgraded by inserting new parts. People also regularly expand their computers themselves by adding on new devices, such as sound and video cards, in order to be able to do more with them. Rather than treating computer users as 'digitally challenged', assigning the control over their machines to the realm of 'men in white coats' who overwhelm them with technical jargon, we just need to use the right approach. Then we can go about getting the best out of this new mode of communication. This will involve getting to grips not only with the technology, but also with the intended and unintended consequences of institutional arrangements and the kinds of relationships that may result from them.

The beginnings of an alternative view

In referring to the *Tractatus*, Turkle ignores the contrast often made between this and Wittgenstein's later work. In *Philosophical Investigations*, Wittgenstein distances himself from his former views and argues that the meaning of social interaction is intrinsically involved with situated social practices.[69] I also want to re-establish this as a central feature in an alternative view of forms of human association created by the internet. For this purpose we need to combine, in a systematic way, a concern for virtual communities and a concern for the socially structured contexts and processes within which individuals constituting these social relationships are situated.

The framework for analysis set out in the previous chapter will help us not only make sense of the emergence of new mechanisms of human association shaped by the internet, but also of the profound processes of the reorganization of time-space involved as the internet prizes social relations free from the hold of specific locales. Moreover, a twin concern for virtual communities and their socially structured contexts will help us register and analyse internet use in terms of differentiated access to forms of self-actualization and empowerment. For while internet use may hold out the possibility of emancipation, we must at the same time be aware of how it might create new mechanisms of suppression. The internet may be a relatively open medium and, as Reid claims, allow for the deconstruction of existing technical and social boundaries, but I want to avoid perpetuating the notion that internet users can, as a general rule, 'appear to be whoever they wish'. Instead, I want to appreciate more fully the social and historical conditions involved in the production, circulation and reception of information and symbolic content. At the same time, though, I want to avoid swinging towards the position occupied by Rheingold and Turkle, where individuals are treated as 'cultural dopes' whose mediated exchanges are somehow no longer transparent to them.

I take the view that when individuals use the internet to establish and sustain communal relationships, they do so as intelligent agents. As such, they know a great deal about the properties of the technical medium and about the constraints and capabilities afforded by the institutional contexts in which they deploy it. Nevertheless, such knowledgeability is always bounded. First, a good deal of their knowledge is tacit and made out of experience. Second, they are neither fully aware of the social and historical conditions of the production, circulation and reception, nor ever fully aware of the consequences of their actions. As Giddens writes, 'every competent member of every society knows a great deal about the institutions of that society: such knowledge is not incidental to the operation of society, but is necessarily involved in it.'[70] An important motivation for recovering 'virtual communities' as situated practices is that we can begin to examine this complex area rather than merely collapsing its complexity.

In drawing on the framework and concepts developed in the previous chapter, I shall focus on #Gay.nl, the IRC channel I mentioned earlier, as this will help illustrate some of the points I make. It must be remembered, however, that #Gay.nl is an example of a publicly accessible IRC channel and differs somewhat from the kinds of 'discursive spaces' which might be found on private internets or intranets belonging to organizations. Although much of what I say here will still be relevant for private internets and intranets, I shall be discussing these kinds of enclosed systems of communication and other forms of human association, such as webpages and newsgroups, in the next chapter.

Any elaboration of the impact of the internet on forms of human association ought to consider how such systems of social interaction bracket time and space. How, for example, do forms of human association, such as #Gay.nl, stretch across time-space? Like all forms of human association, #Gay.nl is produced and reproduced through the knowledgeable practices of its constituent participants. When we address the way in which the internet is facilitating this process, then we are studying how the internet is involved in cultural transmission – a process which is both a condition and an outcome of the regularized coordination of mediated exchanges across time-space. Extracts of routine and mundane dialogue taken from IRC log files will, when carefully chosen, in some part display traces of the complexity of this process. However, taken on their own, such extracts do not exhaust the elaborate organization by means of which these exchanges are produced and received. In fact, taken on their own, any attempt to interpret them becomes a risky and conflict-laden activity. We need, therefore, to recover the situated character of such extracts and recognize the three sets of time-space coordinates across which information and symbolic content are organized, transmitted, and used for the upkeep of these forms of human association. These are the time-space coordinates involved in what is going on online, and the time-space coordinates involved in the two distanciated contexts of production and reception.

In order to illustrate this point, I want to examine the following extract taken from #Gay.nl which goes like this:

* GiO was in barcelona last week
*** Rodger-NL (wiels@ehv0.svw.nl) has left #Gay.nl (Rodger-NL)
<GiO > just as well or it was ban time
<Abaqs18> hi Thunder
<ThUnDeR> I gotta go soon
<ThUnDeR> some guys keeps looking at my screen
*** ThUnDeR has quit IRC (I'm outta here)
<Abaqs18> me too my sister needs to use the phone
<GiO > Thunder: tell them to go away
<Abaqs18> ah she's gone
<Abaqs18> CU L8r guys
*** Abaqs18 has quit IRC (Leaving)

I chose this extract deliberately to show that interaction on IRC can be a lot less tidy than the extracts featured in Reid's work would have us believe. Her examples tend to create the illusion that they can be understood in their own right. The dialogue on IRC is, however, very much like talk and is often similarly fragmented and messy. As with talk, contextuality is the basis on which such encounters are routinely coordinated and extended across time-space. It would simply not be possible to understand the complex processes involved in the opening and closing of engagements taking place in the example above without due consideration of the broader socially structured contexts within which the communication took place. Take *Abaqs 18*, for example. He phones into a local internet service provider in Arnhem which allows him to participate in the interaction on #Gay.nl. The use of the phone, and of the computer, at his home is, however, embedded in the broader social context of his household. Like other aspects of his domestic social life, the use of the phone and of the computer is subject to the relations of power between different members of his family. Another participant on #Gay.nl, *Rodger-NL*, accesses the internet from his uncle's office, but can only do so during the evenings. However, his behaviour on the channel on previous occasions has upset some of the other participants. One of these is *GiO*, a channel operator, who removes *Rodger-NL* from the channel if he detects him. *ThUnDeR*, the last of the four nicknames in this extract, lives in Moscow and accesses #Gay.nl infrequently from a computer lab at the university where she studies. She has heard a lot about life in the Netherlands and hopes to get an invitation to visit Amsterdam after her exams. The computer lab she uses is often busy and sometimes she has to close down her IRC program because she is worried that her fellow students would not understand her interest in chatting on such a channel. Moreover, the systems operator of the lab does not approve of students using the computers for IRC. By viewing extracts of IRC log files as interactionally situated, we are able to study online chat, as Erving Goffman writes, as traces of arrangements 'by which individuals come together and sustain matters having a ratified, joint, current, and running claim upon attention, a claim which lodges them together in some sort of intersubjective, mental world'.[71]

Turkle, as we have seen, exploits the apparent messiness of online interaction to support her case for celebrating the decentring of the subject. I would argue, however, that we need instead to seek a recovery of the subject. Newcomers to an IRC channel may well be rather confused by some of the exchanges and insider jokes. But regular participants, on the other hand, skilfully and routinely draw on shared stocks of knowledge and monitor the settings of their interaction in order to accomplish and make sense of this mediated experience.

Sometimes interaction on an IRC channel can look like this second example taken from #Gay.nl:

```
*** martijn (~noname@p000.asd.euroweb.nl) has joined #Gay.nl
*** martijn has quit IRC (Leaving)
*** Wes20 (waar@vp00-00.worldnet.nl) has joined #Gay.nl
*** KRiZ (~me@sneek.demonet.nl) has joined #Gay.nl
*** indy20 (bilde@gs0.saxo.nl) has joined #Gay.nl
*** |Tim| has quit IRC
*** |ROOX| has quit IRC
*** indy20 (bilde@gs0.saxo.nl) has left #Gay.nl (indy20)
*** jess20 (jess20@hg00.saxo.nl) has joined #Gay.nl
*** jess20 (jess20@hg00.saxo.nl) has left #Gay.nl (jess20)
*** koen (k@i00.ant.euroweb.be) has joined #Gay.nl
<Wes20> hya anyone here?
*** Peg20 (someone@amf0.saxo.nl) has joined #Gay.nl
*** Peg20 has quit IRC
*** Wes20 (waar@vp00-00.worldnet.nl) has left #Gay.nl (Wes20)
```

Like *Wes20*, one might be led to conclude from this kind of apparent non-activity, which can continue for many hours, that #Gay.nl as a community is in decline. Indeed, IRC channels do come and go. But what I want to demonstrate here is that we must not treat an IRC channel such as #Gay.nl as the only arena of circulation involved in forms of human association created by the internet. If we are sympathetic to the idea of a need to recover 'virtual communities' as situated practices in order to understand what is going on online, then we will also accept that there is much more to #Gay.nl than what goes on in the main channel. In this extract, the main channel is acting as a central meeting area where users announce their presence but are not yet engaged in open discussion. Out of public view, some of those present might be engaged in private conversation with others, or they may be chatting on a different channel altogether. Some may even be logged on, but busy writing an e-mail, or making a pot of tea, etc.

Rather than focusing on the main channel of #Gay.nl simply as a source of evidence for the communal activities of participants, we need to look at a much wider range of arenas of circulation of information. These may include a whole range of articulated interactional situations. The development of the integrity, trust and shared stocks of knowledge that are necessary to sustain the social organization of a group may involve a whole variety of online forms of communication, such as the use of webpages and e-mail. Moreover, users frequently also turn to conventional media such as the telephone and, of course, group and individual meetings where #Gay.nl participants meet each other in situations of co-presence. Such face-to-face encounters are not just incidental to what goes on online. They provide an essential boost to the contextual underpinning of mediated experience, even though not all participants may be in a position to engage in face-to-face meetings themselves. We should not view this involvement in various fields of circulation, either on or off the screen, as a series of parallel lives vying for the participant's attention and resulting in the fragmentation of their life experience. We ought to see it as a skilful splicing together of different interactional situations. As such, IRC users' participation in communal activity is a skilled accomplishment that is embroiled in their ability to negotiate effectively between the different arenas of circulation and different interactional situations. This is a process that is both enabled and constrained by the repertoire of possibilities attached to their position within the intersecting sets of institutionalized rules and resources involved.

We need, I think, to look afresh at how individuals might actively draw on the internet to promote new kinds of relationship which assist rather than obstruct their attempts to make sense of a world in which the most intimate and the most distant have become directly connected.

First, we cannot properly acknowledge the opportunity for new modes of relationship if we focus primarily on the attributes of the technical medium while ignoring the structured social relations and contexts within which information and other symbolic content are produced and received. IRC, for example, as a technical medium may very well allow for the deconstruction of social boundaries. But how individuals go about negotiating this loss is a matter that is bound up with complex issues that have to do with their ability to intervene in the ongoing process, and with the interests they may have at stake in doing so. It is therefore not realistic to treat the internet simply as a medium of new opportunities for creating new forms of human association. It is instead a medium of practical social activity. This means that its use is inextricably linked to the kinds of knowledgeability, skills and resources which individuals and groups can bring to these new interactional situations, and to the intentions they have in using it.

Second, we cannot properly acknowledge the opportunity for new modes of relationship if we suggest that individuals come together 'out of nothing' to form new entities in much the same way micro-organisms do.[72] The position-takings of individuals and their repertoires of possibilities within different arenas of circulation do not remain untouched by their association with others. Understanding the direction of change will once again involve due consideration of the contexts of the production and reception of content.

So how might an IRC channel such as #Gay.nl open up new opportunities for new modes of relationship and new forms of human association? Let us consider this matter critically in the light of these arguments. It would be difficult to support the claim that the modes of relationship constituting #Gay.nl can be wholly described in Oakeshott's terms as 'organic, evolutionary, teleological, functional or syndromic'. There are some guiding lights. After all, it is a gay IRC channel, and a channel topic can be set. But this does not mean that the channel is only open to gay individuals who agree tacitly, by their presence, to stick to discussing a set theme. Nor does it mean that all gay individuals who join the channel are at the right address. For example, those who are looking for local information or who are seeking to make dates with others do get advised to go to a different channel. But this is less a question of throwing these participants out and rather more a question of genuinely helping them on their way. The operators do not enact their authority and enforce any kind of common purpose that should contingently be pursued. Not only does the channel have to be run in a way that meets the approval of participants who might otherwise simply move elsewhere, there is also a realization that there are many advantages to be had from a common bond. Fragmentation into an infinitesimal number of splinter channels would mean it would be less easy for individuals to find each other, and small channels would be more difficult to protect from channel takeovers by those hostile to them. These 'virtual communities' give what are otherwise very open mechanisms for human association a degree of predictability and certainty.

The modes of relationship constituting #Gay.nl would therefore seem much more in tune with Oakeshott's idea of spontaneous coordination, as a relationship of intelligent agents which can be evaluated in terms of their capacity to share in a give-and-take experience rather than in terms of some common purpose. As such, the spontaneous coordination involved in maintaining and sustaining #Gay.nl is very much about participants making things happen rather than having things happen to them. Participants, for example, build webpages to inform others about topics ranging from health matters to where to go on holiday. Others organize trips, holidays and parties.

However, this does not mean that #Gay.nl is a snug 'back to the future' type community consisting of 'enough people' carrying on relationships in virtual reality with 'sufficient feeling' and for a 'long enough' period of time! Castells's claims about network culture can be applied to #Gay.nl, which is also 'made of many cultures, many values, many projects, that cross through the minds and inform the strategies of the various participants'.[73] Its very survival, however, attests to the fact that #Gay.nl and its participants have somehow embraced cosmopolitanism as an attitude of mind and as an institutionalized phenomenon. Some individuals fare better at this than others, depending again on the kinds of knowledgeability, skills and resources which individuals can bring to these new interactional situations. Clearly there is a potential here for conflict and new uncertainties. Some participants do occasionally quit the channel in a huff. Others even delete the IRC program from their computers entirely and vow never to return again. Yet the majority of #Gay.nl participants value the channel as a discursive space in which they can develop an attitude of responsibility for the ideas they hold and the practices in which they engage. Moreover, while it is possible to log on to the channel anonymously and adopt an 'anything goes' attitude, most individuals realize that if they want to participate in #Gay.nl communality to the full, they have to adopt a more committed and intelligent mode of participation.

Castells has also advanced the hypothesis that while these kinds of virtual communities can 'go on for a long time, around a nucleus of dedicated computer users, most of the contributions to the interaction are sporadic, with most people moving in and out of networks as their interests change or their expectations remain unfulfilled.'[74] I would argue, however, that the question as to whether or not these communities exist for a long period of time is inextricably linked to the kinds of knowledgeability, skills and resources that individuals and groups have at their disposal, and to their motives for maintaining it. As for forms of human association like #Gay.nl, they persist for a very long time, not so much due to the existence of a tiny core of dedicated users, but, paradoxically, by way of the ephemeral nature of the purposes of doing things together itself. Ephemeral, however, not in the sense that participants somehow 'leave their bodies behind', but in the sense that participants can relate to each other in terms of continually changing practices which they value.

Postmodernity: making the best of our freedoms

If the internet is not, as Reid and Turkle claim, necessarily propelling us into postmodernity at all, then we must urgently consider what other possibilities there may be. My intention is not so much to draw this matter to a firm conclusion, but rather to open up this area to critical debate. With this purpose in mind, let me sketch the outline of an alternative set of ideas put forward by Giddens in his influential work *The*

Consequences of Modernity.[75] In this work he relates a set of arguments which current internet analysis largely ignores.

Giddens writes that ' "modernity" refers to modes of social life or organization which emerged in Europe from about the seventeenth century onwards and which subsequently became more or less world-wide in their influence' (p. 1). He claims that the disorientation and uncertainty we feel today 'results primarily from the sense many of us have of being caught up in a universe of events we do not fully understand' (p. 2). However, contrary to the claims made by Reid and Turkle, Giddens argues that 'rather than entering a period of postmodernity, we are moving into one in which the consequences of modernity are becoming more radicalized and universalized than before' (p. 3). He refers to this period as 'high' or 'radicalized modernity', a state which is characterized by the three sets of related developments which I discussed in chapter 1 above: the influence of intensifying globalization; the emergence of post-traditional forms of organization; and the expansion and intensification of social reflexivity. These processes have, as I explained, resulted in an acceleration and intensification of manufactured uncertainty over the past four or five decades. Nobody intended this state of affairs to come about. It is very much what Giddens refers to as an *unintended consequence* of human activity in general. However, it also has to do with what he calls the *circularity of social knowledge* (pp. 151–73). This means that our modern world can never be very stable because we are continually feeding new information into it. Such information may well make the world more transparent, yet it does not leave it untouched or exempt from further change.

Under these conditions we would seem to have two choices. Either we can throw up our arms and claim that we may as well do whatever we fancy, advising others and ourselves not to take matters too seriously. Or we can follow Giddens's suggestion and attempt to 'seek to further the possibilities of a fulfilling and satisfying life for all' (p. 156).

Rather than claiming that the internet is propelling us into this kind of postmodernity, I propose to opt for the second of these two choices. After all, it offers an opportunity for a more positive and critical approach to finding ways of developing the freedom of individuals to use the internet to participate in engagements which, as explained earlier, emphasize 'the responsibility that individuals and groups have for the ideas they hold and the practices in which they engage'.[76] Moreover, opting for the second choice does not mean that we ought to ignore Bauman when he writes that

> the acceptance of responsibility does not come easy – not just because it ushers in the torments of choice (which always entails forfeiting something as well as gaining something else), but also because it heralds the perpetual

anxiety of being – who knows? – in the wrong . . . It is with such an increasingly uncertain world that its inhabitants struggle to grapple, and it is for living in such a world that they brace themselves and wish to prepare when looking feverishly for the skills of 'making the best' of their perhaps unchosen, yet all-too-real freedom.[77]

Studying the interactional impact of the internet is not about seeking proof that it inherently contributes to the common good of society, or that it leads to the deterioration of human well-being. It is about finding ways to develop skills to use technologies such as the internet to cope in modern conditions. What we may hope for at best is what Thompson describes as 'a greater diffusion of information concerning the activities of powerful individuals and organizations, a greater diversity in channels of diffusion and a greater emphasis on the establishment of mechanisms through which these activities can be rendered accountable and control-led'.[78] In order to cope with the consequences and opportunities of the internet, individuals and organizations need to brace themselves for these developments and develop new skills. To understand how they might do this, we need to study the emergence of new mechanisms of human association. The hopes Reid, Rheingold and Turkle have for mobilizing the opportunities offered by the internet, however noble, will not materialize all on their own. The consequences of internet use, as I argued previously, are the result of a tensionful, contradictory pushing and pulling of different technical and social conditions. We may choose to ignore them, but we do so at our peril.

5

Organizations and the internet

Over the past four or five decades, the broader institutional contexts in which we exist have been caught up in a major cultural transformation. All forms of organization have become engaged in an endless process of negotiating choices among a diversity of options under conditions of intensified globalization and reflexivity.[1] In this altered social, political and economic context, the use of information technology has permeated all forms of organization, from private to public, from local to global, old and new. Parallel to this development, organizations have developed and experimented with new ways of organizing their activities, and devised and applied a variety of social-managerial strategies connecting information technology to their ways of organizing.[2] Within this setting, the deployment of the internet is creating not only a number of new opportunities, but also a range of new uncertainties and burdens. In the present day, all social interaction is embedded in organizations of some sort. In this context, the transmutations introduced by organizations in their attempts to come to terms with an increasingly unpredictable world interlace in a direct way with all aspects of our everyday lives.

Examples of ideal-typical interests and projects which are emerging as nation-states, economic organizations, social movements and more traditional forms of organization, such as the family, the church and the school, attempt to handle uncertainty in our modern world are illustrated in chapter 1. All these interests and projects have taken quite some time to develop, and they are all in some way related to a newly forming generative approach to the control of risk. The internet is now having a considerable impact on this world in transition. We seem to be facing a whole new agenda, complete with its own rhetoric and its own buzz words like electronic community, electronic democracy, electronic business and electronic commerce. With the new agenda seem to come vague promises of new ways of organizing our world.

While organizations are gradually developing the knowledge and expertise they need to cope with the new circumstances, it would be misleading to maintain that they have somehow constructed a set of well-defined purposes and practices within which internet technology might be successfully deployed. Moreover, many of the problems organizations are coping with today are not ones which their members are themselves able to define. The problems are often the unintended outcome of the actions of a whole constellation of individuals, groups and organizations, involving multifaceted clashes of interests and traditions, creating problems which are frequently global in extent. We must therefore conclude that we are still struggling with both the dynamics and the complexity of new organizational practices, and with our understanding of the way in which new technologies such as the internet might help in attempts to manage them.

The challenges of handling uncertainty in the modern world, and also some possible responses, are well illustrated in economic organizations. For example, there are the many efforts aimed at fundamentally restructuring work processes. In recent times, three of these have been particularly prevalent: (1) the implementation of *total quality control*; (2) the *re-engineering of business processes*; and (3) the creation of *market-based organizations*. All three have been used to provide their own rationale for underpinning organizational change.

Total quality control, applied in various guises, is a system whereby organizations focus more clearly on their customers or clients and promote teamwork and participatory management in order to improve the quality of service or products, stimulate innovation and reduce defects.[3]

Business process re-engineering, also applied in various ways, involves the redesigning of organizational practices and a focus on processes rather than on tasks in order to increase productivity and improve customer satisfaction while cutting costs.[4] Whereas total quality control is often described as highly participative, involving bottom-up decision-making to enhance and improve on existing production or service provision, business process re-engineering is typically described as a 'top-down' rethinking of the design of organizational practices.

Market-based organizations are an attempt to move away from mass marketing and towards a situation whereby enterprises target their customers not as market segments but as dynamic groups of competent individuals. To this effect, organizations are encouraged to capture, store, analyse and lever customer information, with the intention of protecting and enhancing customer loyalty. This information also allows market-based organizations to target and identify the more profitable areas of their customer and client base and to shed the less profitable ones. The creation of market-based organizations connects up many of the aspects involved in implementing total quality control and in re-engineering business processes, because the aligning of organizational resources to serve customers more directly calls for both the horizontal and vertical integration of organizational practices.

Despite the high hopes pinned on them, however, a majority of these efforts flounder. They end up producing unintended consequences or they fail to achieve the results the economic organizations desire. Many reasons have been given to explain this widely experienced disappointment. Davenport claims, for example, that organizations do not sufficiently recognize the potential of information technology to enable process innovation. Organizations often use information technology only to replace existing work processes.[5] Using a powerful personal computer merely to type out correspondence, for example, can hardly be considered a process innovation. He also points out that organizations deploying information technology in order to stimulate information flow and eliminate managerial hierarchy often fail in their attempts because they do not manage the politics of organizational information.[6] Because information can be used to mobilize power, those who possess it are not always so eager to share it out.

Stan Davis and James Botkin, for their part, criticize businesses for gathering information and attempting to foster learning organizations while failing to create the kinds of enterprises which might benefit from being knowledge-based.[7] They argue that the last thing you want is a learning organization! In other words, a learning organization may well collect information but it must first develop strategies allowing it to use the information it collects in order to gain competitive advantage. Under conditions of reflexive modernization, however, we might well want to carry the Davis and Botkin critique of learning organizations further. If organizations and their members are to survive and carry on under conditions of intensified reflexivity, being in danger of becoming engulfed by the volume of information they collect, they must foster their ability to both learn and forget.[8]

Barabba suggests that many attempts to create market-based organizations with all their parts working in unison to serve the customer often merely involve turning functionally structured organizations on their side: 'instead of silos we have processes, but they are still disconnected. So how much has really changed?'[9] In his opinion, the foundation of a

> market-based enterprise is neither its physical assets nor the shape of its organizational chart. Its foundation is an open information system that allows a free flow of knowledge shared across functions by individual employees who use common business processes.... Fundamental to this seamless form of enterprise – be it organized horizontally or vertically – is an understanding of industries, customers, and community based on decision-making networks informed by knowledge developed from listening, learning, and leading.[10]

Some commentators have become highly sceptical about the value of information technology altogether, arguing that when not properly used, it can even become a competitive burden. Timothy Warner writes: 'the important thing to realize is that sometimes one can solve an apparent information-processing problem not by throwing computer power at it, but by removing the conditions that caused the need for information processing in the first place.'[11] Moreover, if information technology is wrongly used it can spread erroneous information throughout an organization at lightning speed.[12]

Like new ideas on how to go about reorganizing work practices, ideas on how to use the internet are bandied about by economic organizations with some degree of enthusiasm, yet many of the opportunities and risks involved in its use remain only poorly understood. Put more bluntly, while there is a good deal of literature attempting to explain the 'hands on' use of networks and network applications, and even a growing array of work discussing their potential as a business resource, there is little known about what the interactional impact of the internet will be. Consequently, it is not surprising that some organizations tend to treat the internet, intranets and extranets as no more than hyped-up fads that will eventually disappear, much like other systems they have seen come and go. Others see websites and e-mail systems as accessories which can be simply tagged on to a wider arsenal of communication channels. As such, internet, intranet and extranet applications are often approached merely as alternative ways of distributing information rather than as involving new forms of action and interaction requiring new forms of rationalization and motivational underpinning. On introducing e-mail, for example, some organizations go about explaining its use to their members by comparing it to a conventional postal system. Although this analogy may serve some educational purpose, it is certainly not an appropriate way to go about understanding the internet's impact on organizational culture. An unintended consequence of using such an analogy to understand the internet is that many opportunities offered by internet technology are not utilized and many risks associated with its use remain unacknowledged. The most significant of these risks is an insufficient recognition of how this new technology might give rise to new forms of action and interaction.

The attitudes of many organizations towards the use and role of internet technology in organizational change can be best understood against the backdrop of the business solutions that were applied in the 1980s and most of the 1990s, when emphasis was placed on the economic and technological aspects of organizational problems. Business restructuring often meant lean production and downsizing, doing more with less, and a loss of jobs. Concurrently, information technology, as Castells writes, was supposed to be the magic tool to reform and change the industrial corporation. But its introduction in the absence of fundamental organizational change in fact aggravated the problems of bureaucratization and rigidity. Computerized controls are even more paralyzing than traditional face-to-face chains of command in which there was still place for some form of implicit bargaining.[13]

By viewing the current problems of economic organizations in terms of a crisis in the management of risk, we can attempt to break open the stranglehold that limiting the emphasis to economic and technological aspects tends to place on the way we understand information technology and how it can facilitate change. In many respects, modern organizations face risks and dangers rather than competitors or adversaries. Tackling uncertainty in organizational settings, Giddens argues, calls for an alternative, generative approach to risk.[14] Under conditions of reflexive modernization, coping with risk can no longer be simply initiated from the top of organizational hierarchies or placed wholly within the realm of bottom-up decision-making. Organizations need to jump both ways at once. They must develop generative initiatives at the same time as promoting active trust, to be sustained through intelligent relationships between individuals and groups of individuals whose informed practices constitute the organization. The success of attempts to mobilize internet technology to further new forms of economic organization is dependent on both a proper understanding of the constitution of organizational culture and a proper realization of the importance of technologies, such as the internet, as modalities of cultural transmission.

These preliminary observations are also relevant for other domains of human organization. Nation-states, traditional forms of organization, critical movements and special-interest groups are all engaged in finding ways to cope with the new risk parameters and in refashioning their institutional dimensions. Networks of nation-state agencies, for example, increasingly substitute for traditional centralized state authorities, and networks of people increasingly substitute for traditional social groups. All of these changes are redefining the ways these organizations work, communicate, and regularize their activities across time-space. Here, too, internet use is increasing the organization's range of options, which in turn demands a new involvement of all those who participate in them.

The problems faced by organizations today have led some social and cultural theorists to take a very dismal view. For them, forms of social organization today do not add up to much. Bauman writes for example: 'the momentary explosions of solidary action which may result do not alter the essential traits of postmodern relationships: their fragmentariness and discontinuity, narrowness of focus and purpose, surface-deep shallowness of contact. Joint engagements come and go, and in each case, indeed, the emergent "totality" is no more than "the sum of its parts".'[15] While all forms of social organization are being transformed, the conditions in which they exist have also been substantially altered; but we need to think about this transformation in a different way.

My aim in this chapter is to demonstrate how the theoretical framework developed in the second step of this book might provide us with a greater sense of direction and purpose in understanding how internet technology is used by organizations. This framework allows us to focus on the socially structured contexts and processes of production, transmission and reception as well as on the information and other symbolic content. In more general terms, I wish to examine critically the impact on organizational culture of the structuring features at the core of internet use. I hope to demonstrate how understanding the internet as a modality of cultural transmission might help us see how organizations can steer a more careful and more positive path between their newly acquired autonomy and the responsibilities arising from the practical and situated contexts within which the internet is used.

Distinctive characteristics of modern organizational culture

Any attempt to discover the structuring features at the core of internet use in organizational settings must be firmly based on a general theory of organization. This means that we must begin by asking some fundamental questions about the nature of modern forms of organization.

Modern organizations differ from all preceding forms of organization in respect of their ubiquity and their intensified dynamism.[16] One of the most signal characteristics of modern organizational culture is the tremendous intensification in the gathering, storing and transmitting of information used by organizations for the coordination of activities which take place within their domain. As such, modern forms of organization can best be understood as relatively open social systems in which, as Giddens writes, 'information is regularly used, and its discursive articulation carefully coded, so as to maximize control over system reproduction.'[17] Modern organizational cultures are thus reflexively made, and exist by virtue of the informed practices of individuals who participate in them.

These informed practices do not just happen in time-space, they are fundamental to the relationship organizational forms have to it, allowing them to stretch across greater or lesser spans. Some organizations, for example, have a short timespan and exist for the time it takes to complete a particular task. Others pride themselves on still being in existence many years on from their establishment. As for their spatial dimensions, some organizations span one or two rooms in a single building, while others stretch out over vast areas of space, connecting up various centres of activity. Organizational culture and communication are therefore central to what organizations are. In this context, the internet can be studied as a means whereby discursively available resources are generated by forms of organization for their reproduction in time and space, but also as a means whereby the transmission of organizational culture is achieved.

In his essay on 'Time and social organization', Giddens sets out three distinctive features of modern organizations.[18] Let me focus my argument here by examining critically each of these in turn, for they will act as useful markers for analysing some of the most chronic problems that most contemporary forms of organization face.

The intensification of surveillance   The first distinctive feature of modern organizations, as set out by Giddens, is that these social systems involve the intensification of two combined aspects of surveillance. The first is surveillance as *the accumulation, coding and retrieval of information.* A hotel, for example, is an organization which collects and processes vast amounts of information during a working day. It has to keep track of reservations, cancellations and availability of rooms, but also of stock and inventory, and the activities of competitors. The second aspect of surveillance concerns *the direct supervision of activities* of those participating in the organization. Taking the example of the hotel again, we might think of the supervision of the junior front-office staff, but also of the guests entering the hotel restaurant and waiting to be seated. These combined aspects of surveillance are vital to the power base of organizations because of the control over time-space they allow them to generate, particularly, as Giddens says, 'control over the timing and spacing of the activities of individuals whose behaviour is then made part of the organization'.[19]

Both these kinds of surveillance can involve either 'lower order' or 'higher order' information inputs. 'Lower order' inputs are those signalled, for example, by a drop in accumulated hotel bookings as registered by a reservation system. 'Higher order' inputs are those, for example, involving an individual guest complaining to the hotel manager of a critical incident which might deter them from staying in the hotel again.

The concept of surveillance is also related to organizational hierarchy and procedural rules. Giddens claims that all organizations involve a tendency towards hierarchy, while within these settings, an individual's performance can be monitored against either impersonal or personal procedural rules.[20] Impersonal definition of organizational procedures permits organizations to attain greater time-space distanciation. In this respect, however, there tends to be a distinction between people at the top and those at lower levels of authority hierarchies. Although hierarchy is 'always accompanied by countervailing tendencies towards the recapture of power by those on lower levels', for individuals at the top levels, personalized ties become more significant, allowing them to assert more independent power and follow rules more autonomously and at their pleasure.[21]

A problem with Giddens's use of the concept of surveillance is that it tends to stress the reflexive monitoring activities of authority hierarchies.[22] Surveillance, however, is always a two-way process. For example, it involves those being controlled also monitoring their controllers, and includes both the accumulation and the dispersal of information. The concept of surveillance as reflexive monitoring must therefore be seen as a far broader phenomenon than Giddens suggests, incorporating the many ways in which information and communication is used in the production and reproduction of organizations in time and space.

The association of organizations with specifically designed locales A second distinctive feature of modern organizations is their association with specifically designed locales. Giddens views the locales of modern organizations as 'physical settings which through the interaction of setting and social conduct generate administrative power'.[23] Returning to the hotel example, a hotel building is not simply an expression of accumulated power, it is also integral to it. Its design is relevant to the maintenance of various kinds of supervision over the timing and spacing of organizational activities. On entering a hotel lobby, for example, guests are directed towards a reception desk where their physical entrance into the organization is carefully managed. The architectural concentration of power is the physical manifestation of authority and hierarchy and, as such, extends the possibilities for surveillance.

The relation between locales and the timing and spacing of activities A third feature of modern organizations is what Giddens points to as 'the relation between locales and the timing and spacing of activities through the various sectors of organizations'. Schedules, such as timetables and other charts, are *time-space organizing devices* which coordinate activities involving both the internal and external contexts of organizations. In this respect, Giddens also recognizes a distinction between the organizational and personal dimensions. For participants in low trust positions, personal time-space organizing devices mostly coincide and converge with organizational timetables. For those in high trust positions, greater autonomy means that personal time-space organizing devices tend to diverge, and intersect with organizational timetables only at certain points.

There are two reasons, however, why each of these three distinctive features of modern organization requires further critical elaboration. First, we need to relate them to the changes affecting organizations in late modernity – changes which, as I explained in chapter 1, are largely independent of internet use and generally preceded its introduction. Second, in mobilizing internet technology we must begin to prepare ourselves for these changes to become more radicalized and extensive than ever before.

The internet and organizational culture in late modernity

Under conditions of reflexive modernization, all forms of organization lack fixed horizons of action. Organizational communication and the contexts in which information is produced and received are therefore involved in a process of substantial reorganization. Uncertainty can no longer be confronted by the routine exertions of centralized authorities or be contained within spaces made up of relatively fixed temporal-spatial coordinates.

As modern organizations move into late modernity, major changes are occurring in the nature of their modes of surveillance, the design of their locales, and the timing and spacing of their activities. Organizations that treat internet use in a peripheral way, regarding it as merely an alternative mode of information diffusion, can only partially understand how internet use might impact on these transformations. They are unlikely to recognize properly the opportunities this technology may offer for an alternative approach to handling risk. They may even contribute unintendedly to the creation of new uncertainties, which will tend to appear as negative phenomena rather than as positive organizational challenges.

In the light of these initial observations, let us now update the distinctive characteristics of modern organizational culture with regard to the conditions prevailing in late modernity, and relate them to the possible consequences of internet use.

Surveillance in late modernity

In a universe of high reflexivity, and as a result of globalization, the nature of surveillance within organizations is in the process of being radically transformed. These changes, however are by no means uniform or without contradiction. First, in many respects, centralized organizational authority is being maintained less rigidly than ever before. As organizations 'open out', they facilitate the emergence of relationships which cut across traditional bureaucratic hierarchies. To this effect the means for producing, transmitting and receiving information are being redistributed, even with respect to those in lower echelons of organizations and those in the external arena. At the same time, all those participating in the organization are being given greater degrees of autonomy of action. This allows them more room to be innovative and to develop skills, rather than merely fulfil duties. It is thought that being empowered to act on the information they have will enable them to identify and act collaboratively to solve the day-to-day problems they encounter, and generally to improve the core performances on which the success of the organization depends. As such, alternative developments in organizational control are beginning to focus increasingly on the organization as a constellation of relationships of intelligent agents. The downside of this development is, however, that experience of the uncertainties of the organization is also becoming more commonplace across various supervisory levels.

It is not surprising that the relaxation of centralized organizational authority has prompted some commentators, most notably Castells, to herald the advent of new organizational forms which accompany the sharing of risk and the responsibility for control. Castells writes of these forms: 'Under different organizational arrangements, and through diverse cultural expressions, they are based on networks. Networks are the fundamental stuff of which new organizations are and will be made.'[24] Beck, on a more sombre note, sees the decentralized character of organizational authority as the 'disintegration of institutions' which

> makes room for a refeudalization of social relationships. It is the opening for a neo-Machiavellianism in all areas of social action. Orderings must be created, forged and formed. Only networks, which must be connected together and preserved and have their own "currency", allow the formation of power or opposing power.[25]

Giddens also warns, in similar vein, that the decentralized character of organizational authority may result in difficulties in forging a balance between scepticism and commitment in the practical contexts of day-to-day life.[26] Trust in the organization no longer depends on an almost blind respect for the intrinsic competence believed to be held by a central authority. The decentralized character of organizational authority means that most claims to competence are now revisable.

A second way in which the nature of surveillance is being radically transformed, in stark contrast to the first, involves the intensification of the input of low-level and highly automated information for the co-ordination of activities. There is, for example, a booming market for enterprise resource-planning software. This is used to automate and connect various processes involved in running a business so that managers can obtain more or less instantaneous information about all aspects of their enterprise.[27] However, because hierarchical authority is becoming increasingly negotiable, the consequences of decisions based on low-level inputs of information are now more likely to be reflexively challenged, resulting in new areas of potential struggle and conflict.

Neither of these transformations in surveillance, however, necessarily amounts to the lowering of the degree of overall integration which organizations might hope to achieve. There is no reason to suppose that the stability of organizations requires, or depends on, strictly imposed centralized top-down decision-making, or even consensus or commitment. On the contrary, organizational stability in late modernity depends increasingly on creating conditions which facilitate the accomplishment of tasks and processes amid a diversity of values and norms held in organizations and their environments. Moreover, the decentred character of authority does not preclude the existence of 'authoritative centres', but sets the scene for a complex enactment of authority from a multiplicity of sources. Successful organizations today are those that are able to generate knowledge and adapt its processing and its flow through the organization, and across organizations, as rapidly as their organizational goals and contexts change.

But what about the impact of the internet? The internet can be used to open up a wide range of new opportunities which may be drawn on to facilitate these radical transformations of surveillance. Publishing information on the internet, or on a corporate intranet, can constitute a major shift in opportunities for redistributing information. Whereas once organizations had to race against the public media in order to communicate their version of their news, now they can 'broadcast' it immediately themselves.[28]

Internet technology, however, is not only capable of being used to boost the centralized diffusion of information and the vertical integration of organizations, it can also be drawn on to support networks of decentralized organizational units, cross-organizational networks and delegated decision-making. Dieter Ernst lists five different kinds of networks in this respect: supplier networks, producer networks, customer networks, standard coalitions and technology cooperation networks.[29]

Across all these networks, the internet can be used to support the intensification of both 'lower order' and 'higher order' information inputs. Knowledge sharing and interactive features of the internet, intranets and extranets may be used to support 'intelligent relationships' within and across organizational boundaries. In this respect organizations draw on websites, e-mail, discussion forums and conferencing systems to work collaboratively and share knowledge. Internet technology, however, can also be used to gather, store and transmit vast quantities of low-level information necessary for the coordination of organizational activities. In this respect websites and e-mail can be used for electronic data exchange and the management of electronic commerce transactions.

Given that the internet might seem capable of being used to do virtually anything an organization might wish, it might be seen as a magic tool to support organizational reform and change. Paradoxically, however, under conditions of reflexive modernization this openness is also a major source of concern for organizations. So much so, in fact, that the uncertainties resulting from internet use can sometimes become quite overwhelming. First, the ephemeral and often intangible patterns of network use, the time-space rhythms of connections made, the opening and closing of webpages, the direction and volume of the flow of packets of information across its networks, all these seem to say more about how an organization is run than does a hard copy of its organizational chart. Second, as practices and processes acquire heightened visibility and transparency with the use of web publishing and collaborative tools, organizational outcomes which were once deemed satisfactory may now appear to be reached by methods which are not generally accepted within the organization. Certain unintended consequences of organizational policy might suddenly be revealed, thus fracturing their tacit acceptance by individuals affected by them. Third, activities and practices can also be more or less completely concealed, either deliberately or unintendedly. Networks can sometimes appear to be loaded down with information, with users unable to find the information they need or left in uncertainty as to its status and the value they should attach to it. Fourth, as networks create new opportunities for linkages within organizations, they heighten the decentred character of authority by cutting out traditional 'authoritative centres' through processes of 'disintermediation'. Concurrently, new 'infomediaries' emerge and disappear, allowing for the recombination of knowledge and skills for a given field of action or organizational process.

All the uncertainties listed above are at once liberating and anxiety provoking. Liberating, because individuals or groups can bypass or enter into dialogue with sources of authority which would otherwise hinder their work. Anxiety provoking, because people themselves are also in danger of losing the aura of authority they once held or hoped to enjoy, and because everything they do is governed by decisions which are increasingly taken on the basis of claims to expert knowledge which they can no longer be sure about.

Designed locales in late modernity

Although most organizations still, in one way or another, remain associated with locales where administrative power is concentrated, the architectural concentration of power typically associated with hierarchical authorities is being displaced by very different physical settings in which the concept of *place* takes on a very different significance.

In this respect, Castells describes the advent of what he calls the '*architecture of nudity*', that is, 'the architecture whose forms are so neutral, so pure, so diaphanous, that they do not pretend to say anything'.[30] He writes: 'localities become disembodied from their cultural, historical, geographical meaning, and reintegrated into functional networks, or into image collages.'[31] His views, however, contrast with those of David Harvey, who claims that 'as spatial barriers diminish so we become much more sensitized to what the world's spaces contain.'[32]

The changing significance of place in modern organizations is clearly extremely complex. Sometimes it involves a particular organizational building or a constellation of buildings spread over time-space. At other times it involves locales which are not formally part of organizations but can be drawn into their sphere of influence when necessary. For the sake of clarity, I shall use three examples to illustrate how the changing significance of place is challenging the assumptions of traditional organizational location in modern organizations.

First, let us look at Jameson's seminal account of the Westin Bonaventura Hotel, designed by John Portman, and built in Los Angeles in the mid-1970s. The Bonaventura has three entrances, Jameson writes, 'none of these is anything like the old hotel marquee, or the monumental *porte cochère* with which the sumptuous buildings of yesteryear were wont to stage your passage from the city street to the interior.' He describes the entrances as being 'backdoor affairs', and claims that the architecture is imposing some 'new category of closure governing the inner space of the hotel itself'. The glass skin of the building, for example, 'achieves a peculiar and placeless dissociation'. He continues: 'the lobby or atrium, with its great central column, is surrounded by a miniature lake. I am tempted to say that such space makes it impossible for us to use the language of volume or volumes any longer, since these are impossible to seize ... You are in hyperspace up to your eyes and your body ...' Jameson's describes what goes on within this space as 'milling confusion, something like the vengeance this space takes on those who still seek to walk through it'.[33] Related to the transformation of surveillance in late modernity, however, I would argue that what we see here is not chaos or confusion as Jameson claims, but the changing physical expression of organizational power.

Second, the opening up of self-contained organizational space is not just affecting the design of individual organizational buildings or locations. A high degree of overall coordination with the policies of an organization can also be achieved when sectors of an organization are far removed from each other in time-space. We can elaborate an early example of the transformations taking place in the design of multilocational organizations by drawing on Hanswerner Voss's account of a textile mill which was inherited by Massimo Menichetti in the early 1970s, in the Prato region of Italy.[34] Here, in order to reduce costs, offer lower market prices and create a greater product variety, Menichetti decided to disassemble this large hierarchical company into smaller, functionally specialized, independent groups. He empowered the various sectors of the organization to innovate, and to specialize in whatever they were good at doing. He also founded Italfabrics, a New York-based marketing company specializing in fashion fabrics which would order no more than 30 per cent of its trade from the companies of the group. The disaggregation of this hierarchical organization and the introduction of flexible production and bottom-up decision-making was thus reflected in the physical layout of the organization on a global scale.

Third, while, for example, accommodation such as homes, hotels and modes of transport remain relatively autonomous places, their design is increasingly enabling them to be made part of organizations. Individuals can thus have strong and unprecedented ties with organizations even while they are at home, on the move, or indeed anywhere around the world. Phone calls can be made from aircraft, hand-held computers can be plugged into mobile phones, and individuals can be electronically tagged.

But how might the internet impact on the changes taking place in the design of organizational locales? The answer to this question is also very complex and dependent on particular conditions of time and place. However, for a great many organizations, getting 'wired' is a trigger point for a radical rethink of the design of their physical settings involving the introduction of alternative work arrangements and the creation of virtual offices.[35] Let me now examine for the purpose of this analysis the new head office of British Airways, 'Waterside' at Harmondsworth, England. Like many modern organizations, British Airways is beginning to reward work by output rather than by presence in traditional offices.[36] In place of traditional offices separated from one another in time-space, most of the 'residents' of Waterside work in flexible and open work areas connected by a 175-metre atrium street. There are still some semi-closed areas, though even the workplace of the airline's chief executive has no interior walls. It is hoped that the open-plan architecture will improve work flow and encourage people to work cross-functionally and in teams. The airline claims that the environment is designed to encourage a work culture characterized by openness, with minimal hierarchy and bureaucracy and radically improved access to information. This in turn will deliver decision-making and increased personal productivity. The concept of 'hot desking' has been adopted by many of the airline's departments, which means that the 'residents' choose places to work which are arranged around the processes in which they are currently engaged, sometimes even on a day-to-day basis. Using the intranet enables people to work at a desk, from home, in one of the building's cafés, or outside in the 240 acres of parkland. Moreover, while it allows them to work anywhere, it also allows them to work at any time. A great deal of communication is performed electronically via e-mail and electronic diaries, forms, manuals and shared databases. Besides having a computer-based learning centre, Waterside is linked to a supermarket where employees can shop electronically.[37]

What this example demonstrates is that while internet technology is, as it were, facilitating the emptying of time-space, it is not creating, in Castells's terms, an 'architecture of nudity' whose message is silent or neutral.[38] Rather, it is making possible an architecture which claims to represent 'space without reference to a privileged locale which forms a distinct vantage-point'.[39] It is the substitutability of different places that matters: atriums for corridors, and street cafés for boardrooms. I would argue these new physical settings are not so much silent, but communicate three very important messages which are central to the dynamism of modern organizations. First, they communicate the opening out of the organization to its members. Second, they communicate that for those who are part of the organization, activities and transactions can take place seamlessly, anywhere, at any time. Third, they communicate the organization's idea of *manufactured certainty* through the creation of settings which are safer even than the places they attempt to signify: individuals are unlikely to be mugged in the atrium street, and individuals will always be certain that in the café they will be among people who will know their name. Moreover, these places are 'energizing' in that they are all associated with leisure.

However, all these arrangements are double-edged, for they also have a range of unintended consequences and a range of new uncertainties resulting from them.[40] People who work at home or on the move, with no real place in the organization which they can call their own, may feel alienated. They no longer have a fixed 'place' of work where they can develop shared experiences and a sense of belonging. Alternatively they may also feel overwhelmed by the omnipresence of an organization from which it may seem there are no longer safe areas for them to escape to. Such developments may also result in new kinds of interregional stresses and partition problems. For example, between two people using the same table: one busy preparing a meal and the other engaged in writing e-mail.

On a more abstract level, the internet is thus heightening a process which allows for the exploitation of a wide range of seemingly contingent places, snapping them together as restructured organizational regions. Their uniqueness can thereby be enhanced, abstracted from, or even largely ignored, depending on the conditions which frame the practices within which they are being articulated. Once separated from their local experience, history and specific culture, these places face a new and increasingly turbulent future which may change at a click of a mouse. To complicate matters further, whatever we may believe places to be is often dependent on the signifying services not just of one network, but a constellation of them, and each may focus on widely divergent, and even conflicting interpretations of place.

Time-space organizing devices in late modernity

The swirling conditions of late modernity are blurring the meaningful relationship between rigidly applied time-space organizing devices and the activities taking place both within and outside the organization. Planes are delayed, meetings clash or are postponed or cancelled, announcements are made which are rapidly rendered irrelevant because of unexpected courses of events. All of these happenings are the day-to-day expression of the complex processes which are required to coordinate activities in our world today. This is not surprising given that the activities which constitute organizations take place around the world, across cultures and in a context of rapidly changing conditions. While there is still a growing interest in time-space organizing devices such as just-in-time manufacturing[41] – which uses constantly updated information to make sure supplies of materials and components arrive when they are required, without the need to carry large stocks – these systems continue to rely on all those participating in the organization marching in tight formation, allowing inventories, waiting time and other forms of slack to be drastically cut. It is the failure of such devices, however, which is resulting in a move away from fixed linear time-space organizing devices to more flexible ones which allow for the attainment of organizational goals which may vary according to rapidly changing conditions of time-space.

In this context, I want to advance the thesis that devices such as webpages of organizations are not simply evidence of an organizational internet presence, or even just containers of organizational information. They can be understood as prime examples of new kinds of time-space organizing devices emerging in the late modern age. These multifaceted narratives and virtual experiences created on computer networks interlace with the situated activities and transactions of real people. They provide blueprints which are both the means and the outcome of the cobbling together of activities and transactions which might otherwise seem to be performed in an uncertain social and cultural vacuum.

Dialogue, empowerment and solidarity and the use of the internet in modern organizations

Organizations today are grappling with enormous changes in traditional patterns of organizational values, power and signification. In order to seek out the way in which the internet may facilitate a different approach to the management of risk, we need to connect up some of the ideas which I have discussed over several chapters so far. These involve the distinctive features of organizations as they move into late modernity, the internet as a modality of cultural transmission, and the new mechanisms of human association shaped by the internet. I shall link these ideas by elaborating on four themes: (1) the ambivalent potential of internet technology; (2) the concept of the *inclusive organization*; (3) the patterning of autonomy and responsibility in organizational culture; and (4) the centrality of socially structured organizational contexts within which, and by virtue of which, organizational information and communication is produced and received.

The ambivalent potential of internet technology Never before have organizations had so much say over the ability of a communication technology to store information, the way in which it facilitates its transmission, and the kind of participation it requires. Organizations may well want to use internet technology to facilitate organizational dialogue, to empower people to make things happen rather than have things happen to them, and as a tool for creating new forms of solidarity and cooperation, yet internet technology does not do all these things in and of itself. When organizations deploy internet technology, the complexity of the changes taking place in surveillance, the design of locales and the timing and spacing of activities interlace with the ambivalent potential of the internet as a medium of cultural transmission. Mobilizing the opportunities offered by the internet will therefore always involve unacknowledged conditions, unintended consequences, and a dazzling array of interests which are not only contradictory, but may also be contested by others. The idea that internet technology might somehow bring about benefits automatically, bypassing the forums for managerial decisions and the lines of conflict within organizations, contradicts the self-understanding of modern organizations.

Towards inclusive organizations For organizations to survive under conditions of manufactured uncertainty and against the general backdrop of an expansion of organizational reflexivity, Giddens argues that they have very little choice but to 'open out' and promote *active trust* in their activities and relationships. The 'opening out' of organizations means promoting dialogue and setting standards of relevance which are in keeping with organizations which have less of a *rule-directed* culture and more of a reflexive, *rule-altering* one. Promoting active trust means, as Giddens writes, 'trust that has to be energetically created and sustained'.[42]

These are all formidable challenges and ones which cannot be solved in a traditional way with a mechanical model of equality. Organizational activities would soon come to a grinding halt if the views of all those who are part of an organization would have to be actively canvassed and balanced with respect to every decision made. This does not mean that the sharing out of opportunities is irrelevant to promoting dialogue and trust, but rather that it is not exhaustive as a way of doing it. Individuals and groups of individuals cannot be *made* equal in this way. In this respect, Giddens breaks the mould which such a definition of equality tends to impose on the 'opening out' of organizations by asserting that equality can best be defined as *inclusion* and inequality as *exclusion*.[43] Inclusion refers to the rights and obligations that all members of an organization should have, and exclusion refers to their being shut off from them.

If those at the top of authority hierarchies no longer have all the answers, then the institutional arrangements that organizations should seek are ones which support the 'demonopolizing' of expertise. As such, organizations need to recognize the continuous shifts in available expert knowledge of all sorts.[44] It is not at all surprising, therefore, that webpages and discussion forums that do not facilitate the generation of inclusive forms of community and intelligent relationships fail as inclusive arrangements. The acceleration of reflexivity will mean that they are treated with intense scepticism.[45] The deployment of the internet in facilitating inclusive organizations is about discovering and making use of local knowledge, in all its diversity, and making use of that knowledge for the potential benefit of all.[46]

Autonomy and responsibility in organizational culture   The third theme I want to deal with in connection with the management of risk is autonomy and responsibility in organizational culture. What rights and obligations should those who are part of an organization have? Under conditions of simple modernization, the autonomy of organizational members was curtailed in the general belief that if everyone were to act according to their will, then chaos would ensue. This resulted in a particular kind of moral pressure, one which facilitated the reproduction of selective amnesia concerning the responsibility of the organization as a whole to those members whose views did not coincide with the overall rules and goals of the authority hierarchy.

Promoting greater degrees of autonomy within organizations, however, does not mean that those participating in an organization are free to do as they please. The 'opening out' of modern organizations should be understood as accommodating both autonomy and interdependence within the various spheres of organizational culture.[47] The use of internet technology should therefore be embedded in institutional arrangements which facilitate the balancing of freedom and responsibility. As Dworkin has shown, autonomy is encouraged by the capability of individuals to acquire equal concern and respect for their interests, and by the obligation to resolve clashes of interest through a dialogue which is free from preset overall goals.[48] Viewed from this angle, the activities of modern organizations constitute a non-exhaustive and never-ending flow of self-organization versus congestion, form versus reform, and practice versus struggle, the very process that underpins their dynamism.

The centrality of socially structured organizational contexts   The last of the four themes relating to the management of risk is the centrality of socially structured organizational contexts. Understanding the nature and impact of the internet on organizational culture will always involve locating its use firmly within the particular histories and geographies of the institutional arrangements of its control. As such, patterns of internet use always come about in negotiation with existing patterns of communication. In each case, polity, economy and internet use snap together in different ways. These new communication technologies may well be emerging as spheres for the decentred production and circulation of symbolic forms, but we must be strongly reminded that these processes also characterize the complexity of the structured social relations and contexts within which information is produced and received.

Rather than the internet allowing us to simply forget where we are in time and space, I think Harvey is right in claiming that such technologies are also making us more sensitized and aware of what the world's spaces contain.[49] Knowledge sharing within organizations, for example, is more successful in organizations where individuals are intellectually curious. In organizations where members fear layoffs, people are less inclined to share information which might show up their mistakes. Moreover, while webpages, discussion forums and e-mail afford individuals many new ways of organizing activities and sharing information, they also reflect the attempts which are made to steer events and forms of participation away from them. The degree to which organizations open out, and the patterning of autonomy and interdependence are thus part and parcel of particular privileges dependent on socially stratified institutional arrangements within which internet use is situated. As organizations and individuals attempt to enact authority by way of the internet, an intranet or an extranet, others will call on them to defend the claims they make. In doing so they will develop strategies which allow them to bypass whatever stands in their way, making such factional struggles increasingly difficult to delimit.

Four traits of the development of internet use which support an alternative approach to the management of risk

If the advantages of internet use do not come automatically to organizations, then how might contemporary organizations use internet technology as part of a more positive engagement with risk, stressing the opportunities for innovation it creates? I shall attempt to argue that such a development involves incorporating four related traits into the institutional apparatus governing internet use. Such arrangements must bite deep into all the arenas of circulation, thus engaging with the three interlocking sets of time-space coordinates described by Thompson and set out earlier: those involving the contexts of the production of information, those involving the transmission of information, and lastly those involving the contexts within which individuals, groups and organizations act as recipients of information. The four related traits are: (1) the use of internet technology to encourage reflexive engagements; (2) the use of internet technology to develop generative intervention; (3) the use of internet technology to promote organizational inclusiveness; and (4) the use of internet technology to limit damage.[50]

The use of the internet to encourage reflexive engagements   Organizational authorities have been slow to understand that many others, both within the organization and in the external arena, are tending to use internet technology to generate power which enables them to push to the fore issues which once remained unheard. Internet use heightens this spread of engagement and activism, giving other organizations, individuals and collectivities choices which were not open to them before.

If organizations are to use the internet as part of a more positive engagement with risk, then they must mobilize it to facilitate intelligent relationships and promote dialogue both in their external and in their internal communication. Only then will they stand a chance of making the best of the talents and capacities of all those involved. By shunning active participation, and by neglecting to monitor the unfolding of networked opinion, they may find that their interests are damaged and that trust in their activities is undermined.

Websites on the internet, or on an intranet or extranet, must be understood as reflexive projects which are intricately involved in what organizations are making of themselves. The engagements which they encourage can involve interaction which is top-down, bottom-up, sideways, or which takes place in arenas of circulation which are outside the organization altogether. Interaction can be one-to-one, one-to-many or many-to-many, conducted in real-time or with some delay. Interaction may also involve automated information transfer systems, for example databases or automated e-mail answering devices.

Websites that carry organizational information while failing to deploy the medium's interactive potential will tend to be weak on community. The ability of an organization to mobilize such pages in order to develop strong bonds of trust will be severely hampered. They will not appear as the pages of a 'listening organization', for the organization will have difficulty in displaying to users that their visit makes a difference. Consequently, such websites are more likely to contain information that users do not need, or in a form which users will have great difficulty in relating to. Websites like these are also often difficult to find. This is not only due to their failure to interact with users, but because their weakness on community also shows up in their lack of linkages with other websites, and in their failure to develop reciprocal relationships of recommendation. These websites are thus often highly internally focused, sometimes with no links leaving the website at all.

The use of the internet to develop generative intervention   The second trait that organizations need to incorporate if they are to use internet technology as part of a more positive engagement with risk is the ability to develop generative intervention. Organizations must mobilize the internet to allow groups and individuals to make things happen, rather than to have things happen to them, in the context of overall social goals. At the same time, however, the advantages of internet use will not materialize if individuals or groups are abandoned to sink or swim in the bustle of such an organizational culture. In some respects, network organizations need more management, not less. Organizations need to help individuals participating in them to confront risk in a productive fashion, while taking measures to protect them against the new scenarios of risk. Consequently, while those at the top of authority hierarchies may no longer know what is best, they must adopt an active role and invest in human resources and in infrastructure in a way that is sensitive to local demands.

Mobilizing internet technology thus constitutes a considerable challenge for both contemporary organizations and all those participating in them. While individuals and groups often register frustration regarding the outcome of problems solved in an actuarial way, they are not yet experienced in taking the initiative themselves and sharing in control. In the past, individuals and groups within organizations have become all too accustomed to having a wide range of solutions imposed on them in a way which has not paid due respect and consideration to their needs and circumstances. Rather than being presented with intranets or websites as a *fait accompli*, those who will be using them need to be actively involved and consulted in designing, implementing, evaluating and improving them. In network organizations tradition is changing its role.

In developing opportunities for generative intervention, organizations will need to redistribute the possibilities for decision-making and redefine the repertoires of possible strategic position-takings people have within the various fields of circulation. In doing so, organizations will open up new uncertainties. Most of these, I would argue, have to do with how organizations choose to organize their internal and external processes in a participatory way. The guiding tenet is to allow individuals and groups to use internet technology so that they may competently share knowledge, monitor and engage with the differing ideas of others, and make decisions on the basis of that information.

Examples of how the development of opportunities for generative intervention might translate to a more practical concern can be gleaned from the design of those organizational websites and intranets which are not developed as closed circles of expertise. Given that authority hierarchies no longer know what is best, no intelligent communication department, not even one consisting of the most insightful body of experts, can hope to determine and generate successfully the information that those participating in the organization might need. While some sort of control is necessary, for example, to filter out erroneous information or to bring an intranet or website back to manageable proportions, any sort of directive control can damage its functioning. In this respect, the intranets and websites of organizations that take up this challenge appear as ongoing living activities involved in continual cycles of rejuvenation and decay. Their webpages are not so much designed to give their users 'all they might need to know' about a particular subject, but are rather more concerned with facilitating users' decision-making regarding 'where to go next'. Even this is a relatively open process rather than a deliberate move to colonize the future.

The use of the internet to promote organizational inclusiveness The third trait that organizations must incorporate if they are to use the internet as part of a more positive engagement with risk is the ability to mobilize it to allow organizations, collectivities and individuals to establish more inclusive forms of organizational community. These must facilitate the forging of new kinds of strategic alliances and solidarity based on intelligent relationships. Tackling modern organizational problems in the whirlpool of ever-changing conditions demands autonomy of action combined with the active involvement of all those who are part of the organization. Under these taxing conditions, those at the top of contemporary organizations will retain power only if they succeed in using technologies such as the internet to actively collaborate with others, both within the organization and in the external arena. Moreover, as the dynamism of contemporary organizations continues to undermine traditional forms of authority, organizations will need to deploy technologies such as the internet to facilitate and incorporate active bottom-up alliances which come about in response to new risk scenarios.

Endowing participants in strategic alliances with both rights and responsibilities facilitates the generation of active commitment. As such, creating more inclusive organizational communities not only poses the technological problem for an organization of creating equal opportunities to get members connected. It also poses the problem of getting them integrated into the processes in a way which recognizes their rights and responsibilities relating to real and comprehensive participatory involvement in organizational practices.

The necessary redefinition of possible strategic position-takings within organizational communication has prompted some internet analysts to define several relevant communication roles which were once specific to particular specialized position-takings within organizations.[51] Using internet technology, however, means that most individuals are now likely to play more than one of these roles in the course of their interactions. First, more inclusive forms of internet use must promote the role of individuals as *users* who access and view the information. Second, individuals must be encouraged to act as *authors* who produce content for others. Third, individuals must not only be called upon to produce content, they must also act as *publishers*, making it available to others. Lastly, technology that facilitates both the prolific and the autonomous creation of information will create inefficiencies for users trying to find it: individuals must therefore be encouraged to take on responsibilities as *information brokers*. As such, they develop a number of skills and procedures to assist others in finding the information they need, often involving a range of filtering activities such as the collecting, evaluating, signposting, republishing and annotating of networked information.

Any organization using the internet, or an intranet or extranet, to successfully endow its participants with both rights and responsibilities would be recognizable by a number of characteristics. First, it would positively contribute to processes which enabled those interested in it to use it. This might involve creating infrastructure, and would certainly involve instructing people on how to use it. Thus webpages which allow their users to 'get lost' do not promote inclusion. It also means, for example, that the organization would take note of how users might go about finding its webpages. Sometimes this would involve using media other than the internet to inform people that a particular website existed. Second, the organization would ensure that the information contained on its website, and on the trajectories which could be followed through, and even out of it, took account of users' interests. This might involve updating pages regularly and checking for broken links. Third, the organization would demonstrate that users of its intranet or visitors to its website on the internet could make a difference and that they mattered, even though this might sometimes be limited to giving users an e-mail address to which they might send feedback. Allowing users to make a difference regarding an intranet, for example, will require an organization to adopt an inclusive attitude which allows users to produce content and publish information themselves. Fourth, if the organization were forced to limit the freedom of users to participate in certain ways it would produce reasons for doing so, which could of course then become part of a heated debate. Each of these characteristics would play its part in promoting inclusiveness in the organization.

The use of the internet to ensure damage limitation   The current interest in facilitating organizational dialogue, autonomy and new forms of solidarity demonstrates once again the importance of acquiring a proper understanding of the complex mechanisms of human association which are shaped by the internet. Of equal importance, however, are the problems and tensions which might be encountered in doing so. If organizations are to use the internet as part of a more positive engagement with risk, then they must incorporate a fourth trait: that of using the internet to ensure damage limitation and control. Organizations, collectivities and individuals will have to develop ways of mapping and monitoring the various time-space edges that transect arenas of circulation, and of sensitizing themselves to the stresses and strains which may be associated with them. They must not only find ways of using the internet to cope with damaging events once they have happened, but also of dealing with the sources of network violence and conflict before they erupt.

The topic of network violence and conflict is a very complex one. Clashes of values between those using the internet or an intranet are often still dealt with only in a limited way. First, individuals may actively disengage or shun one another. Second, on an institutional level, organized segregation can shield hostile individuals and groups from one another, for example, by using security systems to block direct interaction. However, in an intensely globalizing society, and given the characteristics of internet technology, these options are significantly reduced. Even though in some cases we might be able to produce a sharp separation electronically, no organization, collectivity or individual can isolate themselves with much success.

These limitations bring us back to the possibility of settling such conflicting dispositions through dialogue and other deliberative arrangements. Laura Garton and Barry Wellman explain how 'e-mail's reduction of nonverbal cues and suppression of status information can hinder a group's movement to consensus by fostering nonconforming behavior and disagreement. Even in experimental task groups e-mail is often blunt, with uninhibited "flaming" language such as swearing and insults.'[52] I would argue, however, that in situations where there is a high degree of anonymity among participants, pressures to reconcile differences are very different from situations where participants' time-space paths frequently intersect, either on a network or in situations of co-presence. Settling conflicting dispositions through dialogue and other deliberative arrangements depends on the degree to which individuals and institutional contexts can be encouraged to embrace cosmopolitanism and openness, and pursue active trust and commitment.

Damage limitation must not, however, stifle and smother dialogue and deliberation. In modern organizational culture, risk and uncertainty cannot be so easily defined, let alone be listed, ranked and assessed. Under such conditions, network conflict can play a central role in converting practical and mostly tacit knowledge into discursive knowledge, and may even enhance and improve arguments underpinning particular courses of action. Conflict can also ultimately result in individuals, groups and organizations gaining recognition and mobilizing support for their activities.

An organization that was successful in translating its concern for damage limitation to a more practical level of internet use would be recognizable, for example, by its ability to openly address sensitive subjects on its website. An organization that was less successful in this might instead take a detached position. In this case, the discussion would most likely be conducted elsewhere, sometimes even on other webpages or in newsgroups, and the organization would appear increasingly irresponsible and unaccountable. Discussion forums on an organization's webpages might provide early signals of an emerging conflict, and organizations cannot afford to take a back seat when contributors start treating each other with little respect. They cannot be seen to condone prejudice, for example, where a participant in a discussion makes moral judgements about others based on a belief that belonging to a particular group automatically deserves less respect.

These four traits point to how internet use can be purposefully directed to foster new forms of action and interaction in organizational settings. Using the internet as part of a more positive engagement with risk cannot be achieved if we treat it merely as an alternative way of distributing information. These new forms of action and interaction will undoubtedly involve new kinds of risk and uncertainty, yet they also demonstrate that risk is not always a negative phenomenon. Internet use which embraces these four traits will help redefine and establish risk as an *energizing principle*.[53] For organizations that have broken away from traditional forms of surveillance, traditionally designed locales and traditional time-space organizing devices, these traits help stress the opportunities for organizational innovation that internet technology creates. They also help us to focus on the kinds of problems which might threaten the progress of such endeavours.

Above all, the use of internet technology as part of a more positive engagement with risk will mean that face-to-face contact will remain an essential part of organizational communication. Edward Hallowell writes: 'The absence of the human moment – on an organizational scale – can wreak havoc'; and he stresses the importance of combining 'high tech and high touch'. Such moments of face-to-face interaction are, he argues, fundamental for creating trust and commitment.[54]

Using the internet strategically

So far, I have been mainly engaged in putting theoretical flesh on the structuring features at the core of internet use by organizations. Now I want to demonstrate that this theoretical reflection can be placed in the service of empirical work, providing our understanding of the use of internet technology by organizations with a greater sense of direction and purpose. In order to render this discussion more concrete, I shall consider in detail a number of contrasting examples of internet, intranet and extranet use by organizations.

All the examples I discuss here relate directly to the ideal-typical interests and projects which are central to the way in which nation-states, economic organizations, social movements and more traditional forms of organization, such as the family, the church and the school, are attempting to manage risk and uncertainty. My aim is to demonstrate how approaching the internet as a modality of cultural transmission enables us now to steer a more careful course between celebration and dismissal, one which allows us to see where dangers lurk and where we might break the connection between unacknowledged conditions and unintended consequences. The following analysis is not for the purpose of making normative comments, but rather to draw out some of the consequences which particular forms of internet use may have for our institutional contexts.

Internet use by nation-state agencies

Today, most governments and agencies of state use internet technology and do so for a great variety of reasons. They may use it, for example, for inter- or intrastate communication, or they may do so in order to communicate with their citizens or other organizations. To illustrate, I have chosen to examine the use of two websites: the Singapore government's website and the United Kingdom government's 10 Downing Street website. Both aim to inform their users about their key activities. Each site reveals a great deal about the cultural context in which it is set and the very different ways in which this medium can be deployed by government.

The Singapore government's website: automating information transfer
The website of the Singapore government supports the delivery of information and the provision of services to the public and businesses across the full range of government departments.[55] As such, it is a 'one-stop shop' for multiple government services, giving people access to services with speedy, sometimes instantaneous responses to their requests, twenty-four hours a day and seven days a week. It provides for the simplification and automation of a large number of routine processes so as to reduce the need for manual operations and paper-handling, particularly in the areas of information transfer. It is a clear-cut example of how governments are organizing their information holding in a systematic fashion so that

publicly available data is readily accessible electronically, in forms which are meant to display government competitiveness and openness.

However, while this website might be considered as the acme of governmental actuarial awareness and efficiency, it does very little to encourage reflexive engagements in the form of anything approaching dialogue or discussion. The user may be able to fill out automated forms and send e-mail to government ministries, yet the site does not provide them with any means to take part in discussing government policy and activities. Individuals can only send private e-mails to ministries and departments of government concerning their opinions and views, and these may remain unanswered. Even the webpages of the Prime Minister's office provide nothing more than a formal description of the role of this office in government. For their part, the webpages of Prime Minister Goh Chok Tong focus on his life history and career. Other than providing users with vital government information, it is difficult, therefore, to imagine how this website relates to the Ministry of Information's mission: 'to help inform, educate and entertain, as part of our national goal to make Singapore a hub city of the world and to build a society that is economically dynamic, socially cohesive and culturally vibrant'.

The 10 Downing Street website: letting you have your say Like the Singapore government's website, the 10 Downing Street website also provides users with information about the Prime Minister and about the United Kingdom government.[56] It likewise furnishes links to many other organizations and institutions on the world wide web which are connected to the work of government departments. These links map out the publicly endorsed strategic alliances which the United Kingdom government claims to maintain. An e-mail news service expands the information transfer in that it automatically sends users regular updates on the government activities in which they have expressed an interest.

Unlike the Singapore government's website, the 10 Downing Street website not only provides information and permits e-mail feedback; it positively encourages dialogue in a number of different ways. As the Prime Minister's welcome statement suggests, 'this site lets you have your say. Take part in a discussion forum, or pose a question to be answered in one of our live broadcasts . . .' The website also includes a questionnaire with questions like: 'are there any other improvements that you would like to see made to the Number 10 website?' The first live broadcast involved an interview with the British Prime Minister. He responded to questions submitted by e-mail, some of which were posted while the broadcast was in progress. The discussion forums allow for a far wider and more active participation in the public debate on government policy and activities. Users can view existing discussions by clicking on a topic, respond to points made by others, and even open up new topics of their own. In order to take part they must register some personal details. Regarding their participation, users are asked to 'provide useful, relevant and respectful postings that add value to open debate on government issues. In the event of any defamatory or libellous text being posted, the registrant and his/her postings will be deleted from the forum.' Exactly what constitutes defamatory or libellous text is not made clear.

Let us focus now on one of these discussions, concerning the Crime and Disorder Bill and the fate of the government's amendment to make the age of consent for homosexuals the same as that which applies to heterosexuals. While the House of Commons overwhelmingly endorsed an equal age of consent on 22 June 1998, the House of Lords rejected it on 22 July. This led to the amendment being removed so that the remaining bill could receive royal assent.

The first contribution to this debate was posted to the website on 22 July and more than a hundred other contributions soon followed. However, given that the website lists only 'health, welfare, international affairs, the economy and education' as categories for indexing discussions, the discussion unfolded rather uneasily under the category 'health'. This in itself sparked off conflict, with one contributor remarking: 'I thought this category was about health. To me, all these letters from queers are extremely unhealthy. Why don't they stick to their own sites and leave this one to decent people' (26 July). To which another contributor responded: 'I am puzzled by the idea that this site doesn't "belong" to me. I meet the most obvious criteria: I was born and live in the UK, work and pay taxes here, am answerable to the laws of the country, vote and so forth . . . I would rather post comments in a category on "Human Rights", but there isn't one' (28 July). Given that this debate was not deleted from the forum, this is a struggle for access to the human imagination that this social group obviously won.

Most of the contributors, however, concerned themselves with the subject of equalizing the age of consent itself, urging the House of Commons to take a strong stand and overturn the vote by the House of Lords. Some contributors also volunteered personal accounts of their own experiences at the ages of sixteen and seventeen. One wrote:

> most of my friends started 'dating' during this period leaving me more lonely and isolated. The only information available to me at this time was a local newspaper article relating to a police raid on a public convenience and nearby park 'a known haunt for homosexuals'. I foolishly went to this area with the hope of finding someone I could talk to. (24 July)

Others pointed out that the House of Commons's conflict with the Lords was not just a gay problem: 'the entire issue of an unelected and unrepresentative body having the ability to influence democracy should strike concern in every man, woman and child in Britain' (24 July).

Given the aim of the Home Office, 'to build a safe, just and tolerant society in which the rights and responsibilities of individuals, families and communities are properly balanced and the protection and security of the public are maintained', it is odd that politicians did not undertake to participate in this discussion forum themselves. Moreover, there is no clear evidence that the Home Office made use of the website to limit the negative consequences of this damaging discussion. The government has since committed itself to introducing a new bill to equalize the age of consent and to implement the will of Parliament as expressed in the House of Commons vote.

With respect to the opportunities afforded by the 10 Downing Street website, one contributor commented sceptically: 'no one in any position of authority actually reads any of the comments! So my answer to you, is don't bother!' (19 June 1998). This point of view, however, stands in stark contrast to that of Prime Minister Tony Blair, expressed in an open discussion which he himself initiated in October 1998. This discussion focused on 'Forging closer links between China and the West', and Gerhard Schröder, the German Chancellor, also posted several contributions and responses during the three weeks it ran. In closing the discussion, the Prime Minister remarked: 'I have read your views with interest. . . . We will now produce a summary of the discussion which will be published on this site.' There is a problem, however, with both these points of view. The first displays disappointment that an assumed general right to be heard is being denied. The second displays impractical optimism. While the relationship between China and the West is a global issue, and the internet a fitting place to discuss what should be done, the discussion in this format was only able to be summarized because few people realized it was taking place and because many more are not yet connected to the network.

All this does not imply that websites like these would do best to limit themselves to automated information transfer only. Nor does it mean that we should return to the situation of early broadcasting when, in referring to the suitability of speakers in broadcasts, Lord Reith wrote: 'I see periodically men down to speak whose status, either professionally or socially, and whose qualifications to speak, seem doubtful . . . only those who have a claim to be heard above their fellows . . . should be put on the programme'.[57] What it does mean is that the way in which governments use the internet to learn from individuals, groups and other organizations, the way in which they react to the issues raised, and the way in which they negotiate with them must somehow be reconstructed to embody all four of the traits discussed above. The emergence of the internet interlaces with the emergence of a more reflexive citizenry. Democratization, Giddens writes, 'is outflanking democracy, and the imbalance must be addressed'.[58] In the age of the network state, moving towards a more cosmopolitan nation and a more inclusive notion of citizenship also means taking more positive steps to improve citizens' access to websites like these. With the United Kingdom having 18 per cent and Singapore 15 per cent of their population using the internet by the end of the millennium, there is still some way to go.[59]

Internet use by economic organizations

Like governments and agencies of state, a wide range of economic organizations are exploring and developing the opportunities of internet technology. The first two of the four examples which I shall discuss in this section are drawn from the field of electronic commerce. The electronic marketplace is extremely complex and internet use touches all aspects of it. Electronic commerce can, for example, be understood to refer to the business-to-business market. It might also refer to the market for business information services, for example services that capture customer information and sell it to others for marketing purposes. Sometimes, e-commerce even refers to the advertising we see on webpages and search engines. The e-commerce examples I have chosen to discuss here are concerned with web-based retailing. The first concerns an Italian online shopping mall: the Best of Italy. The second concerns one of the many electronic outlets for books which may be found on the internet: Blackwell's Online Bookshop.

Following on from this, the third example of internet technology use by economic organizations which I shall discuss here concerns intranets and extranets. Here I shall discuss a number of ways in which internet technology is being deployed by the British Petroleum oil company.

In the final part of this section on economic organizations, I shall study how the Shell oil company uses its website to display a sense of corporate responsibility and to engage in dialogue with a number of critical movements and special-interest groups.

Best of Italy website: generating trust   A growing number of websites belonging to economic organizations are in use as virtual store fronts, and some of them are grouped together to form virtual shopping malls. The Best of Italy website is set up as a mall where space is rented to a number of suppliers.[60] The basic idea behind the website is to eliminate intermediaries such as agents, importers and retailers in order to facilitate the competitive pricing of goods and attract the consumer.

The website facilitates the creation of both a supplier network and a customer network. The 'shoppers' can browse through the webpages of products on sale, most of which are Italian luxury products, and can electronically fill their shopping baskets with the merchandise of their choice. They can also pay online using their credit card and have the goods dispatched to them anywhere in the world. The suppliers, on their part, benefit from the services offered by Best of Italy and from a part-nership which allows them to generate a greater degree of visibility than they would have if they stood alone.

The Best of Italy website raises a number of interesting issues regard-ing electronic commerce. First, the success of any such website depends heavily on its ability to develop strong bonds of trust with its customers. Given that the Best of Italy website and the group backing it are not at all well known, this presents considerable problems and it attempts to address them with, for example, a 'money back guarantee', various security systems for payments, an address and telephone number in Italy, etc. Even a relatively well-known retailer such as Waitrose, the British supermarket chain, prefers to offer its services to employees connected up to an internal web rather than on the open internet. This is because it allows them to deliver locally optimized solutions in a safe and trusted environment.[61] Many retail services on the web sink or swim according to the experiences of customers who, using the internet, can relate what they have encountered to a great many others.

The second issue raised by the Best of Italy website is the way it attempts to gather information about customers and generate repeat visits and future sales. The better the information that can be gathered from visitors to the site, the more effectively the visitors can be targeted and served. The gathering of information, however, has to be balanced against the issue of customer privacy. Towards the end of the millen-nium, many commercial websites were still gathering very little informa-tion about their visitors. While some used 'cookies' or electronic tags which are placed on the visitor's computer to monitor the pages they visit and access, many commercial sites failed even to provide an e-mail address, making it very difficult for customers to volunteer information even if they so wished.[62] Such a situation begged improvement. The Best of Italy website addresses the privacy worries of customers and invites them to register as site-shoppers, a necessary act if purchases are to be made. In return, customers can join various discount programmes. How-ever, the information customers are asked to give is very limited and they are not told why it is relevant. An additional feature of the site is a selection of links to tourist information about Italy. But this information broker feature is not really used to the full, and many of the links pro-vided can be accessed by internet users in numerous other ways. More-over, for a page which is attempting to appeal to a fashion-conscious clientele, the lay-out and design of the website are rather dull. The con-tent is presented in the form of lists, and no attempt has been made to recreate symbolically the experience of a shopping mall, or to exploit the fact that the 'shopper' is likely to be ensconced in the relative certainty of their home. Websites like these not only have to display trust and integrity, they also have to actively convince both the suppliers and the customer of their benefits. On the web, competitors are only a 'mouse click' away.

The Blackwell's Online Bookshop: strengthening an established reputation   Blackwell's online bookshop is an interesting case for two reasons. First, it demonstrates how an established retailer can draw on its long-standing reputation and turn it into a strategic advantage on the web. Benjamin Henry Blackwell opened a bookshop in Oxford in England in 1879. By 1913, overseas custom accounted for 12 per cent of Blackwell's sales. Today, Blackwell's online bookshop allows it to vastly increase the number of customers it reaches, to collate more information about them, to target them more effectively, and to provide them with more services. It also demonstrates how a 'new medium' like the internet is not replacing a traditional one which involves the publishing and selling of books, but is extending and enhancing it.

While Blackwell's can build on its secure reputation, using the internet to gain unprecedented visibility for its practices and skills as a bookseller, this does not mean that it can adopt a cavalier attitude with respect to actively generating trust in its activities. Blackwell is but one bookseller among many others on the internet. It can only retain its power by successfully using new technologies to create value for itself and its customers, and prevent such leverage shifting to its competitors. Blackwell attempts to do so in a number of ways. First, the online bookshop forms part of Blackwell's corporate website where it also offers services to library users, libraries and publishers, and information about its bookshops around the world.[63] Second, the online bookshop allows customers to search or browse for books themselves, and obtain information about availability and prices. Third, an online magazine informs customers about new books and even displays extracts from some of them. Fourth, a wide variety of services is offered, ranging from an out-of-print book service to the gift wrapping of books to be sent as presents. Fifth, an alerting service allows the online bookshop to construct customer information profiles, allowing Blackwell not only to get to know its customers, but also to notify them about new books in subject categories they have selected.

The growing numbers of virtual store fronts and virtual shopping malls on the internet are giving both competitors and consumers access to comparative pricing information. Moreover, these services are letting customers

> see farther and farther upstream, with access to inventory, order status, backlog, and other previously hidden or proprietary information. As

customers know more and more about market offerings, options, and alternatives, their expectations rise accordingly: multiple aspects of trans-actions – order speed and timeliness, quality, customization, configurability, compatibility with the existing environment, and of course price – are being negotiated harder than ever.[64]

In this respect, it is also interesting to study the differences in the pro-ducts Blackwell and the Best of Italy are attempting to sell. There is a big difference between choosing to purchase a book and choosing to purchase an espresso coffee machine via the web. While espresso coffee machines are cultural phenomena they are objects that cannot be constituted as symbolic forms in the way that books can. Checking out an espresso coffee machine via the web, we would still like to know the feel of operating it and the taste of the coffee that it makes. Moreover, in the future, books, videos and CDs may increasingly be delivered digitally, while goods like expresso coffee machines will still need to be delivered physically. The ability to deliver such goods anywhere and at any time will become an important feature in the struggle for competitive advantage.

An apparent lack in both these examples of electronic commerce is their failure to implement discussion forums. While neither of these organiza-tions may have the resources to engage actively in such forums themselves, creating facilities that would allow customers to interact with each other might attract users to these sites. The Best of Italy website could, for ex-ample, allow customers to meet up and discuss Italian fashion or exchange accounts of other experiences that interest them. Blackwell's could facilit-ate discussions about books and even invite authors to participate. Such discussions might provide interesting information which could be used to improve service performance.

The British Petroleum oil company intranet/extranet   In discussing Brit-ish Petroleum's use of internet technology,[65] I am shifting the focus of this discussion from electronic commerce towards business applications on intranets and extranets. By the century's end, following link-ups with Amoco and the Atlantic Richfield Company of Los Angeles, the com-pany had become one of the world's two top oil majors.[66] Like many chief executives of large corporate structures, Sir John Browne was very concerned about the nature of the organization's knowledge base and decided to turn the oil company into an 'agile learning organization':[67] the BP Amoco and Atlantic Richfield link-up demanded new business processes and the use of communication and information technology. Let us examine the advent of a number of examples of intranet and extranet use which have allowed individuals who are part of this organ-ization to work together, to share knowledge and to solve problems across company boundaries.

When employees are scattered everywhere around the globe it is easy to lose sight of the skills and expert knowledge they have. Unable to locate the leading experts on a particular topic, BP often had to hire in external consultants and pay their fees. Now a worldwide contact and skills database has been created which will enable the BP organization to capture these details of all its employees. Accessed via an intranet, the system allows users to do a search and locate this vital corporate data. While it has clear benefits, the new database also gives rise to new problems. For example, experts might not always be available or willing to be detached from one part of the organization in order to solve a particular problem in another. However, the system is expected to save the company several million dollars a year in consulting fees.[68]

A BP project for sharing knowledge between employees was already in existence. The Virtual Teamwork Project initiated in 1995 is intended to encourage different business units to exchange information using an intranet that incorporates a videoconferencing facility. The system has facilitated collaboration across organizational boundaries between designers, fabricators and construction workers and has substantially reduced the amount of time employees spend travelling. Users also claim that it has reduced the time spent searching for information and making decisions. The leader of BP's knowledge management team, Kent Greenes, argues that the videoconferencing facility generates more commitment and trust than when telephones are used. A training programme has been set up for staff to learn how they can benefit from the system and also avoid its pitfalls. For example, individuals often tended to interrupt their work immediately to deal with video calls. Sometimes people would become inundated with calls from others requesting their advice.[69]

A further BP project is the Charter-Ring extranet site. The company previously used a centralized ship-chartering planning department that coordinated the transportation of chemicals on a global level. Members of this planning team orchestrated a complex set of arrangements which involved travelling around the world, coordinating the various BP business departments, and communicating with shipping brokers. The shipping brokers would fax information concerning the movement of ships to the team, who would then enter this into reports which were forwarded to the relevant business departments.

Today, most of this work is done using an extranet. This allows the BP organization to track the position and movement of ships and cargo around the world.[70] As project manager Colin Frost explains,

> the lifecycle of a shipping movement starts way before any ships are chartered. The individual business looks at what needs to be moved at some future date and places a request in the forward programme in the Charter-Ring system. This shows the shipping brokers what the business is thinking

of doing, allowing them to plan ahead and check availability of vessels. Eventually a date comes when brokers have to nominate a ship and businesses have to commit to it, whereupon it is placed on the Position List. From here, the shipping broker takes control of the updates and the updating process amends records of movements every day, in real time.[71]

British Petroleum uses many other intranet and extranet applications to improve the way it does business. There is, for example, a website which allows Chevron, Mobil, Texaco and BP to share project data. There is one intranet application that allows the BP Marine sales department to monitor the global marketplace for fuels and lubricants for shipping. There is another intranet application that allows administrators to publish news and information and that facilitates the automated e-mailing of news items. There is a failure incidents database that allows access to the entire failure data, allowing for more complex analysis and an overall reduction of failures. There is a website that collates and disseminates research findings on major oil and gas fields and thus reduces the need for symposiums. Lastly, there is a website register which allows the Intranet Management Team to oversee the number of websites and their usage, to allocate responsibility and provide a framework for the listing of 'approved' intranet sites and their tables of content.[72]

The Shell oil company website: limiting damage   The final example of internet use by economic organizations to be examined here is the Shell oil company website.[73] In recent years, the Shell oil company has been discussed by many commentators reflecting on the way some organizations are coping with the spread of activism and engagement among critical movements and special-interest groups. In Nigeria, for example, Shell became entangled in human rights abuses in oil-rich Ogoniland. In 1995, Shell was accused of failing to use its influence when the government executed Ken Saro-Wiwa and other activists who had been engaged in a struggle for environmental clean-up and Ogoni rights. Another key episode in that same year involved Shell's plans to dump the redundant Brent Spar oil rig by sinking it to the ocean bed. Environmental and human rights groups protested against Shell's activities, and many consumers stopped using their service stations.

Against a background such as this, the internet offers a powerful platform for critical movements and special-interest groups to voice and debate their concerns. In 1995 these groups were already far more aware of such opportunities and quicker to make use of them than companies like Shell were.[74] Since then, however, considerable changes have taken place in Shell's attitude to corporate responsibility and accountability. In 1998, Shell published *Profits and Principles – Does There Have to be a Choice?*,[75] a report expressing and detailing a new accountability map, a set of guidelines for sustainable development and a willingness to engage in dialogue with groups critical of their activities.

Today, the Shell website forms a central part of its strategies aimed at displaying organizational responsibility and accountability. Shell uses internet technology in an attempt both to avoid and to manage any damage resulting from the unintended consequences of its actions. The website invites users to

'Tell Shell' . . . let us know what you think of us, how you would like us to improve and how you might tackle some of the issues we face on a daily basis. We might not always agree with your views, but I promise they will be taken seriously . . . We want to put your concerns, knowledge and priorities onto the table when we make necessary business decisions.

The company describes its 'Speaker's Corner', a conference area on its website, as a 'listening post'. There is a webpage that 'lists other people's sites, all ones that we think can make an interesting contribution to the debates surrounding our business. We don't necessarily agree with all of them, but you might have a different view.' The company attempts to explain how it is trying to 'balance business with active citizenship': 'if we can balance the needs and legitimate demands of people and planet, we will be doing it better. What Shell cannot do, however, is ignore the laws of economics. Profits matter. Just as poverty is the cruellest form of environmental degradation, so bankruptcy destroys the ability to make balanced business decisions . . .' Lastly, Shell devotes a number of pages on its website to giving its own account of its involvement in Nigeria and to listing how it contributes to the communities where it operates.

But what is Shell to do with what it is 'told'? 'Decisions in the real world', Shell's website suggests, 'are always judgements based on imperfect data . . . Shell has many technically expert people familiar with data – and its imperfections – that underpin their decisions.' Yet the problem is not just about listening harder: it is about coming to terms with the loss of final authorities who were once able to stifle or smooth the rough edges of such debates. These debates are becoming very intense and are questioning existing definitions of the legitimate demands of people and what is required to protect the planet. Shell thus needs not only to limit or manage damage, but to find new ways of doing so.

Internet use by traditional forms of organization and social movements

In this final section, I want to examine two websites which have been created by two very different kinds of organization. The first is the Family

Research Council website set up by a group based in Washington DC.[76] There are few countries where the future of the family is not in question. Towards the end of the millennium, only 23 per cent of US households were considered to be 'traditional families'.[77] Many suggest that the exposure to modern media has played a decisive role in the break-up of these traditional forms of organization.[78] However, while there is a good deal of substance to this suggestion, we must not neglect the way in which traditional forms of organization might also deploy new communication networks for their transformative potential.[79] The second website which I shall examine here also relates to changes taking place in sexuality and emotional life. It belongs to Stonewall, a London-based national civil rights group, working for legal equality and social justice for lesbians, gay men and bisexuals.

Family Research Council website: promoting the traditional family　The Family Research Council (FRC) profiles itself as a non-profit, educational organization, and aims to reaffirm and to promote nationally, and particularly in Washington DC, the traditional family unit and the Judeo-Christian value system upon which it is built. The Council claims to be an 'unparalleled organization which focuses its efforts solely on defending the interests of America's families'. It promotes and defends traditional family values in print, broadcast and now also by using the internet.

The members of the FRC team present themselves as experts on all aspects of family life: the media, the military, government relations, family culture, etc. In this context, the page is used to disseminate their views on a number of issues. The 'Military Readiness Project', for example, opposes 'efforts to lift the ban on homosexuals serving in the military, to place women in combat roles, and other "social experiments" that threaten to degrade our military's ability to preserve our national security'. In its culture section, the website claims to track 'the strategies and rhetoric of America's powerful "gay" lobby and its ongoing campaign to redefine marriage and family and propagandize children'. This intense anti-gay attitude is continued in a section on 'Family: friends and foes', where the FRC names and criticizes what it calls 'the twelve top corporate sponsors of homosexuality'. These include AT&T, American Airlines, American Express, the Disney Corporation, IBM, Kodak and Levi-Strauss, all accused by FRC of pro-homosexual activism. The private addresses are given of some of the presidents, chairpersons and chief executives of these companies, and users of the website are urged to let them know what they think. The same list, however, is also used by homosexuals to voice their support of corporate diversity programmes and non-discrimination policies.

In their frequently asked questions section, the FRC further attends to matters such as: 'What can be done to restore the sanctity of human life?'; 'What should be done to relieve the excessive tax burden on families?'; 'Should China's "Most Favored Nation" trade status be revoked?' and 'Should the war on AIDS be redirected?'

While organizations such as the Family Research Council can use the internet to promote their particular interpretation of traditional family values, they cannot remain unaware that an individual's choice to join their fold is but one option among a plurality of possibilities open to them.[80] The questioning of the traditional family has provided an opening for individuals to explore other forms of family. The FRC website, however, does very little to acknowledge this, or even to anticipate the kind of unintended consequences that their mode of exclusion may produce. For example, they do not produce reasons for excluding homosexuals from family life. Instead, they simply claim to speak on behalf of the 'American family' in denouncing all homosexual behaviour as inherently 'lethal and immoral', implicitly claiming that this needs no further explanation. This kind of moral position-taking is extremely vulnerable when practised on an interactive medium such as the internet, where its arbitrary nature is soon revealed in discussion. It leaves the FRC's own moral position on a very slippery slope.

The Stonewall website: working for inclusion   Stonewall was established in 1989 and now has over 20,000 members.[81] It works alongside government, the media, employers, a range of social organizations and grassroots groups. Its aim is to combat discrimination and prejudice, not regarded as the province of any one political party or any one group. Stonewall claims 'that lesbians, gay men and bisexuals exist throughout society and we support the efforts of lesbian and gay groups to achieve visibility within their own cultures and traditions'. Moreover, 'lesbians and gay men are now visible in all walks of life and Stonewall has played a fundamental part in forcing this change.'

The Stonewall website is an attempt to extend and intensify such visibility by using the internet. Thus it informs users about its many campaigns, including the activities it undertakes to equalize the age of consent, to end workplace discrimination, to lift the ban on gay men and lesbians serving in the armed forces, to protect lesbians and gay men from being victims of attack and to end all forms of exclusion of lesbians and gay men from public life. 'We cannot be a part of society', Stonewall argues, 'if we are excluded from the military or if we can be sacked from our jobs.' In a different section of the website, a series of fact sheets discuss a wide range of issues covering 'gay sex and the law', 'lesbian and gay parents', 'same-sex couples and pension schemes', 'public opinion of lesbian and gay rights', 'same-sex couples and the law', and 'discrimination in the workplace'.

Stonewall is not using its website to struggle for the exclusion of particular individuals or groups. For unlike the Family Research Council, it is not disqualifying anyone. Instead, Stonewall is using its website in a positive struggle for the right of equal respect, the right to form what it calls a 'family of choice' which it sees as 'one of the most fundamental human rights'. Stonewall aims to 'begin the process of reshaping society to recognize same-sex relationships. Whether it be parenting or immigration, pensions or inheritance we must set our claim for full citizenship.' As such, Stonewall's use of the internet does not square with Castells's rather dismal claim that such social movements are in danger of remaining subdued and fragmented in their consciousness, creating 'tribes' and 'cultural communes'. Nor has it stooped to excluding its excluders on emotional, arbitrary or prejudicial grounds and thus distorting the possibility of a reasoned debate.

Examining these examples of internet use by organizations, we might conclude that the internet is rather a mixed blessing, both for organizations themselves and for all those who participate in them. We might, for example, support Stuart Hall's claim that we do not yet have an alternative means by which we 'can benefit from the ways in which people have released themselves from the bonds of traditionalist forms of living and thinking, and still exert responsibilities for others in a free and open way'.[82] However, while some of these examples may serve to reinforce some of our fears about organizations today, I hope to have demonstrated that studying the internet as a modality of cultural transmission provides us with a more privileged vantage point to attempt to understand and possibly steer what is going on.

Two observations are particularly relevant here. First, all those who use internet technology also 'stand in a position of appropriation in relation to the social world, which they constitute and reconstitute in their actions'.[83] While internet technology is undoubtedly expanding the realm of organizations, allowing them to penetrate deeply into our day-to-day lives, it is also providing us with possibilities of reappropriation well beyond those ever available before.

Second, while organizations using internet technology are becoming increasingly unconstrained by their location, opening out both internally and externally, their activities are also becoming ever more open to scrutiny and debate. In order to generate trust in their activities, they must be seen to be trying to encourage this. As best they can, they must steer a careful path between their newly acquired autonomy and the responsibilities arising from the practical and situated contexts within which the internet is used. In finding such a balance, they are not obliged to implement the four traits set out above, but in an increasingly uncertain world, it might be the best option they have.

6

The internet, the self and experience in everyday life

In the previous chapter I examined questions concerning the internet and how its use is transforming organizational culture. In this chapter I want to focus on how the internet might enrich and transform the nature of the self and experience in everyday life. Some of the distinctive features of the self and experience today are the outcome of a set of fundamental transformations that began in the early modern period. With the advent of modern society, and parallel to the institutional contexts in which it exists, the self has to be reflexively made. Individuals must, as Beck writes, 'produce, stage and cobble together their biographies'.[1] As Thompson explains, throughout modernity this process of self-formation has become 'increasingly nourished by mediated symbolic materials, greatly expanding the range of options available to individuals and loosening – without destroying – the connection between self-formation and shared locale'.[2] Today, under conditions of reflexive modernization, individuals are faced with having to use communication technologies such as the internet in their attempts to refashion the project of the self and attempt to steer it through an increasingly uncertain world of baffling complexity.

While my focus here is on the individual, the changes of the project of the self and the institutional transformations within which they occur must be understood to be interdependent processes. The self is, therefore, not being transformed by forces that operate exclusively behind the backs of individuals. On the contrary, the project of the self is one in which individuals are actively and intelligently involved. Nevertheless, as I stressed in my analysis of virtual communities, such knowledgeability is always bounded, such that the unintended consequences of their activities may always result in yet more uncertainty. Given that organizations exist by virtue of the informed practices of the individuals who participate in them, a proper understanding of the project of the self is an essential prerequisite for understanding and restructuring the way in which these broader institutional contexts are produced and reproduced in time-space.

On a broader institutional level my starting point is clear. In late modernity, individuals are participating in forms of social organization which are increasingly open-ended. The demise of final authorities means that people are having, as Thompson explains, to 'fall back increasingly on their own resources to construct a coherent identity for themselves'.[3] However, while the expanding networks of communication are giving them unprecedented access to forms of information and communication almost anywhere and at any time, individuals remain endowed with varying capacities and resources on which they may draw to construct their sense of self. The ability to enrich and transform the process of self-formation is thus unevenly spread. These conditions undoubtedly have far-reaching consequences for individuals' social involvement and well-being, for the way they communicate, for their experience of everyday life, and for their ability to construct who they are. However, in our attempts to understand this process, we must steer clear of accounts that tend to freeze human autonomy and see individuals ending up living broken lives, or of accounts that tend to celebrate a future based on naive visions of human empowerment.

I want to begin this chapter by examining how in late modernity we might view the self as a symbolic project. In doing so, I shall draw out some of the distinctive tensions and difficulties which people have to resolve in order to preserve a coherent narrative of self-identity. These are what Giddens describes as 'dilemmas of the self'.[4]

While some accounts of new and positive mechanisms of self-formation are now beginning to emerge, other accounts, lurking particularly in the literature associated with postmodernism, seem to dismiss the idea that individuals might actively resolve 'dilemmas of the self'. In the second section of this chapter I want therefore to explore critically what Bauman has dubbed 'intertwining and interpenetrating postmodern life strategies'.[5] I shall relate each of these strategies to types of 'personality' which in some form we might well come across on the internet. But adopting such life strategies in communication via intranets or the internet would severely curtail the choices that individuals might otherwise have had open to them: we do not have to agree with Bauman's claim that 'the fragmented bones of postmodern contention do not fit together to form a skeleton around which a non-fragmentary and continuous, shared engagement could be wrapped.'[6]

Against the analytical backcloth of the first two sections of this chapter, I shall explore in the third section what empirical research has to say about these matters by examining two empirical studies. Each of these studies attempts in its own way to focus on how the development of the internet might be transforming the nature of the self, experience and communication in everyday life. Then, in the concluding section, I shall explain how, by approaching the internet as a modality of cultural trans-mission, we might generate more potential for developing an under-standing of the impact of the internet on the self as a symbolic project. Parallel to the traits of an alternative approach to the management of risk in the broader institutional contexts, I shall tease out some similar traits which may guide a more positive use of the internet by individuals in their day-to-day communication.

The dilemmas of the self as a symbolic project

With the increasing availability of mediated experience, the project of the modern self has in many respects become a symbolic project. As Thompson explains,

> it is a project that the individual constructs out of the symbolic materials which are available to him or her, materials which the individual weaves into a coherent account of who he or she is, a narrative of self-identity ... To recount to ourselves or others who we are is to retell the narratives – which are continuously modified in the process of retelling – of how we got to where we are and of where we are going from here.[7]

By examining an individual's biography through time-space we can con-struct what Giddens calls a 'trajectory of the self'. As such, the narrative of the self forms a 'trajectory of development from the past to the anticip-ated future. The individual appropriates his past by sifting through it in the light of what is anticipated for an (organized) future. The trajectory of the self has a coherence that derives from a cognitive awareness of the various phases of the lifespan.'[8] Social relations and social contexts are thus reflexively incorporated into the forging of the project of the self.

  Under conditions of simple modernity, a number of mechanisms acted to diminish anxiety and diffuse worries about how an individual might live in the world. While identity, Bauman writes, entered the modern mind and practice dressed from the start as an individual task,

> putting the individual responsibility for self-formation on the agenda spawned the host of trainers, coaches, teachers, counselors and guides all claiming to hold superior knowledge of what the identities they recom-mended consisted of and of the ways such identities could be acquired, held, and shown to be acquired and held.[9]

The development of internally referential expert systems provided the basis for individuals to counter uncertainty and to pick out relatively coherent trajectories for the development of the self. Moreover, as Giddens argues, 'the ontological security which modernity has purchased, on the level of day-to-day routines, depends on an institutional exclusion of social life from fundamental existential issues which raise central moral dilemmas for human beings'.[10] In effect, this involves processes of *experiential segregation* and the concealment of certain unsettling phenomena in order to reduce the anxieties related to life planning to manageable proportions.[11] Day-to-day life thus became sequestered from experiences to do with, for example, madness, criminality, sickness and death, sexuality and nature, in an attempt to bracket out unlikely experiences and turns of events in people's lives.[12]

Today, under conditions of reflexive modernization, however, Giddens argues that radical doubt has filtered into most aspects of day-to-day life and is having important consequences for the self as a symbolic project. The abandonment of final authorities means that at any given moment in time there are no longer any clear-cut answers telling individuals how the project of the self must proceed. Internally referential systems are being continually questioned, weakened and sometimes even broken down. Statements communicated to us via the media such as: 'British beef is best: this beef is British so it must be safe to eat' no longer cut much cloth. Moreover, as Thompson explains, 'the profusion of mediated materials can provide individuals with the means of exploring alternative forms of life in a symbolic or imaginary mode; it can provide individuals with a glimpse of alternatives, thereby enabling them to reflect critically on themselves and on the actual circumstances of their lives.'[13]

Living in the world of late modernity involves what Giddens has identified in *Modernity and Self-Identity* as four 'dilemmas of the self' which have to be resolved if the individual is to attain a coherent narrative of the self.[14] Let us now look at each of these in turn.

Unification versus fragmentation   Modernity, writes Giddens, 'fragments; it also unites' (p. 189). On the one hand, individuals have to negotiate choices among a diversity of options. On the other, mediated experience is heightening the degree to which individuals can become integrated into distant frameworks of experience. These distant frameworks may even provide them with experiences that are more easily available as resources to create a coherent narrative of the self than those nearby. While Giddens does not deny that localized trust relations continue to play an important role in promoting integrated projects of the self, the mere fact that happenings are distant and mediated does not necessarily mean that they are opaque. Nor are projects of the self that interlace with such distant frameworks necessarily doomed to disintegrate into a multitude of disconnected 'selves'.

Powerlessness versus appropriation   It is often claimed that individuals experience feelings of powerlessness in relation to distant, often large-scale happenings outside the spheres of their day-to-day life. In describing his second dilemma of the self, Giddens argues, however, that we would be 'hard pressed to substantiate an overall generalization that, with the coming of modern institutions, most individuals either are (or feel) more powerless than in preceding times . . . all forms of expropriation necessarily provide the possibility of reappropriation' (p. 192). Moreover, participation in small communities does not necessarily guarantee that individuals are more powerful, and in most cases tradition has an unchallengeable hold over scope for independent action.

Authority versus uncertainty   The third dilemma of the self that Giddens identifies is that under conditions of reflexive modernization, there are no determinant authorities yet plenty of claimants to authority (p. 194). However, while the experience of doubt as a background phenomenon may enter into most aspects of daily life, individuals who worry about risk all of the time are not regarded as 'normal' (p. 183). Most individuals develop strategies to cope with uncertainty. These *compromise packages*, as Giddens calls them, involve a mixture of routine behaviour and commitment. They might, for example, contribute to a particular choice of lifestyle, and vest trust in particular choices of expert systems. People thus succeed in bracketing out anxieties and getting on with their day-to-day activities. Someone with a fear for flying, for example, might routinely incorporate flying into what they do, but only at a cost of overcoming their anxiety by flying only with particular airline companies, or by never leaving their seat while in the air.

Personalized versus commodified experience   Giddens's fourth dilemma of the self is that between personalized versus commodified experience. He writes: 'modernity opens up the project of the self, but under conditions strongly influenced by the standardizing effects of commodity capitalism' (p. 196). More broadly, modernity opens up the project of the self to the standardizing effects of all forms of authority hierarchy. However, these standardized influences do not impact on the project of the self in a direct way. Individuals may draw on standardized influences in an active and creative fashion, and the degree to which individuals can appropriate them is, of course, a source of tension and conflict and dependent on their ability to master appropriate responses.

In the light of these dilemmas confronting individuals in the turmoil of our modern world, we might conclude with Giddens that 'achieving control over change, in respect of lifestyle, demands an engagement with the outer social world rather than a retreat from it' (p. 184). Yet, in so far as the internet is intensifying these dilemmas of the self, it is more than ever an engagement which involves developing skills and strategies for actively fending off threats of meaninglessness and repression.

Life strategies and the internet

The internet, together with intranets and extranets, is resulting in a tremendous expansion of information available to individuals. It incorporates contextual happenings on a global scale and creates new opportunities for both mediated and quasi-mediated interaction. Individuals charting a course through these options and burdens have to create a compromise package that allows them both to construct and to protect a coherent narrative of the self. But what options might we as individuals be said to have when preparing and bracing ourselves and developing the necessary skills and strategies for using this new mode of communication in order to 'make the best' of our projects of the self? I have explained that under conditions of reflexive modernization, new mechanisms of self-formation are beginning to emerge, and these are directly related to the ongoing process of resolving the 'dilemmas of the self' in everyday life. Yet some of the recent literature of cultural and social theory is highly sceptical, characterizing the self as being dissolved as a coherent entity. In this section I want critically to examine four types of 'postmodern identity' as elaborated by Bauman in his book *Life in Fragments*. He introduces these personalities as *the stroller, the vagabond, the tourist* and *the player*. All four of these 'postmodern personalities' are developed against the backdrop of a modern type of personality, *the pilgrim*, which he says has been displaced by the uncertainties we face today.

But how convincing are Bauman's 'postmodern personalities' as the only ingredients from which we can blend a cohesive lifestyle? If we were to use these as blueprints, how successful would we be at mobilizing the internet in our attempts to chart a path through the dilemmas of the self? Let me examine the personality of *the pilgrim* first, and go on to elaborate the others in turn while relating them to internet use.

The end of modern life strategies   In *Life in Fragments* Bauman describes the pilgrim as 'the most fitting allegory of modern life strategy' (p. 91). Not that pilgrims are a modern invention, but modernity reshaped and gave them a new kind of prominence. In line with what he considers to be the essence of a pilgrim's being in the world, Bauman argues that the process of producing and cobbling together a biography for modern individuals was very much a 'living-towards-project' (p. 87). 'For the pilgrim, for the modern man, this meant in practical terms that he could/should/had to select his point of arrival fairly early in life with confidence, certain that the straight line of life-time ahead will not bend, twist or warp, come to a halt or turn backwards' (p. 87). The pilgrim thus walked with a purpose and for this walk to be orderly, time and space had to be emptied of all obstacles which might get in the way, and had to be made to measure the goals which had been pre-set. However, as Bauman argues, the world we live in today has become inhospitable to the pilgrim. Both the pilgrim's way and their final destination have become uncertain. The pilgrim's progress has become fragmented and rendered meaningless by a lack of shared journeys. In our contemporary world, Bauman explains, 'the real problem is not how to build identity but how to preserve it' (p. 88).

Bauman's description of the modern-day pilgrim might appear to fit a great many people who are left baffled by the possibilities of the internet. For them, too, the internet is a placeless and obstacle-ridden world without a clear purpose, one in which walking becomes dislocated and the walker is continually tempted to divert from the chosen path, forever postponing or even forgetting their destination. As such, it is a confusing world in which websites appear from nowhere and vanish again without notice, and seldom exist long enough for the modern-day pilgrim to find their way about them. From the pilgrim's perspective, it would be difficult to envisage how the internet might ever facilitate and support a coherent narrative of the self. For the pilgrim, the internet creates an unreal world inhabited by fake and untrustworthy people who can adopt, and experiment with, any identity they like.

Reading Bauman's subsequent account of the emergence of new life strategies from the experience of conditions of intensifying globalization and social reflexivity, and his description of the emergence of post-traditional forms of organization might only serve to substantiate the pilgrim's worst fears. Today, Bauman writes, the life strategy of the pilgrim has given way to that of *the stroller, the vagabond, the tourist* and *the player*. All of these life strategies 'offer jointly the metaphor for the postmodern strategy moved by the horror of being bound and fixed'. From their experience of the world, Bauman claims, nothing much emerges but mostly negative rules of thumb (p. 91). If we followed Bauman's negative rules of thumb through to internet practice and the way we use it to communicate, then the rather depressing result would read something like this:

1 'Do not spend too much time surfing the WWW or enterprise-wide web. The shorter the time spent online, the greater the chance of completing what you set out to do.'
2 'Do not get too fond of people you meet on IRC – the less you care about them, the easier it will be for you to move on.'
3 'Do not commit yourself too strongly to particular webpages or IRC channels – you cannot know for how long they will remain available or whether they will continue to justify your commitment in the future.'

4 'Do not invest too much time building a homepage – once it has been seen by others it will lose its value fast and become a liability.'
5 'Do not delay gratification. If you can download a file or print a webpage, do it now; you cannot know for sure whether it will still be there tomorrow or whether that what you want now will be what you will want in the future.'

Each of Bauman's four types or styles of 'postmodern identity' in *Life in Fragments* interprets these rules of thumb in their own way.

The stroller and the internet   The experience of the stroller is one of going for a stroll, 'finding themselves among strangers and being a stranger to them . . . taking in those strangers as "surfaces" – so that "what one sees" exhausts "what they are", and above all seeing and knowing them episodically' (p. 92). For those who adopt this strategy, the internet is both an ideal haunt and a means to elevate their style of communication to an even higher level of perfection. They can stroll uncommittedly from webpage to webpage, from IRC channel to IRC channel, from newsgroup to newsgroup, choosing to accept or to decline incoming chat requests from ICQ – in so doing, they are immersed in the ultimate freedom of being present, but out of reach.

The vagabond and the internet   The experience of the vagabond is that of a stranger. As Bauman writes, 'he can never be "the native", the "settled one", one with "roots with the soil" – and not for the lack of trying: whatever he may do to ingratiate himself in the eyes of the natives, too fresh is the memory of his arrival – that is, of his being elsewhere before' (pp. 94–5). Vagabonds on the internet will often have a string of dormant or disused e-mail addresses. They will be registered as users of websites for which they have long since forgotten their passwords. They will have started to build homepages and then abandoned them. They roam the internet, snapping up offers of free internet accounts, only to be struck off or evicted for not having used them.

The tourist and the internet   The experience of the tourist, Bauman argues, is that of 'a conscious and systematic seeker of experience . . . of the experience of difference and novelty – as the joys of the familiar wear off quickly and cease to allure. The tourists want to immerse themselves in the strange and bizarre element . . . on the condition, though, that it would not outlive its pleasure-giving facility and can be shaken off whenever they wish' (p. 96). For those adopting this life strategy, the internet offers the space they need. It allows them to participate in strange and bizarre experiences which they end at a click of their mouse. They can escape their familiar world and enter into dialogue with others having very different outlooks on life. They can view webpages which frighten, shock and question their expectations. At the same time, however, such a strategy heightens their confusion over which place they might choose to call their 'home' and which place they might be said to be 'just visiting'. Their nightmare consists of getting caught up between a fear of homesickness and homeboundedness.

The player and the internet   The experience of the player, the last of Bauman's 'postmodern identities', is that of a succession of games. The player's world, Bauman writes, 'is the world of risks, of intuition, of precaution taking . . . the game has also a clear, uncontested ending . . . Whoever does not like the outcome, must "cut his losses" and start from scratch . . . The game is like war, yet that war which is a game must leave no mental scars and no nursed grudges' (pp. 98–9). From the viewpoint of this strategy, the internet might be approached as an extended computer game; a mediated experience entered into out of choice and one which can be terminated at any time, leaving participants untouched but for the loss of time elapsed during play. The aim of the player is to win at all cost while protecting themselves as best they can against danger. Having engaged others in conversation on IRC and gained their trust, the player will often just quit the 'game'. The only reasoning to be given would be that 'all good things must come to an end at some time.' To the dismay of others who are not players, the players are seldom willing to suspend disbelief and play the same game again.

Each of Bauman's types or styles of 'postmodern identity' thus appears to have its own practised life strategy, often with a 'generous pinch of schizophrenia' (p. 99). More importantly, Bauman argues, all four of these strategies further human disengagement and commitment-avoidance and necessarily render community fragmentary. As such, Bauman concludes,

> each society sets limits to the life strategies that can be imagined, and certainly to those which can be practised. But the kind of society we live in leaves off-limits such strategies as may critically and militantly question its principles and thus open the way to new strategies, currently excluded for the reason of their non-viability. (p. 104)

If these conceptions of contemporary life strategies exhaust all possibilities of communication on the net, then this would preclude projects of the self that are capable of standing in a position of appropriation in relation to the social world. For each of Bauman's 'postmodern identities', social life results only in impoverished social action. The stroller, the vagabond, the tourist and the player are all personalities whose participation in the world is mainly constituted through the defensive rejection of more positive and open social engagements. As such, each of these personalities tends in the direction of more narrowly defined and sceptical personal realms.

Regarding the internet and its impact on life strategies, its use may well impoverish certain aspects of individual action and Bauman's ideas draw our attention to these very well. Yet it would be difficult to deny that the internet is also furthering the appropriation of new possibilities. Communication via the internet is alienating yet at the same time it is opening up new possibilities of reappropriation which extend well beyond those available to individuals before. So while I believe Bauman is correct in suggesting that the self has been transformed under conditions of reflexive modernization, I want to argue in the next section that we need to think about this transformation in a different light. Bauman's postmodern life strategies certainly do not exhaust all the options open to us.

Transforming the process of self-formation

Having viewed the project of the self in late modernity from the perspective of a number of social and cultural theorists, I want also to look critically at the connected topics of the internet, communication and the self and experience as pursued in contemporary empirical studies. What do they have to offer in the way of knowledge as to how people might best deploy the internet to actively fend off threats of meaninglessness and repression? Is there any evidence to suggest that people are successfully mobilizing the internet to communicate as part of more positive life strategies?

I shall examine two contrasting studies of internet communication. First, an investigation by Robert Kraut et al., 'Internet paradox: a social technology that reduces social involvement and psychological well-being?'.[15] Second, a research project described by Daniel Chandler in his paper 'Personal home pages and the construction of identities on the web', published on the web. Chandler examines the process of fashioning personal and public identities as communicated by homepages.

Both these studies are path-breaking and provocative in many respects. However, I shall also try to demonstrate that they do not provide a satisfactory account of how individuals might deploy the internet to enrich and transform their processes of self-formation. While the investigation conducted by Robert Kraut et al. does not draw directly on Bauman's postmodern life strategies, it does reflect some of their central aspects. And while Chandler's study offers a more suitable starting point for examining how the internet might help to enrich and transform the process of self-formation, it also has its weaknesses, as I shall explain.

The internet paradox: loneliness and depression versus friendship and happiness

The first of these two empirical studies is intended to contribute to the debate on whether the internet is improving social involvement and psychological well-being or whether it is harming it. It reports the results of a two-year study, the HomeNet project, which began in March 1995 and involved 169 individuals in 73 households. Research of this nature is crucial if we are to form an understanding of the impact of the internet on the self and experience. The researchers, Kraut and his colleagues, complain that empirical evidence about the impact of the internet on social relationships and social involvement is sparse, speculative and anecdotal. It is this information gap that sparked off their study.

The HomeNet project   The families in the study come from eight diverse neighbourhoods in Pittsburgh, Pennsylvania. The families were given a computer, software, a phone line and free access to the internet. At least two family members were given training in the use of the computer, electronic mail and the world wide web. In return, the families allowed the researchers to monitor their internet use and they agreed to participate in a number of interviews. Demographic characteristics, social involvement and psychological well-being were measured at the outset, and social involvement and psychological well-being were measured again after between twelve and twenty-four months of internet use in order to make a comparison over time. During this period, internet use was monitored automatically using a logging program.

The research findings   According to the study, 'greater use of the internet was associated with subsequent declines in family communication.' Greater use of the internet to communicate was also associated with declines in the size of both the local and the distant social circle. Individuals who made greater use of the internet also reported larger increases in loneliness. Moreover, the researchers write, 'greater use of the internet was associated with increased depression . . . and disengagement from real life.'

While their findings are based on statistical associations, the researchers adamantly believe 'that in this case, correlation does indeed imply causation'. At the same time, however, they are cautious about how far their research findings can be generalized. For example, the experiences of the families studied may change over time. They discovered, for example, that for some teenagers the internet lost its appeal when they 'became immersed in the more serious work of college'. Moreover, the internet is continually changing too – ICQ, for example, was not available during the early days of their study. ICQ is a programme which allows individuals to monitor the presence of selected other users and may have benefited users in finding online friends and acquaintances.

'Some plausible and theoretically interesting mechanisms' While Kraut and his colleagues do not mention the processes through which their findings occur, they do refer to 'plausible and theoretically interesting mechanisms'. In doing so, they start from a comparison of the internet with earlier communication technologies such as television and the telephone. It is plausible, they argue, that television caused a reduction in social involvement and psychological well-being. Television 'reduced social participation as it kept people home watching the set. . . . That is, the time people spend watching TV is time they are not actively socially engaged.' They argue that the internet, when used for obtaining information via the world wide web, is similar to television. Both television and the internet thus displace other forms of social activity. On the other hand, when the internet is used for interpersonal communication, they claim that the impact of the internet may be more like that of the telephone. The telephone, in their view, 'turned out to be far more social than television'.

Much however depends, according to the researchers, on how a communication technology 'shapes the balance of strong and weak network ties that people maintain'. Generally, they argue,

> strong personal ties are supported by physical proximity.' The internet 'potentially reduces the importance of physical proximity in creating and maintaining networks of strong social ties . . . the internet offers opportunities for social interaction that do not depend on the distance between parties. People often use the internet to keep up with those with whom they have preexisting relationships. But they also develop new relationships online. Most of these new relationships are weak.

The internet may therefore result not only in the displacement of other forms of social activity, but also in the displacement of strong social involvement. Online friendships, these researchers write, 'are likely to be more limited than friendships supported by physical proximity'.

This first study ends by giving the advice that 'until the technology evolves to be more beneficial, people should moderate how much they use the internet and monitor the uses to which they put it.'

Shortcomings of the HomeNet project While Kraut et al. are right to draw our attention to the importance of studying the impact of the internet on the self and experience, there are a number of problems with their account. I shall elaborate this argument by briefly considering six important aspects of their study: their interpretation of the consequences of internet use; the idea that their study implies causation; their conceptualization of the internet; their arguments concerning the displacement of social activity and strong relationships; their account of the software that was used and the training that was given; their advice that individuals should moderate how much they use the internet to communicate with others.

In their interpretation of the consequences of internet use for social involvement and well-being, Kraut et al. describe these as tending towards the opposite poles of either harm or improvement. While this may be an indispensable starting point, it is also too elementary an approach. In order to understand the consequences of internet use we need to go beyond these either/or descriptions and recognize the ambivalence of this technology. The internet can both harm and improve social involvement and well-being at the same time.

The researchers are careful to point out that 'people can use home computers and the internet in many different ways and for many purposes' and that the internet in their view is merely 'associated' with a reduction in social involvement and well-being. Yet there is also more than a hint of technological determinism in their work. First, they have a clear conviction 'that in this case, correlation does indeed imply causation'. Second, their idea that we ought to sit back and wait until the technology 'evolves to be more beneficial' is suggestive of the internet as some kind of external force that develops beyond our control. Third, their advice that 'people should moderate how much they use the internet' clearly smacks again of a conviction that this technology in its present form is inherently harmful. However, given their strongly worded warnings, it does seem rather odd that they did not identify any mechanism through which causality occurs.

Kraut and his colleagues are aware that the internet as a medium is made up of a whole range of different applications. However, in their conclusions concerning the reduction in social involvement and well-being, they continually refer indiscriminately to 'the internet' as one medium or one application. Moreover, the nature of social interaction may be affected both by the very form of the technology and by the content of messages conveyed. Consequently, claims that 'the internet was associated with declines in participants' communication with family members' and so on become so vague as to be meaningless. Are the researchers referring to the technology or the message?

Kraut et al. also perpetuate the idea that when individuals use the internet, they are somehow disengaging from 'real' life. Of course, such approaches do filter into lay opinions about the internet, for example when participants report that they reduced their use of the internet when they had more serious things to do. However, this does not mean that researchers should perpetuate such a view.

Not having been able to identify any mechanism through which causality occurs, Kraut et al. engage in precisely the kind of speculative debate they set out to avoid. What they refer to as 'plausible and theoretically interesting mechanisms' turn out to be based on very partial and uncritical understandings of other media such as television and the telephone. They claim, for instance, that television reduces social participation and negatively affects social relationships. Yet the idea that recipients of mediated experience are passive consumers of that experience has long been laid to rest.[16]

A more sensitive appraisal of the social uses of television is brought out well in the writings of James Lull.[17] He distinguishes between structural and relational uses of television in this respect. The structural use of television may be environmental, by which he means it is switched on, providing only a background noise and companionship against which other activities such as conversation may take place. The structural use of television may also be social in a sense that social activities may be organized, coordinated and regulated around its use. As for the relational uses of television, television may act as a facilitator of communication. It might, for example, provide illustrations for discussing experiences, give participants a common ground for conversation and set an agenda for talk. Television use may also create a setting for displaying social affiliation or avoidance. Watching television together, for example, may provide family members with opportunities to display mutual interests and affection, and relieve tension. It might also be used to display avoidance as individuals become immersed in watching and so exclude all others. A further relational use of television described by Lull concerns social learning. Television use may help people solve problems or legitimize certain decisions. Lastly, television use often involves households having to negotiate what they want to watch, a process that sometimes ends in conflicts, reinforcing or challenging patterns of authority. Kraut et al. ignore these dimensions, and equally ignore Ithiel de Sola Pool's interesting writings concerning the telephone.[18]

The case that the internet may act to displace social activity and strong relationships cannot therefore be so simply put. Many of the researchers' claims as to the harmful nature of the internet lack a real basis of understanding either of the technology or of the social contexts within which, and by virtue of which, information and symbolic content are produced and received.

The researchers describe the software given to the participants in the HomeNet project as consisting of 'MacMail II, Netscape Navigator 2 or 3 for web browsing, and ClarisWorks Office'. However, their account of this software package, and the opportunities it opened to participants, is confusing in many respects. The time spent on the internet is reported to have included time spent using internet relay chat. However, we were not told that this programme was included in the original package. Are we therefore to conclude from this that participants could download additional software? Would this not have affected the measurements of the impact of the internet on well-being and social involvement? The internet would mean many different things to many different participants. If, on the other hand, individuals were not permitted to download additional software, would this not also have frustrated their efforts to use the internet in the way they wanted?

Moreover throughout their account, Kraut et al. describe the world wide web solely as a place for retrieving electronic information or engaging in web chat. Nowhere do they mention that it is also a place where individuals can actively engage in creating and communicating information via their own homepages. The opportunities for building homepages were available and being enjoyed by many at the time the researchers were conducting their study. Are we therefore to conclude that while participants received some form of training, this did not include training in how to construct webpages? The opportunity to build webpages is very important for the way in which individuals might use the internet to communicate and enrich and transform the nature of the self and experience in everyday life.

The researchers advise people not to spend too much time on the internet. Yet if someone makes friends with a person living some distance away, but lacks the means to travel and meet up with them face to face, is that a problem 'caused' by the internet? Suppose individuals using the internet to communicate with others discovered information which allowed them to see their own lives in a new light. Imagine also that this experience affected their feelings of well-being because they discovered that the life they were living was unacceptable in the light of this new knowledge. Are we then to turn to them and say: 'Sorry but you'll just have to moderate how much you use the internet from now on.' Such a response perpetuates the idea of the individual as a minimal self, who can do little else but passively wait for whatever will happen next.

Positive experiences   In stark contrast to the negative findings of this study, positive experiences were also revealed during the interviews with participants. These included, for example, parents keeping in contact with distant children, friends rediscovering each other, individuals consoling each other during times of tragedy, and friendships between classmates being continued after school. Events like these may be outnumbered quantitatively, but qualitatively they can be of life-changing importance. The researchers seem to have a clear-cut vision that the internet causes too much disengagement from 'real' life. Yet their study helps us to discover how individuals as 'real' people might be more positively engaged in using the internet to develop strategies and skills to actively fend off meaninglessness and repression in their everyday lives.

The construction of identity on the web

The investigation by Chandler adopts a phenomenological approach which results in a mainly ethnographic account of the construction of identity on the world wide web.[19] His study is full of detailed and rich description of the reasoning behind people's use of the internet to construct projects of the self and to share these with others. The individuals in Chandler's study are treated as clever people who have a purposeful and knowledgeable penetration of the WWW and the opportunities for communication it offers them. However, his writings do have other shortcomings which we will need to examine critically.

The WWW and the presentation of self   When people build homepages they are not just constructing webpages. As Chandler writes, 'personal homepages can be seen as reflecting the construction of their makers' identities.' He likens homepages to the collages of symbolic material we might see on an individual's wall in the home. However, the WWW 'is incalculably more widely accessible for self-presentation'. While most of his investigation focuses on how individuals use homepages to constitute their identities and frame their experiences, he is also aware that this medium of communication is not universally accessible. Moreover, the images individuals present of themselves on the web also have unintended consequences in the way they may be interpreted by others independently of their builders' intentions or presence. Thus, Chandler writes, homepages 'may involve both intentional and unintentional disclosures (as well as sometimes leading to misinterpretation)'.

Content, form and context   The content of homepages may reflect the private or professional interests and biographical details of their authors. Subject to people's skill, experience and resources, they communicate meaning through text, graphics and sound. 'Individual "pages" ', writes Chandler, 'vary from short screenfuls to long scrolls, and one individual's personal homepages may range from a single page to many interconnected pages.' Most homepages provide visitors with the person's e-mail address and sometimes even a 'guest book' where they may leave their comments. Some homepages have 'access counters' which give their creators some idea of how often others visit them.

The form of the homepage also allows individuals to present themselves in different ways. Some pages thus reflect their creators as 'arty types' or 'science types', etc. The use of interconnected webpages allows individuals to separate out different aspects of their personality and manage their communication with others more effectively.

However, it is not only the content and the form of the homepages that reveal much about their builders. The links made to other webpages, for example to homepages of friends or other places of interest on the web, are all part of the individual's quest to use this communication technology to collage an identity. Such links work to contextualize the homepage and thereby contribute to its meaning. This process of contextualization also works in the other direction. The interpretation of a particular homepage would change, for example, according to whether it was accessed from a link on a webpage belonging to an individual's place of work, or from a link on a webpage belonging to a relative or friend.

Constructing identities   Some commentators dismiss the value of a homepage as just 'a fan club to oneself'. To this, Chandler responds: 'Even if some of these pages may be practically worthless to anyone other than their authors, their value to their authors may be considerable.' Not only does the WWW allow individuals to experiment with shaping their identity, it is a communication medium ideally adapted, Chandler argues, 'to the dynamic purposes of identity maintenance'. He also comments, however, that 'the rewriting of identities in homepages wipes out those formulations which preceded it', unless the author adopts the 'diary form'.

Chandler's study reflects individuals' active and discursive involvement regarding how and why they create their homepages in the way they do. Tristan, one of the people in Chandler's investigation, for example, comments on his homepage: 'It helps to define who I am. Before I start to look at/write about something then I'm often not sure what my feelings are, but after having done so, I can at least have more of an idea.' David, a gay man in Chandler's study, reports that his homepage allows him 'to give a complete definition of how I see the gay scene and my place in it, as well as a lot of stuff about my life which people are not going to guess by just looking at me across a crowded room'. In much the same way, Rob explained that his homepage provided 'a very easy way for me to come out. I could say, "check out my website" and knew they'd come across the gay part. More importantly, they could find out in my own positive terms and think about it before reacting.' Some individuals reported having several unconnected homepages which they had created for different 'audiences', allowing them to manage more effectively the enclosure and disclosure of aspects of the self.

The shortcomings of the homepage study   Chandler's study into the construction of identities on the web illuminates many interesting aspects of this communication process. The activities of the individuals he studies do not slot easily into any of Bauman's postmodern life strategies. Moreover, for participants in Chandler's study, the advice at the end of the 'internet paradox' study would probably go in at one ear and out at the other: being told to moderate their internet use would be an unacceptable response to their different kinds of experiences in day-to-day life.

My criticism of Chandler's investigation is that it gives insufficient attention to the structured social relations within which the construction of homepages is always embedded. As such, it suffers from what Giddens describes as the basic difficulties of '"interpretative sociology" – the failure to cope with the problems of institutional organization, power and struggle as integral features of social life'.[20] This is not to say that Chandler completely ignores the fact that individuals have varying capacities and resources on which they may draw to construct their sense of self as individuals. Rather, it is to say that the broader institutional features of late modernity are poorly developed in his work. They 'do not appear as "negotiated", as themselves the product of human action, but rather as the backdrop against which such action becomes intelligible'.[21] Chandler mentions the unintended consequences of constructing homepages, but he fails to connect them up to the way in which individuals cope with the 'dilemmas of the self' and the challenges they must face in order to develop a coherent narrative of the self.

The internet and enriching the process of self-formation

In late modernity, individuals are facing profound changes in their personal and emotional lives. Within this context internet use is altering the very texture of their experience. In this final section of the chapter I shall focus on four traits of internet use which might help individuals deploy the internet within more positive life strategies. We can only understand how the internet might enrich and transform processes of self-formation, however, if we treat it as a modality of cultural transmission. Internet use is not just a matter of individuals adding yet another device to their arsenal of modern communication technologies. The internet is shaking up the way they live.

If individuals do not want internet use to contribute to a feeling of being thrown into a world of overwhelming complexity, then they must attempt to incorporate the four related traits into all the arenas of circulation involved in internet use. These traits are related to the contexts within which individuals act as producers of information, the contexts involved in the transmission of information, and lastly the contexts within which individuals act as recipients of information. I do not want to balance these traits against Bauman's 'rules of thumb', for although I intend them to give individuals a particular direction in their use of the internet, they do not necessitate a particular outcome. The four related traits are: (1) the use of internet technology to negotiate mediated experience; (2) the use of internet technology to reappropriate knowledge and skills; (3) the use of internet technology to forge commitment and mutuality; and (4) the use of internet technology to track risk and uncertainty and transcend conflict. All four relate directly to the 'dilemmas of the self' identified by Giddens and described above. They must also be understood in the context of the changes taking place within modern organizations described in chapter 5. Individuals cannot be expected to successfully take up the challenges of new communication technologies such as the internet all on their own.

I shall conclude this chapter by relating each of the four traits to an example of internet use and demonstrate how approaching the internet as a modality of cultural transmission will help us see ways in which the internet can help us regain some mastery over our life circumstances. I shall also use this example to develop an awareness of how the use of the internet to actively fend off threats of meaninglessness and repression will always involve the creation of new risks and uncertainties.

Let me now look at each of the four traits in turn.

The use of internet technology to negotiate experience

Intranets and the internet vastly increase the opportunities for negotiating mediated experience, that is, for making information and other symbolic content available to others and actively acquiring mediated content and re-embedding it as part of the project of the self. The negotiation of mediated experience must always be understood within the socially structured contexts in which it is generated. Mediated experience is thus, as Thompson writes, always 'recontextualized experience'.[22] Studying the use of internet technology helps reveal how its use interweaves with the priorities and experiences which are relevant in people's particular spatial-temporal contexts. Individuals are not just merely connected to intranets or the internet: they always participate selectively in their use. Some information and some forms of interaction are relevant to their projects, while others are not. Probably more than with any other medium, individuals using intranets and the internet have to actively negotiate mediated experience and endow it with structures of relevance to the self. Moreover, their interests are formed and reformed over time.

At one end of the spectrum, the internet or intranets extend standardized influences. Without the standardized influences of, for example, technological design, intranets or the internet simply would not exist. Such networks also extend and intensify the standardized influences of institutional arrangements. Examples include the standard questions answered in a list of frequently asked questions, the standardized interaction made possible by dialogue boxes on a webpage, or even a particular version of events encoded on a webpage. At the other end of the spectrum, however, the internet vastly extends an individual's ability to control, filter, personalize and shape the content of mediated experience themselves.

While the internet vastly increases the opportunities for individuals to negotiate mediated experience, it can also heighten their awareness of the limits of their ability to do so. Sometimes, people complain because they feel they are being swamped by the amount of information which is available. Other times, they complain that they cannot find or access the information or the person they need. Sometimes individuals send e-mail which is not replied to. Other times, they are confronted with information which is useless because they cannot relate it to their own priorities and experiences. They may also have created a homepage which has simply vanished into the digital wilderness. Internet use can thus make individuals aware of the limits of their ability to negotiate mediated experience, but it would be ridiculous to suggest that intranets and the internet always do so.

Actively negotiating mediated experience can also be a positive experience. Someone using internet relay chat, for example, may communicate with a person on the other side of the world and have a more intimate relationship with this person than with somebody living next door. Alternatively, someone may acquire information from a webpage which allows them to participate more competently in face-to-face communication and even discover proximate others with whom they share an interest.

If intranets or the internet were deliberately designed to be opaque, to cause loneliness and depression, they would look rather different. Instead, there are many communicative arrangements which can assist individuals in their attempts to negotiate mediated experience. Internet browsers, for example, allow people to personalize them by adding bookmarks to webpages they enjoy visiting. Some webpages allow users to customize the information conveyed to them. Some individuals take it on themselves to help others to actively negotiate mediated experience by taking on the responsibilities of an information broker, collecting together information and recontextualizing it in such a way that it becomes relevant to others' lives.

Individuals with access to an intranet or the internet must not, and do not, just sit back and wait until the technology evolves to be more beneficial. In most cases, they can use internet technology to actively negotiate and participate in creating the kinds of mediated experience they want. If they are not yet aware of the parameters of their freedom to do so, if they lack the necessary skills or if they cannot agree with each other, then that is yet another matter.

The use of internet technology to reappropriate knowledge and skills

If intranets or the internet are to be used to enrich and transform processes of self-formation, then strategies must be developed to use them to reappropriate knowledge and skills which in modern society have been passed on to external agencies or particular expert systems. This is the second trait people need to incorporate into all the arenas of circulation involved in their internet use. An individual's ability to draw on the internet to reappropriate knowledge and skills must again be understood within the socially structured contexts within which such attempts are made. Reappropriating knowledge and skills often involves learning to actively shed, forget and transform other knowledge and skills that have become inappropriate under conditions of late modernity.

Internet technology is vastly increasing the individual's ability to intervene in events that are not normally 'within reach'. Most expert systems now realize that sharing knowledge is an important way of actively gaining trust at a time when the quality of their performance is continually questioned. The internet and intranets can also be used to compare and assess claims made by rival authorities. However, one of the most important ways in which individuals reappropriate control is by using intranets and the internet to bypass certain intermediaries or gatekeepers who once managed and limited their access to information and their channels of communication.

While people may, for example, complain about how they or their lives are portrayed and represented in the mass media, the internet offers them a platform to frame their own experiences and take control over their own symbolic projects. In order to do this successfully, much of the new knowledge and many of the skills that have to be acquired relate to using internet technology itself. Learning how to build homepages and how to draw attention to them are of central importance. Varying degrees of competence and ability will again prevail. An individual may, for example, reappropriate information from another website by merely linking their homepage to it. An individual who has mastered the use of frames, however, can recontextualize and reappropriate mediated experiences from other sources in a more sophisticated way. Frames allow people to divide their homepage window into separate windows. They can thus 'reframe' external information while at the same time continuing their own presence in the surrounding windows. This gives them a more powerful platform for providing critical comment.

The use of internet technology to forge commitment and mutuality

The internet and intranets can undoubtedly increase a person's aware-ness of the unpredictability of daily life and the threats and dangers which are felt to be outside their control. Yet it would be rather one-sided and pathetic to suggest that their only response can be to take a negative and sceptical outlook which results only in paranoia or par-alysis. In order to enrich and transform processes of self-formation, indi-viduals must actively draw on intranets and the internet to establish new patterns of commitment and routine. This is the third trait they need to incorporate into their internet use. While these new *compromise pack-ages* may indeed be fragile and precarious, at least they are not oppress-ively parochial. Moreover, active involvement with the outer social world increasingly means articulating the nature of individual commitment and routine so as to be able to assess their implications for others whose interests and outlook may be very different.

The internet and intranets offer a great many opportunities for forging new alliances, entering into new social engagements and monitoring the differing opinions of others. Again, individuals do not relate indiscrim-inately to all potential dialogic spaces and all potential interconnections with others. Instead, they orient themselves selectively in terms of priorit-ies and interests that are part of their tasks and projects. In some cases, the relevance of particular patterns of individual commitment and rou-tine remain largely unquestioned for long periods of time. We can find evidence of such routine and commitment in the lists of bookmarks that people create when surfing the WWW. We can also find them in the files containing information about regular e-mail contacts or internet relay chat friends they communicate with. Moreover, an individual's e-mail address and homepage location can remain unchanged, offering stabil-ity even though they themselves have moved to another city or country. Equally, internet and intranets offer a great many opportunities for indi-viduals to shift their alliances according to changes in the social and material conditions of their life projects and tasks, in their socially struc-tured contexts.

The use of internet technology to track risk and uncertainty and transcend conflict

Given the increasingly diverse contexts connected together by internet technology, there are very wide variations in available and potential experiences. The internet will increasingly bring individuals into contact with events and experience which take place in contexts far removed from their own, involving people of conflicting dispositions or cultures which may be hostile to one another. Of course, one reaction could be to disengage from such situations. However, internet technology also offers a great many new ways of dealing with conflicting dispositions under a more positive sign. Taking advantage of these opportunities is the fourth trait individuals need to incorporate into internet use.

There are four ways in which internet technology offers new ways of dealing with conflicting dispositions. First, it can be used by individuals to monitor the development and nature of conflicts and assess their safety. As such, it may allow them to manage their fears and responses more consciously. Second, internet technology allows individuals to cope with cultural differences through dialogue. Third, more communication may, in potential at least, lead to a greater mutual understanding and there-fore to cosmopolitanism as an attitude of mind. Fourth, the internet may confront individuals with experiences which are normally excluded from the regularities of their day-to-day lives. They may find some of these experiences shocking or disconcerting, but it is not impossible for them to manage their use of it in such a way as to filter these out. As always, the potential for clashes of interest and the ability of individuals to cope under such circumstances are conditioned by the socially structured contexts within which they have to, or are seeking to, get along.

The internet and the day-to-day life of 'Kate'

Let me apply some of these ideas to the daily use of the internet by 'Kate', a student in her late teens living in Chicago. Kate's life changed dramatically when her parents split up and her father moved to Vancouver, where most of the rest of her family live. College had instructed her how to use e-mail and the WWW but it was Jeff, a fellow student, who had introduced her to IRC and creating her own webpage. Until she started using the internet regularly she had felt 'hidden away'.

Chatting on IRC opened up a new world to her. She was surprised at how freely she began to discuss intimate details of her life and her feelings with people she hardly knew. Sometimes she and Jeff would team up for a bit of fun. Once at an internet café they saw a guy using IRC and noted the nickname he was using. While Kate sat on guard, Jeff logged on using a girl's nickname and started exciting the guy with a flurry of messages. The guy suddenly stood up and started looking around eagerly. Kate went to warn Jeff. 'I know,' he told her, 'I let him know I was here!'

Late one night, Kate started chatting with Jane, who happened to live in Vancouver. They got on well and following many long chats they decided to meet up during the winter vacation. They decided to meet at a café that a webpage described as being 'gay, lesbian and mixed'. Kate knew the street but would never have gone to the café on her own. She recognized Jane immediately from the photographs on her webpage. They knew so much about each other. There was no chance that they would not get on, but it was like they had to start all over again. Back in Chicago Kate felt that Jane had become a real person and she could not wait to see her again.

Such vignettes say something about our modern world and the way in which individuals are using the internet to cope with both the disruptive and the more positive sides of their lives. Our modern lives may well be fraught with anxieties and we may well feel in the grip of circumstances over which we have little control, yet the internet offers individuals many new ways of reimposing new forms of control that are more appropriate to our global age.

Community, organizations, individuals and the internet: some general considerations

In this and the two previous chapters of this book I have been examining the internet and its role in the formation of communities, how it is affecting organizational culture and how it might enrich and transform the nature of the self and experience in everyday life. In particular, I have pursued ways in which internet technology might be used as part of a more positive engagement with the conditions of reflexive modernization. Although I have raised a number of questions of a moral-practical character concerning the internet and its role in organizations and in the day-to-day lives of individuals, this discussion now needs to be placed in a wider context. What new forms of publicness do the internet and intranets create? Will existing inequalities not be eased but just become further entrenched? How will the internet affect the cultivation of diversity and pluralism on a global level? What possibilities might we have to regulate mediated publicness created by the internet? These are some of the questions I want to pursue in the final three chapters of this book.

7

Publicness and the internet

Prior to the development of the internet most of us were largely invisible to most other people in the world. Internet users, however, have to adapt their activities to a new kind of publicness. When we consider the nature of this transformation we have to bear in mind that the concept of *publicness* has been adopted by different social and cultural theorists in different ways. Moreover, the current developments involving the internet are taking place in an environment which has already been profoundly altered by the advent of radio, television and other forms of communication.

In this chapter, I want to focus on the kind of 'publicness' which Thompson describes as the *space of the visible*: namely, as space constituted by actions and events that through processes of symbolic exchange have been made available and visible in a public domain.[1] Such a space features as the realm in which members of a society, organization or group may be held to give an account of, and morally account for, their perspectives and opinions. It is in this context, Gouldner claims, that they may be asked to reveal what they have done and why they have done it.[2] In what ways is the use of internet technology changing this kind of publicness?

I have already discussed Habermas's account of the emergence and subsequent disintegration of the 'public sphere' and Thompson's criticism of his work. While it is easy to get excited about the new kinds of 'dialogic spaces' created by the internet, many commentators are rather sceptical about the idea that we might use this technology to reinvigorate critical public spheres today. They argue that while internet use may well be allowing new opportunities for social interaction, the new forms of togetherness it creates are equally characterized by processes of fragmentation and 'reparochialization'.[3]

While the examples of internet use which I have discussed so far might not substantiate such fears, they do beg certain questions. For instance, organizations inviting individuals to 'talk' to them using their websites want to display that there really is somebody there behind the slick facade of their corporate webpage. But how should they respond to the multitude of responses they receive? How might they instil confidence in those who believe these 'talks' to be nothing but a sham? Moreover, the various discussion forums which can be found on the internet or intranets, particularly those taking place in real-time, often appear as a cacophony of dissident voices, obstructing rather than facilitating a process of unrestricted debate.

My aim in this chapter is to focus on the kind of publicness created by the internet and to try and tease out some of the opportunities for, and the limitations on, the renewal of 'dialogic spaces' and the consequences this may have for moral-practical thinking. I shall begin by examining the way in which the internet and intranets mediate visibility. These communication networks are not only challenging traditional conceptions of public life: they are also confronting the way we have come to think about the kind of publicness created by the mass media. Drawing together these arguments, I shall conclude this chapter by reflecting critically on the possibility of a different model of the 'space of the visible' as created by internet use and illustrate it with an example. In doing so, I shall again make extensive use of Thompson's concepts and ideas and extend them to an analysis of the internet.

Visibility and the internet

Thompson argues in *The Media and Modernity* that the way we think about publicness today has been inspired by a traditional model of publicness derived from the assemblies of the classical Greek city-states, 'a model in which individuals come together in the same spatial-temporal setting to discuss issues of common concern'.[4] Publicness at this time was constituted by dialogical interaction and tied to particular spatial-temporal locales. The development of communication media – in particular electronic communication such as radio and television – has facilitated the advent of new kinds of publicness which deviate profoundly from the traditional model. We now live and work in very different institutional contexts, ones in which individuals acquire information, encounter differing views of others and form reasoned judgements mostly by means of a mediated publicness. Such a publicness involves individuals and organizations using communication media to make information and their points of view visible and available to others. It is thus, as Thompson calls it, 'a publicness of openness and visibility' (p. 236).

In an earlier chapter we considered how he dismisses the traditional model of publicness as 'co-presence' as inadequate, given the social and practical conditions in late modernity. Mediated publicness, he claims, has for the most part been *non-dialogical* in character. This is because media such as radio and television, on which he focuses his argument, create a fundamental break between the producers and recipients of information. Moreover, the scale and complexity of the institutional contexts in which we live today make implementing the traditional model of publicness impractical.

Thompson argues on the basis of these considerations that two responses to *non-dialogical mediated publicness* need to be avoided. The first response consists of attempts to retain as an ideal the traditional model of publicness as co-presence. He rejects this response because it would only result in our continually focusing on the fragmented nature of contemporary mediated publicness, and viewing further developments of mediated publicness as yet another step on a slippery slope.

The second response consists of attempts to treat non-dialogical mediated publicness as some kind of extension of the traditional model. He rejects this second response because it would involve understanding the communication taking place on radio and television, in newspapers, etc., as a kind of 'conversation writ large' (p. 245). Thompson argues that given the fact that most participants in such a conversation are only recipients, any sense of a 'conversational' relationship with the producers of information is just an illusion.

Thompson's preferred response to non-dialogical mediated publicness is to put aside the traditional model of publicness altogether. In this way, he argues, 'we can focus our attention on the kind of publicness created by the media and seek to analyse its characteristics. . . . We can try to refashion our way of thinking about public life.' On the basis of this move, Thompson then proceeds to reconstruct the new kind of publicness created in the era of mass communication as 'the non-localized, non-dialogical, open-ended space of the visible in which mediated symbolic forms can be expressed and received by a plurality of non-present others' (p. 245).

Let us consider the features of Thompson's new kind of publicness in detail and examine how the advent of the internet might affect each of them. What kind of publicness is created by the internet or intranet use?

'Non-localized space'   Thompson argues that mediated publicness is a non-localized space in that it is not bounded by a particular spatial-temporal locale. In this sense we can also approach the internet and intranets as spheres of possibilities in which mediated information can be made available without individuals having to share a common locale. While users of intranets might share a particular organizational place of

work, their co-presence in time-space is by no means a necessary condition for the creation of a shared space for the circulation of symbolic forms. Moreover, while most mass media are still only potentially global in scope, the WWW involves making information availability worldwide.

'Non-dialogical space'   Mediated publicness as created by radio, television, newspapers, etc., Thompson argues, is mostly non-dialogical, with participants engaged in forms of mediated quasi-interaction. Mediated publicness created by the internet and intranets, on the other hand, is a 'dialogical space' for the circulation of symbolic forms.

'Open-ended space'   Mediated publicness, Thompson claims, is a creative and relatively uncontrollable space in which previously absent information may be made available and where the content of symbolic forms cannot be entirely fixed in advance. The advent of the internet has resulted in the intensification of the open-ended character of mediated publicness, which, as I shall explain later, has also become even less controllable in many respects.

'A plurality of non-present producers and recipients'   In his study of conventional mass communication, Thompson consistently argues that most participants in non-dialogical mediated publicness are only recipients of information. The advent of the internet, however, means that individuals can now participate in a form of mediated publicness in which, in principle, none are deprived of the option of providing feedback.

All of the features of mediated publicness described above relate to the transformation of what Thompson calls *struggles for visibility*. Before the advent of mediated publicness, individuals who wanted to express their views or concerns had to make themselves heard in contexts of co-presence. Today, writes Thompson, 'struggles for recognition have increasingly become constituted as struggles for visibility within non-localized space of mediated publicness.'[5] However, in the case of mediated publicness created by radio, television, newspapers, etc., struggles for visibility are very much about getting views and concerns recognized by the producers of mass communication. Most individuals are unable to contribute directly to mediated publicness on their own.

I would argue that the essence of mediated publicness created by the internet and intranet is different from the one Thompson describes in many respects. Their development has contributed to the creation of new forms of mediated publicness which do not replace 'non-dialogic' forms, but which supplement them with spaces constituted by the to-and-fro of argument between a plurality of participants who do not share a common locale. The new communication technologies are thus challenging and transforming the ways in which we understand how individuals acquire information, encounter differing views of others and form reasoned judgements. Let us consider this challenge and transformation of the *space of the visible* in more detail.

Towards a renewal of mediated publicness

From a moral-practical point of view, the internet and intranets offer interesting opportunities for furthering participatory forms of symbolic exchange and opinion formation. They tempt us once again to turn back for inspiration to the traditional model of the assemblies of the classical Greek city-states. Participants might not share a spatial-temporal locale, yet the internet and intranets do create 'dialogical spaces' where they can come together and discuss issues of common concern. However, while the internet and intranets undoubtedly open up new opportunities, two fundamental problems still remain. First, the scale and complexity of the institutional contexts in which we live today continue to render a dialogical mediated publicness a rather remote ideal. Second, the processes of dialogue are still 'mediated' in the sense that a great deal of the information produced and transmitted is done so independent of any response. This paradox of isolation and visibility means that those using the internet and intranets must still treat distant others on peculiar terms of equality.

In this section I want to consider how we should respond to the new forms of publicness created by the internet and intranets. I shall argue that the mechanisms by which the internet and intranets facilitate public spheres continue to have a great deal in common with the mechanisms deployed in *non-dialogical mediated publicness* as set out by Thompson. Those who think that internet technology will create a *dialogical mediated publicness* will be inclined to be disappointed by any practical implementation in this direction. I shall argue therefore that, following through Thompson's ideas, the internet is facilitating a *space of the visible* that can best be characterized as a *deliberative mediated publicness* rather than a dialogical one. Such a space shares features related to dialogical forms of symbolic exchange, but it does not privilege them in any way.

Let us examine first why a deliberative conception of mediated publicness is so crucial to understanding how internet technology might enrich public spheres today. I shall then go on to conclude this chapter by discussing critically the various mechanisms by which the use of internet technology might facilitate the incorporation of individual judgements and moral positions into collective decision-making processes. I want to consider the complexity of such a communication environment in the next chapter, when I shall elaborate the connection between the internet and globalization.

A deliberative conception of mediated publicness

The idea of a deliberative conception of mediated publicness focuses attention on the processes by which individuals can come together in non-localized space and acquire information, encounter differing views of others and form reasoned judgements. I base this idea on Thompson's deliberative conception of democracy in which 'the legitimacy of a decision stems from the fact that the decision is the outcome of a process of generalized deliberation.'[6] The way in which individuals deliberate over and weigh up arguments using the internet or intranets does not presuppose dialogical forms of communication but rather a whole range of interactional situations which I described in detail in chapter 3.

Not all attempts at dialogical communication are successful. The website of British Petroleum, for example, contributed to the process of informing its shareholders and customers about its link-up in 1998 with Amoco, but this can hardly be seen as 'dialogical communication'. The 10 Downing Street website for its part may allow the British Prime Minister to participate in various discussion forums, yet it is not a space where issues that affect people's lives can be actively discussed in dialogue with all those involved. However, both these examples form part of deliberative arrangements and processes that are designed to contribute to people's understanding of what is going on.

The advantage of adopting a deliberative conception of mediated publicness with respect to the kind of publicness created by internet and intranet use is that such a conception is not vulnerable to the kinds of critique that can be raised against dialogical models. The mere fact that an organization or an individual does not answer all their e-mail or does not enter directly into dialogue on every conceivable occasion does not in itself spell out failure. The challenge lies in finding ways of using internet technology to enhance the scope of deliberative processes. This can be achieved by encouraging reflexive engagements and by increasing opportunities for the negotiation of mediated experience. The general aim of all deliberative arrangements should be that the opinions and moral positions of all those involved have perceptible consequences for the resulting decisions and the way they affect their lives.

Deliberative processes, the internet and reflexive modernization

What, then, are the moral-practical implications of the idea of deliberative mediated publicness for internet and intranet use in the era of reflexive modernization? And what conditions would favour the creation of successful deliberative arrangements on these networks of communication? I want to discuss four related conditions here which I think contribute in some way. First, care must be taken to see that controversial questions are kept open. Second, the 'facticity' of the logical integration and the empirical content of acts or projects must be allowed to be put to the test. As such, the internet must be used to explain and give reasons as to why particular activities, opinions and courses of action are appropriate so that they may be adjudged to be adequate or inadequate. Third, the rights of participants to equal concern and respect in wishing to use the internet to inform themselves or others comprehensively must be recognized. Fourth, methods and skills must be developed for recognizing moral positions in order to distinguish these from prejudice, personal aversion or taste, arbitrary stands, and the like.

Keeping controversial questions open   Over the years, broadcasters and broadcasting authorities have built up considerable experience with matters concerning mediated publicness and we can learn a great deal from them. Writing about the responsibility of broadcasting towards society as a whole, for example, Kurt Sontheimer sets out that forms of mass communication such as television are essential preconditions in providing a forum in order that citizens may arrive at an awareness of society and of their own position within it.[7] As a modality of cultural transmission, television works to provide the frames of experience within which people organize and interpret information.

Sontheimer recognizes that the assumptions built into the organization of television culture are of significant importance in any understanding of the ability of television to provide a platform for the presentation of social issues. He argues that the real problem of television lies in the dilemma that broadcasters face. On the one hand, they cannot lose sight of the aspect of the possible unity in the diversity of interests and opinions. On the other, they are supposed to show the variety of people, interests and opinions which provide the social foundation for pluralism. In confronting this dilemma, Sontheimer suggests, we ought to retain respect for the principle that television ought to be employed as a means of better informing society about itself and about the goals it pursues or should pursue. The media, in his view, should constantly renew their contribution towards keeping controversial questions open, so that opinions can be objectified, enriched by new information, and corrected. The television viewer is not only a member of an audience, but also a participant in a political community in which the competent forming of opinion and the making of decisions depends on the availability of information and the monitoring of differing ideas of others.

Thompson also argues that 'deliberation thrives on the clash of competing views; nothing is more destructive of the process of deliberation than an orchestrated chorus of opinion which allows for no dissent.'[8] By securing the conditions of openness in internet and intranet use we can establish a framework within which deliberative mediated publicness can be practically developed.

Criticizable rationality   While processes of deliberation should be open-ended, deliberative mediated publicness would not amount to much if participants were unable to criticize the rationalization underpinning the actions and projects of others. This existence of criticizable rationality is the second condition favouring the creation of successful deliberative arrangements. Much of the literature concerning this issue draws on Habermas's more recent work on communicative rationality. Let us examine some of his ideas now.

Habermas's ideas on communicative rationality have displaced his earlier work on the emergence and transformation of the public sphere. However, he continues to be interested in problems of legitimation and communication and in the idea of a public sphere in which individuals participate in rational critical debate. He sees the attainment of the conditions of rational-critical debate as being bound up in a self-controlled learning process. His main concern in latter years lies in the discovery of procedures which would 'ground the presumption that the basic institutions . . . of society and the political decisions would meet with the unforced agreement of all those involved, if they could participate, as free and equal partners, in discursive will-formation'.[9] An interesting contribution to this discussion is his work on the two related concepts of *communicative competence* and the *ideal speech situation*.[10]

It is not my intention to offer any sort of comprehensive analysis of Habermas's notion of communicative competence, but a discussion of a few of its aspects may help us consider the problems involved in attaining the conditions of what Habermas calls an 'ideal speech situation.'[11] Habermas argues that successful everyday communicative practice is underpinned by a rational foundation. He tries to uncover and analyse the procedures by which rationally motivated agreement is attained. Although he does not claim that such procedures will ever guarantee consensus once and for all, he does assert that there are procedures which facilitate communicative competence resulting in rationally motivated agreement. He develops the thesis that when one person communicates something to another, that person makes a series of claims: (1) that what is communicated is intelligible; (2) that the propositional content of whatever is communicated is true; (3) that the individual is justified in communicating whatever is communicated; and (4) that the individual communicating is sincere. All four claims may be contested by the other, but in everyday interaction, the validity of these claims is mostly taken for granted.

Sometimes, participants' expectations are fractured and claims are questioned. Should the validity of one or more of the claims be contested, then successful communication can only continue if the claim is redeemed. As such, the communicator can be called on to elaborate why a certain claim is true or normatively justified. A claim is only adequately redeemed if it is possible to enter freely into discourse and where there is complete symmetry between participants, such that discourse is free from force or constraint. Habermas formalizes such a situation in his idea of the 'ideal speech situation'. Three main features are necessary for an ideal speech situation to arise: mutual understanding must be attained in an unrestrained manner; mutual understanding must be reached solely through the force of better argument; and all participants in the dialogue must do so as full and equal partners.

Habermas argues that the 'ideal speech situation' represents only an ideal, and that communication in real-life situations is often not like this. Even so, he argues, the ideal speech situation is not just an arbitrary construct, but one which is inherent in all communication. Thus this concept must be understood as an attempt to provide a universal critical measure against which we might reveal the shortcomings of communicative procedures.

Habermas's work on communicative rationality and discourse ethics has not gone unchallenged. It raises much the same questions as his earlier ideas concerning the 'critical public sphere'. Seyla Benhabib argues, for example, that positive moral duties cannot be deduced from Habermas's idea of the ideal speech situation alone, 'but require contextual moral judgement in their concretization'.[12] A second challenge to Habermas's work is raised by Thomas McCarthy, who questions whether it is realistic to think that individuals can ever reach rational consensus by transcending the interest-oriented and value-based perspectives they have. He argues that when individuals enter a public debate, they often do so with a variety of expectations, of which reaching a rational consensus is but one. He writes: 'this diversity in types of agreement and expectation is reflected in the diversity of forms of political conflict resolution. A public sphere whose institutions and culture embodied this diversity would . . . be a more realistic ideal than one embodying, in however detranscedentalized a form . . . the rational will.'[13] A third challenge to Habermas is raised by Thompson, who continues his earlier criticism and writes:

> in principle it may seem plausible to suggest that an action would be correct or a norm would be just if and only if everyone affected by it, having had the opportunity to discuss it together under conditions free from domination, were willingly to assent to it. But what could this possibly mean in practice in a world where many actions and norms affect

thousands or even millions of individuals who are widely dispersed in space (and perhaps also in time)?[14]

Given these challenges to Habermas's work, how then might the concepts of communicative competence and the ideal speech situation provide us with a theoretical pointer towards what it might mean to affirm and implement a critical principle within the kind of publicness created by the internet? In many respects, the internet and intranets serve only to aggravate the problems signalled by Benhabib, McCarthy and Thompson. How might we encourage communicative competence and create ideal speech situations in communication environments which are 'made of many cultures, many values, many projects, that cross through the minds and inform the strategies of the various participants'?[15] The prospects of this happening seem rather dim.

What we must salvage for our purposes from Habermas's recent work, I would argue, is that in deliberative mediated publicness, in certain situations, participants must submit to having the 'facticity' of the logical integration and the empirical content of their acts or projects put to the test. Keeping controversial questions open is not just about allowing competing views to clash. It is also about facilitating the questioning of certain grounded principles of action.[16] I want to suggest that nothing is more destructive to the process of deliberation than participants who continually defend the rationalization of their actions in a traditional way. The traditional form of defence they adopt is to assume, often inconsistently, a taken-for-granted attitude towards what is 'right' and 'proper' and to safely underpin this with uncriticizable and internally referential frameworks of justification.

Having achieved the first two conditions necessary for creating successful deliberative arrangements – keeping controversial questions open and maintaining criticizable rationality – the third condition is the preservation of overall goals, principles and rights.

Overall goals, principles and rights Processes of deliberation using the internet or intranets would not amount to much if participants were continuously involved in strife and bickering. How might participants weigh up each other's arguments and draw processes of argument and counterargument to a temporary but practical closure while at the same time keeping them open-ended? In order to examine this third condition for the creation of successful deliberative arrangements we must relate the idea of deliberative mediated publicness to the conditions of reflexive modernization. Some of the most salient features of reflexive modernization are the absence of final authorities, the decentred character of expertise and the questioning of formulaic truths.[17] How might internet and intranet use have a positive impact on processes of deliberation under these conditions? What kind of 'grounding' might provide a justifiable basis for decision-making within the kind of publicness created by the internet?

I want at this juncture to consider some of the ideas developed by Dworkin. I will not go into his writings in detail, nor deal exhaustively with the criticisms they have met. My aim is simply to draw his provocative and thoughtful ideas into the debate. Dworkin recognizes two major grounds of political justification: *arguments of policy* and *arguments of principle*. 'Arguments of policy', he explains, 'justify a political decision by showing that the decision advances or protects some collective goal of the community as a whole.'[18] The argument that a particular webpage should be removed from an intranet and that the removal of such information will protect an organization's integrity is an argument of policy. 'Arguments of principle', he explains, 'justify a political decision by showing that the decision respects or secures some individual or group right.'[19] The argument that a particular webpage should be removed from an intranet, and that the removal of such information respects the right of women employees to equal respect and concern is an argument of principle. 'Arguments of policy' and 'arguments of principle' are thus relevant to particular theories of pacification and the way in which we choose to deal with clashes of interest and values in the public sphere.

While 'arguments of policy' worked tolerably well in a world of simple modernization, they do not survive so well in a world of reflexive modernization – in a universe of high reflexivity and cultural diversity. We can illustrate this by examining a major transformation that has taken place in broadcasting: the move away from broadcasting 'in the public interest'.[20] In many countries where there is a public service broadcasting system, the 'space of the visible', created first by radio and later by television, was organized in the 'public interest'. This way of organizing went a long way towards pacifying conflict over how broadcasting should be controlled in the best interests of its recipient population and survived relatively unchallenged for many decades. Although there were disputes concerning what was in the 'general interest', there was also a moral centre ground, a shared orientation towards the 'general interest'. From the 1960s onwards, however, deep fissures opened up in this goal-based policy. Broadcasting authorities and broadcasting institutions seemed unable to adequately recognize and represent the ever changing richness of moral positions and discourse available over time-space. Organizing broadcasting 'in the public interest' took on a certain arrogance which resulted in considerable resentment among those who felt that they were being unjustly excluded from the 'space of the visible'. Two issues proved catalysts in the ensuing debate: first, the question of how to allocate new broadcasting resources to a baffling variety of competing broadcasting voices; second, how to enhance accountability in the management of communication.

Dworkin discusses two strategies that have developed in response to the failure of traditional 'arguments of policy'. These strategies create more room for discretion in recognizing the legitimacy of decisions. As such, they are an attempt to accommodate the idea that 'how a society develops is itself an important part of the value of that society.'[21] However, both these strategies are essentially just different versions of goal-based arguments of political justification. Moreover, their departure from the rigidity of traditional 'arguments of policy' creates new problems.

The first of the strategies Dworkin discusses involves an attempt to calculate the future consequences of decisions in order to justify a more permissive attitude towards change and cultural diversity. Policy-makers using this strategy would argue that even if a particular decision is bad for the community as a whole, considered only in itself, the consequences of trying to block the decision would in the long run be even worse.[22] For example, the presence of gay webpages on an internet service provider's server may offend some internet users and a provider may be considering removing them because some users are threatening to terminate their accounts. The provider, however, may argue that while these pages are not in the general interest of its subscribers and may even make some of them unhappy, the longer term consequences of banning such pages will be far worse. The problem comes in ascertaining whether or not we would indeed be better off in the long run if a particular decision were tolerated and legitimized. This is, however, Dworkin argues, an extraordinary way of justifying decision-making because it places the grounding of such decisions on a slippery slope. The calculation of future benefit or harm results only in an arbitrary recognition of different interests and values.

This can be illustrated again by returning to the example of public service broadcasting. From the 1960s onwards, in most countries the 'space of the visible' was opened up due to a more liberal interpretation of what was in the 'public interest'. In the Netherlands, for example, the transformation of the public sphere was quite spectacular. From its early beginnings in the 1920s, the Dutch broadcasting system had only five licensed public broadcasting organizations. Following broadcasting legislation introduced in 1969, however, some thirty organizations were allocated broadcasting time. This outcome was heavily criticized because a decision taken to include or exclude a new organization was often experienced as being rather arbitrary. Moreover, the situation was aggravated by the fact that the legislation had also made the broadcasting authorities more accountable and the nature of their decision-making more transparent.[23]

The second of Dworkin's strategies developed in response to the failure of traditional 'arguments of policy' involves the weighing up of different arguments. If a majority is persuaded of the merits of a particular decision, then that decision carries legitimacy for all those concerned. This supposes that when an individual or institution must make a decision,

> the members of the community will each prefer the consequences of one decision to the consequences of others . . . If it can be discovered what each individual prefers, and how intensely, then it might be shown that a particular policy would satisfy on balance more preferences, taking into account their intensity, than alternative policies. On this concept of welfare, a policy makes the community better off . . . if it satisfies the collection of preferences better than alternative policies would, even though it dissatisfies the preferences of some.[24]

We can illustrate this too by returning to the example of broadcasting. From the 1980s onwards, in many countries where there are public service broadcasting systems, changes in policy meant that broadcasters had increasingly to orientate their actions towards consumer preferences coordinated through the market. Organizing the 'space of the visible' in this way results in some annoying consequences. Dworkin argues, for example, that '. . . the preferences of an individual for the consequences of a particular policy may be seen to reflect, on further analysis, either a personal preference for his own enjoyment of some goods or opportunities, or an external preference for the assignment of goods and opportunities to others, or both.' Moreover, market-based broadcasting addresses individuals as consumers who may be denied preferences because these are unattractive to profit-seeking enterprises.

The kind of grounding offered by 'arguments of policy' in its various guises thus merges the impact of decisions into overall goals, totals or averages. It takes the improvement of these totals or averages as desirable while disregarding their impact on any one individual. The kind of grounding for decision-making offered by 'arguments of principle', however, is very different. Here decisions are not justified through rules dictated by general goals but through arguments which concern the *rights* of the particular individuals or groups that they benefit.

'Arguments of principle' would claim, for example, that information and other symbolic goods must be made available or withheld because of their impact on particular people, even if, as a whole, the participants in the public sphere may be worse off in consequence. Such arguments are not goal based because they merely state 'a reason that argues in one direction, but does not necessitate a particular decision'.[25] Individuals have rights when, for some reason, 'a collective goal is not a sufficient justification for denying them what they wish, as individuals, to have or to do, or not a sufficient justification for imposing some loss or injury upon them.'[26] Mediated publicness organized in this way would, for example, involve individuals and groups being obliged to recognize the right of others to equal concern and respect in wishing to inform themselves comprehensively.

On the basis of Dworkin's ideas, we might argue that processes of deliberation using internet technology under conditions of reflexive modernization can only be successful if participants in the discussion strip goals of general significance of their primacy and their self-explanatory status. Not goals, but individuals, groups of individuals, organizations, etc., are the key. Participants would then have to explain why it is an essential or highly desirable condition for human flourishing that they should be allowed to use the internet in a particular way. Or at least why it is a desirable condition that others who have an interest in using the internet in a different way be told that they may not. Participants might have to explain why particular decisions are of 'general interest' and simply require referral to pre-set overall goals for their justification. Alternatively, they might have to explain why, in certain cases, the existence of a 'general interest' is not sufficient justification for denying what participants wish as individuals to have or to do. Or that the existence of a general interest is not a sufficient justification for imposing some loss or injury upon them. Participants would then be obliged to recognize the right of others to equal concern and respect in wishing to use the internet to inform themselves or others comprehensively.

In practice, however, individuals, groups of individuals, organizations, etc., do not always have clear-cut 'ends' in mind when they use the internet or an intranet. Most decision-making takes place within the flow of day-to-day routine and does not involve recourse to formal decision-making procedures. However, Dworkin's ideas have the considerable merit of focusing our attention on the way we ground the legitimacy of our decisions during public debate. They are particularly useful when our normal expectations are fractured or when we are confronted with controversial opinions and have to decide on issues which have moral-practical consequences. Given that the communication environments created by the internet and intranets connect up many cultures and different experiences, the chances of our expectations being challenged now are greater than ever before. If we are to allow processes of deliberation to thrive on the clash of competing views then we need to think of positive ways of dealing with such situations.

Having discussed the first three of Habermas's conditions for the creation of successful deliberative arrangements: the need to keep controversial questions open, the need to maintain criticizable rationality and the need to preserve overall goals, principles and rights, we are now ready to move on to the fourth condition: the recognition of moral positions.

The recognition of moral positions   What arguments enforcing the difference between moral positions should we respect, even if a particular 'community' as a whole might be in some way worse off as a consequence? And what moral positions should we not respect because they offend some principle of moral reasoning? Dworkin provides us with some valuable insight into how the decision-making processes might differ when we take the rights of others seriously.[27]

We can try to explore Dworkin's ideas here by pursuing a line of argument through an example. Suppose the moderator of the 10 Downing Street website, which I discussed in chapter 5, is called on by a number of participants in the discussion forum on 'health' to remove all contributions made by 'gay' individuals concerning the debate on the age of consent. How can the moderator best go about arguing that such contributions 'provide useful, relevant and respectful postings that add value to open debate' and recognize the right of these participants to equal concern and respect in wishing to inform themselves and others comprehensively? By applying Dworkin's ideas, we would arrive at the following:

1   Those requesting the removal of the contributions made by 'gay' individuals must produce some reasons for their demands. They may claim, for example, that these contributions promote human behaviour which their religious faith prohibits, or that gay lifestyles result in the break-up of the family as the basic social unit of society. However, not every reason they might give will do. Dworkin argues that there are four important criteria which stipulate the kinds of reasons which do not count:

   (a)   Those requesting the removal of the contributions made by 'gay' individuals cannot ground their request in the belief that any member of such a group of recipients inherently deserves less respect. For example, they could not claim that 'all letters from gays are unhealthy', as this would constitute prejudice.

   (b)   Those requesting the removal of the contributions made by 'gay' individuals could not ground their request on personal emotional reactions. For example, they could not complain that 'gay contributions to the discussion make me sick', as emotional involvement does not demonstrate moral commitment.

   (c)   Those requesting the removal of the contributions made by 'gay' individuals could not ground their request on arguments and facts which are so implausible that they frustrate the minimal standards they themselves would generally impose on arguments and evidence from others. For example, it would be unacceptable for them to claim that 'gay contributions corrupt other internet users.'

(d) Those requesting the removal of the contributions made by 'gay' individuals could not ground their request on arguments which appeal to a moral authority, such as the 'general interest', and so automatically make the issue of 'gay' contributions to a discussion forum an immoral one.

2 The moral position of those requesting the removal of the contributions made by 'gay' individuals must be sincere and consistent. They would have to demonstrate that their conduct is consistent with their beliefs on other occasions. For example, if their religious faith is cited as the basis for their disapproval of the contributions made by 'gay' individuals, this position should be consistent with their views when they consider contributions made by individuals who are divorced or have sex outside of marriage. Of course, some individuals might argue that the latter is now so common that they would not wish to ban such contributions. But if no better reason is forthcoming than 'if enough people engage in immoral acts, immoral acts will be considered moral', then those objecting to the contributions made by 'gay' individuals cannot successfully defend the moral position that religious faith forbids these, and that their views ought therefore to be respected.

3 Those requesting the removal of the contributions made by 'gay' individuals cannot base their moral conviction on the grounds that it is in some way self-evident that contributions made by 'gay' individuals are immoral and then go on to claim that no further reason is required to support such a position. This would be arbitrary and they might as well claim that the internet is itself immoral and should be banned altogether.

Such deliberations, Dworkin argues, 'enforce the difference between positions we must respect, although we think them wrong, and positions we need not respect because they offend some ground rule of moral reasoning'.[28] While the internet and intranets connect up many cultures and different experiences, increasing the likelihood of clashes of interest, they also increase the visibility and transparency of prejudice, arbitrary stands and the like. Given the interactive potential of internet technology, such views are easily challenged and revealed for what they are.

Examining the interlacing of deliberative processes, the characteristics of internet use and the conditions of reflexive modernization brings home how crucial it is for us to develop some sense of responsibility for our collective fate. We must, as Thompson writes, 'create a sense of responsibility which is not restricted to localized communities, but which is shared on a much wider scale'. However, our deliberative frameworks are cultural phenomena, and as such always express asymmetries of power. The outcome of deliberative processes cannot be regarded simply as the collaborative work carried out by peers. Internet use always involves asymmetries of power and the justification of decisions has to be successfully 'brought off' by those using it. The transformative capacity of internet use in deliberative processes is dependent on the characteristics of the individuals and organizations involved, their location in time-space, the institutional arrangements within which they act and the means they have at their disposal. Whether we will succeed in using internet technology to enhance moral-practical reflection is difficult to say. However, given that internet use makes us more aware of our capacity to *act at a distance*, and of the consequences of such action, we are morally obliged to use such understanding to develop a sense of responsibility as best we can.

8

Globalization and the internet

Globalization is an inherent feature of the modern world. Under conditions of simple modernization, globalizing processes were limited. Over the past four or five decades, however, these processes have intensified and accelerated significantly.[1] Globalization is now a major source of dynamism; it reorders time and space, facilitates the intensification of social reflexivity and enables what Giddens calls 'the excavation of most traditional contexts of action'.[2] Given its pervasiveness, therefore, it is not surprising that globalization raises many questions and difficulties. First, what exactly is globalization? For while globalization has been understood almost solely in economic terms it is also cultural, involving the way in which we produce, store and circulate information and other symbolic material. Second, what implications does globalization have for our lives? Giddens argues that globalization is often treated as if it were an external force and outside our control, but it is not.[3] The activities of economic organizations, agencies of state, other forms of organization, and individuals all contribute to its expansion and to its consequences. Third, is globalization a project of the rich industrial nations or transnational organizations based in those countries? Although it is obvious that many forces promoting the internet as a global communications network are dominated by individuals and organizations in rich countries, globalizing tendencies affect all of us, rich or poor.

In this chapter I shall focus on the internet and the ways in which it is contributing to and being transformed by the process of globalization. We can begin by recalling some earlier points. Throughout this book I have been drawing attention to the way in which the use of internet technology is transforming the complex relationships between local activities and interaction across distance. Indeed, many features of the internet point directly to its deep involvement in globalizing processes.

Yet the term 'world wide web', for example, does not simply imply that connections are literally worldwide. Rather, the WWW allows distant events to affect us more directly than ever before. Conversely, the way in which we use the WWW has global implications. It allows the consequences of our actions to be more decentred than ever before. Behind the transformations in the relationships between what is local and what is distant lie the three aspects of dynamism elaborated in Giddens's work and which I linked to the internet earlier: time-space distanciation, disembedding and re-embedding mechanisms, and the reflexivity of late modernity.

My main aim in this chapter is to examine how we might use the internet to achieve greater control over globalizing influences. I shall begin by analysing the characteristics of globalization and of the globalized processes of communication in the world today. I shall then examine some influential ideas and theoretical interpretations concerning the cultural consequences of global communication flows. I shall argue that while we must recognize the importance of the structuring qualities of the internet as a global arena of circulation, we must also recognize the way in which global communication flows intersect with the situated contexts within which activities are carried out in a knowledgeable and creative way. Against this backdrop I shall also examine and discuss some of the key issues which are currently being considered in debates concerning the internet and *cultural imperialism*. The contours of this debate have been well documented by Thompson but not yet related to the internet. In the final section I shall argue that although the consequences of globalization are often uneven, fractured and disruptive, it is not utopian to suppose that the internet can be used in projects to combat global inequality.

Globalization as action at a distance

Globalization is not a new phenomenon. Its origins can be traced far back in time, yet it was not until the seventeenth, eighteenth and nineteenth centuries that it took on many of the characteristics we associate with it today. Globalization arises, writes Thompson, when: '(a) activities take place in an arena which is global or nearly so . . . ; (b) activities are organized, planned or coordinated on a global scale; and (c) activities involve some degree of reciprocity and interdependency, such that localized activities situated in different parts of the world are shaped by one another.'[4] As such, globalization is distinguishable from terms such as *globality* which, as Bauman explains, 'means merely that everyone everywhere may feed on McDonald's burgers and watch the latest made-for-TV docudrama'.[5] Globalization is more than this: as Giddens explains, it is about the reordering of time and space facilitated by *action at a distance*.[6]

At first sight, as Giddens argues, globalization seems to be an *out there* process, involving the development of social interaction that influences our everyday life but is far removed from it. However, he writes, globalization has always been 'a two-way process; now, increasingly, however, there is no obvious "direction" to globalization at all, as its ramifications are more or less ever-present.' Today, Giddens claims, globalization is 'an "*in here*" matter, that affects, or rather is dialectically related to, even the most intimate aspects of our lives'.[7] Focusing on globalization as action at a distance allows us to understand how we are all actively involved in these processes.

What makes globalization so complex is the dialectical relationship, evident in the reciprocity and interdependency, that connects the local and the distant. Bauman argues that 'the *globalization* of the economy and information and *fragmentation* – indeed, a "re-parochialization" of sorts – of political sovereignty are not, contrary to appearances, opposite and hence mutually conflicting and incongruent trends; they are rather factors in the ongoing rearrangement of various aspects of systemic integration.'[8] Giddens attempts to capture the reciprocity and interdependency connecting the local and the distant in terms of globalization 'pulling away', 'pushing down' and 'squeezing sideways'.[9] Globalization 'pulls away', for example, in the sense that the powers once held by agencies of state or large economic organizations have been weakened by global developments. Globalization 'pushes down' in the sense that it creates new burdens and new options for local identities and interaction. Finally, globalization 'squeezes sideways' in that it reorders time and space, cutting across old boundaries and creating new horizontal alliances. Often, existing institutional contexts seem to get caught in the middle of these processes of pushing, pulling and squeezing; they are, as Daniel Bell has argued, too small for big problems, and too big for the small problems of life.[10]

Communications and information technology facilitate action at a distance and are deeply bound up with the intensification of globalization. Instantaneous global electronic communication has profoundly altered the relationships of reciprocity and interdependency: we now live in a 'global society' in which we can no longer avoid other individuals and alternative ways of life. New communication networks, in Thompson's words, increase the possibility of *global scrutiny* and *global visibility*, but also the possibility of *mutual interrogation*.[11] We no longer merely exist 'side by side' with other intelligent cultures but interact with them in many different and ever-changing ways.

As global communication networks reorder time-space, they facilitate shifts in the global flows of symbolic goods and in the concentrations of symbolic power. Given the complexity of the structured character and the patterns of transmission, it is unlikely that our understanding of these features will ever be more than partial. However, this has not halted scholars in their attempts to raise concerns regarding new concentrations of power and the emergence of new 'power elites'. Bauman, for example, argues that localities are in danger of becoming little more than transit stations in the worldwide flow of information.[12] Castells warns us about the 'structural schizophrenia between two spatial logics': the space of flows created by the global flow of symbolic goods on the one hand, and the space of places made up of the local situatedness of everyday life on the other. Like Bauman, Castells argues that 'we may be heading toward life in parallel universes whose times cannot meet.'[13]

If we take the idea of 'structural schizophrenia' and the possibility of 'parallel universes' seriously, however, it becomes exceedingly difficult to imagine how, in Bauman's case, we might ever be able to 'tempt touring capital to book a stopover in a given locality'.[14] Or how, in Castells's case, we might ever be able to build 'cultural and physical bridges . . . between these two forms of space'.[15] I want to argue, however, that both Castells's and Bauman's elaborations of the likely consequences of structured patterns of global communication are too pessimistic. Their ideas are rooted in accounts of cultural globalization which prioritize the power of commercial and political elites at the expense of those in subordinate positions in these global systems. According to the accounts of Castells and Bauman, those in subordinate positions appear unable to convert whatever resources they have into some degree of control.

Cultural globalization and communication

The literature of cultural globalization, as Thompson points out, has been enormously influential in studies of mass communication. Let us examine two accounts that feature prominently in Thompson's analysis: first, Max Horkheimer and Theodor Adorno's account of the *culture industry*, and second, Herbert Schiller's account of *cultural imperialism*.

The culture industry and the commodification of cultural forms

Horkheimer and Adorno are two of the earlier members of the Institute of Social Research which was established in Frankfurt in 1923. Like Habermas, who later became a member of the institute, they sought to take account of the role of mass communication in modern societies. Their critical examination of the rise of 'mass culture' and the 'culture industry' constitutes one of the earliest attempts to study the mediazation of modern culture in a systematic way.

In their conception of the 'culture industry', Horkheimer and Adorno stress the belief that mass culture does not arise spontaneously. According to Horkheimer, popular culture is evoked and manipulated as a result of the large-scale commodification of cultural forms.[16] The culture industry produces and circulates cultural forms for mass consumption and contributes significantly to the shaping and moulding of their consumption. The overall purpose of the culture industry, Adorno writes, is to 'reproduce the status quo within the mind of the people'.[17] It thus 'impedes the development of autonomous, independent individuals who judge and decide consciously for themselves'.[18]

In *Dialectic of Enlightenment* Horkheimer and Adorno posit capitalism as 'an iron system' which 'is uniform as a whole and in every part'.[19] They argue that the culture industry serves to make the individual 'all the more subservient to his adversary – the absolute power of capitalism' (p. 120). The goals of the culture industry are profit and social control; it follows a 'necessity inherent in the system not to leave the customer alone, not for a moment to allow him any suspicion that resistance is possible' (p. 141). Its job is to 'defend society' and it provides something for everyone 'so that none may escape' (pp. 144–5). 'The stronger the position of the culture industry becomes, the more summarily it can deal with the consumer's needs, producing them, controlling them, disciplining them, and even withdrawing amusement' (p. 144).

For Horkheimer and Adorno, Thompson writes, 'the development of the culture industry is an intrinsic part of the process of increasing rationalization and reification in modern societies, a process which is rendering individuals less and less capable of independent thinking and more and more dependent on social processes over which they have little or no control.'[20]

Cultural imperialism and the manipulation of human minds

During the last three or four decades, accounts of international communication have extended Horkheimer and Adorno's thesis to the study of 'cultural imperialism', most notably in the work of Herbert Schiller.[21] 'Cultural imperialism' develops, Schiller argues,

> in a world system within which there is a single market, and the terms and character of production are determined in the core of that market and radiate outward. . . . The cultural-communications sector of the world system necessarily develops in accordance with and facilitates the aims and objectives of the general system. A largely one-directional flow of informa-

tion from core to periphery represents the reality of power. . . . A rapid, all-encompassing communication technology (satellites and computers) is sought, discovered, and developed. Its utilization exhibits a close correspondence to the structure and needs of the dominant elements in the core of the system'.[22]

The dominating centre of the system, Schiller argues, has a substantial American component yet also includes Great Britain and other West European states, while the peripheral region mostly includes countries in the developing world.[23]

However, Schiller not only perpetuates Horkheimer and Adorno's view of the rationalization of the promotion and distribution of cultural forms, he also perpetuates their understanding of the capacity of individuals as consumers of symbolic goods. 'The man in the market', Schiller argues, 'has become a message receiver beyond all imagination.'[24] America's media managers, he writes,

> create, process, refine, and preside over the circulation of images and information which determine our beliefs and attitudes and, ultimately, our behavior. When they deliberately produce messages that do not correspond to the realities of social existence, the media managers become mind managers. Messages that create a false sense of reality and produce a consciousness that cannot comprehend or willfully reject the actual conditions of life, personal or social, are manipulative messages.'[25]

Schiller describes a permanent division of the society into two broad categories of 'winners' and 'losers'. The winners enjoy private ownership of productive property and are 'the dominant shapers and molders of the community'. The losers, 'the others, the majority, work on as mere conformists, the disadvantaged, and the manipulated; they are manipulated especially to continue to participate, if not wholeheartedly, at least positively, in the established routines.'[26] Commenting on the emergence of satellite television and the computer, Schiller warns, 'it is possible, and even likely, that the future may be more manipulated than the already considerably managed present'.[27]

However, in a retrospective written in 1992, Schiller is forced to adapt some of his earlier views, arguing that the concept of cultural imperialism needs to be recast. He explains that 'powerful US companies have used their considerable resources, in collaboration with their overseas counterparts, to achieve internationally the operational arrangements they enjoy at home.' The corporate-dominated channels of information are no longer 'American' but rather 'huge, integrated, cultural combines . . . American cultural imperialism is not dead, but it no longer adequately describes the global cultural condition. Today it is more useful to view transnational corporate culture as the central force.'[28]

Prioritizing the power of commercial and political elites and the fate of individuals in the modern era

The claims associated with the conception of the culture industry and cultural imperialism proposed by Horkheimer and Adorno and extended by Schiller have not gone unchallenged. For Thompson, two problems in particular make these frameworks unsatisfactory. First, they contribute to an overly exaggerated view of the rationalization of the promotion and distribution of symbolic forms. Second, they contribute to an overly pessimistic view of the fate of individuals in the modern era. Let us look at these problems in more detail.

The rationalization of the distribution of symbolic forms While the accounts of Horkheimer and Adorno and Schiller focus on mass communication, it is difficult to imagine, for example, how the developments of either public service broadcasting or commercial broadcasting might fit neatly into an 'iron system' that is uniform as a whole and in every part. From the 1960s onwards, there was an enormous expansion of available broadcasting resources, radically opening up the rationalization of the promotion and distribution of symbolic forms. Regarding public service broadcasting in Great Britain, Eberhard Wedell writes:

> the restrictive approach to broadcasting which has characterized the first forty-five years of its development no longer seems appropriate ... This need to move away from a restrictive attitude applies as much to the control of broadcasting hours, as to the multiplication of channels. The time has come to reduce and simplify the restrictions to the minimum compatible with the liberty of the subject.[29]

Regarding commercial broadcasting, Douglas Kellner argues that it does not always privilege the values and interests of the commercial and political elites. Programmes are often produced which are strongly critical of forms of economic domination and dependency.[30] Neither Horkheimer and Adorno's thesis of the culture industry, nor Schiller's account of cultural imperialism is capable of adequately explaining the shifting field of complex global power relations in mass communication.[31]

View of the fate of individuals Both accounts fail to acknowledge the complex social processes by which individuals receive and appropriate mediated symbolic forms and their ability to act in an autonomous and critical way. Horkheimer and Adorno's thesis strongly influences Habermas's later arguments concerning the refeudalization of the public sphere, which also treat the recipients of mediated cultural forms as passive individuals. While Schiller suggests that his views on the 'winners' and 'losers' in the circulation of symbolic goods must not 'be taken to imply a frozen and unbridgeable separation of the two groups', it is difficult to see how individuals might cross the divide.

The complex social processes by which individuals belonging to different cultural groups receive and appropriate mediated symbolic forms are uncovered in a more satisfactory way by recent research such as that carried out by Tamar Liebes and Elihu Katz.[32] In their work *The Export of Meaning*, they examine how audiences in Israel – consisting of Arab citizens, Russian immigrants, Moroccan Jews, and residents of a kibbutz – and audiences in Japan and on the west coast of the United States relate to an episode of *Dallas*, the American television soap series. They conclude that these audiences each draw on very different processes and resources in order to make sense of the programme. Liebes and Katz are particularly interested in uncovering the ways in which audiences help each other to relate to the programme, a process they refer to as *mutual aid*. They set out four ways in which mutual aid is displayed: *legitimation, orientation, interpretation* and *evaluation*. First, *legitimation* describes how members of the audience support each other in justifying the decision to watch the programme. Second, *orientation* describes how audience members help each other understand what is going on in the plot. Third, *interpretation* describes how members of the audience guide each other's reading based on their own experience and knowledge of life affairs. Fourth, *evaluation* describes how the audience members work together to form an opinion about the characters in the programme and their actions. Neither the account of the 'culture industry' nor the account of 'cultural imperialism' makes any attempt to consider these complex processes.

While Horkheimer and Adorno, Schiller, Bauman and Castells help us to think about the dangers which may accompany globalized communication, they seem to forget that often new centres of symbolic power can only wield their power in active collaboration with localities and regions, organizations and communities, and groups and individuals. An informed account of the cultural consequences of the globalization of communication must, therefore, be based on two sets of considerations. First, the *in here* character of these communication flows: without real people and real organizations situated in real localities, the global flow of symbolic goods would simply not exist. Second, the reciprocity and interdependency connecting the local and the distant: 'however wide-ranging the control which actors may have over others, the weak nevertheless always have some capabilities of turning resources back against the strong.'[33]

As long as mass communication predominantly involves a one-way flow of messages from large-scale producers of symbolic forms to 'situated local communities', the reciprocity and interdependency between producers and receivers is relatively simple. Yet the internet involves a two-way flow of messages. Moreover, while the transmission of such messages via the internet may involve large-scale communication organizations, the production of content does not. As such, the internet is set to reshape the range of institutionalized forms of control, together with the range of control that individuals have over their own lives and over the lives of others. Such transformations will involve not only the intensification of the reciprocity and interdependency connecting the local and the distant. They will also involve the intensification of the degree of discursive penetration of the conditions governing the way in which such control is recovered and maintained.

The transformations enabled by the internet require an account which recognizes both the structured character of global communication and the contextualized, hermeneutical character of the production/reception processes. Such an account will provide a more plausible attempt to understand the impact of the internet on the globalization of communication and the modern world. The idea that networks such as the internet will necessarily result in a range of dualisms – 'self-programmable labour' versus 'generic labour', 'space of flows' versus 'space of places', the 'connected' versus the 'unconnected', the world 'out there' versus the world 'in here', the 'powerful' versus the 'powerless', etc. – does not provide us with such a framework. Furthermore, any suggestions that such dualisms would characterize a new society go against the nature of the internet as a modality of cultural transmission. They come just as we are about to end an era of traditional mass communication which institutionalized a fundamental break between producers and receivers of information. Even if, in certain situations, the internet results in a loss of autonomy for individuals as against institutionalized forms of control, this loss will be offset by an increase in the scope of control for individuals in other situations. The diagnosis that in the face of all-embracing globalizing tendencies individuals are necessarily rendered powerless denies them the hope of ever mastering a basic understanding of the problems that affect their lives. It dashes any hopes they may hold of using the internet as a way of making a difference.

We must rise to the challenge and not simply apply ourselves to documenting how the 'weak' are overwhelmed by the 'strong' in the structured contexts of global internet use. We must analyse how particular kinds of participation in internet use might actively perpetuate the conditions which help to limit the few chances the 'weak' might have. We should indeed study the complexity of the structured character and patterns of transmission, but in doing so we must also remember that the internet conditions which keep individuals 'in their place' mostly do not involve powerful commercial and political elites telling them what to do. They involve the drab routine of unquestioned day-to-day internet use.

The internet: globalized diffusion and localized appropriation

The debate concerning cultural imperialism is now being extended to the study of the consequences of the internet. Here I want to pursue critically a number of issues raised by a conference which took place in May 1996, now represented by a book, *The Harvard Conference on the Internet and Society*.[34] The panel debate on Cultural Imperialism on the Net (pp. 464–82) involved exchanges, debates, speculation and prediction that continue to illuminate some of the theoretical arguments and issues which I raised above. Let us examine in detail some of the claims the speakers set out.

Jacques Attali: 'The internet is really a very marginal element of . . . cultural imperialism'

Jacques Attali, a French economist, dismissed the internet as a very marginal element of cultural imperialism (p. 468). Cultural imperialism, he argued, takes place in the core areas of the media, in politics and diplomacy, but not on the internet. His somewhat remarkable point of view must, however, be understood against the backdrop of the history of Minitel. Minitel was an information system introduced in 1984 by the French telephone company which allowed users to access services, such as banking, shopping, theatres and chat-lines, over the telephone system. Information services were also developed for businesses. The French government and private service providers were highly committed to the success of the system and viewed the internet as competition. Thus this French communication network predated and substantially slowed down the development of the internet in France. However, referring to the internet as a marginal phenomenon in the creation of an arena which is global, or nearly so, seems to greatly underestimate the transformative potential of such a medium. It is also difficult to see how we might separate internet use from other media or from politics and diplomacy, as it is increasingly deployed by all of them.

A more valid point made by Attali was that 'it's not in the interest of the American community . . . to go toward a world of uniformity' (p. 469). In other words, there would be no likelihood that the internet would facilitate the delivery of the kinds of benefits which living in a modern society requires if it did not reflect different cultures.

Nathan Gardels: 'The net is inherently anti-authoritarian because it is unmediated, and it is a liberating technology'

Nathan Gardels, editor of a number of American publications, dismissed the idea that traditional and local cultures will be destroyed through the intrusion of Western values via the internet, though he did so on different grounds from Attali. Gardels claimed that the internet, unlike the mass media, is inherently 'anti-imperialist' because 'it is unmediated, and it is a liberating technology' (p. 468). The problem with such a perspective is that it is a very broad-brush conceptualization of the nature of the internet and is overly optimistic.

I have tried to demonstrate throughout this book that the internet, much like other modalities of cultural transmission, is a complex technology incorporating dual potentialities. The internet may indeed open up new opportunities for the globalized diffusion and localized appropriation of information and other symbolic goods. Yet in certain situations it may also result in the loss of autonomy. This is why I have argued that it is important to take note of the material conditions and consequences of internet use and of the social constraints which are imposed on and flow from it. As a modality of cultural transmission the internet involves a *technical medium of transmission, an institutional apparatus of transmission* and a certain kind of *space-time distanciation involved in transmission*. To suggest, in the way Gardels does, that communication facilitated by the internet is somehow 'unmediated' is to surrender an opportunity to examine the structured character of global communication and the contextualized, hermeneutical character of the production/reception processes involved in internet use.

Douglas Rushkoff: Networked communication is like 'a global organism that respects the individuality of each member of each culture'

Douglas Rushkoff, a media specialist, argued that the problem of cultural imperialism and the internet is one which is created by those who fight information technology because it allows a 'very natural, freeform, liquid relationship between human beings to take place' (p. 472). I have already argued in chapter 4, regarding Rheingold's analysis of virtual communities as colonies of micro-organisms, that such perspectives are seriously flawed. If we want the internet to play a crucial role in cultivating some sense of responsibility for our collective fate, then we must work to make this happen. How this might be accomplished if, as Rushkoff suggests, 'we don't have to do a thing' (p. 472) is rather difficult to imagine.

Anne-Marie Slaughter: 'The real problem is not cultural imperialism, but rather a problem of two cultures'

Anne-Marie Slaughter, a lawyer at Harvard Law School, championed the idea that it is not cultural imperialism we should be worried about, but rather the 'divide between those who are privileged and online, and the rest of the world' (p. 470). I have already discussed the untenable nature of such dualistic approaches. Being 'unconnected' or 'weakly connected' to the internet is a problem which must be understood in the context of the dialectical relationship, evident in the reciprocity and interdependency connecting the local and the distant. Moreover, the internet involves the transmission of a plurality of cultures which cannot be collapsed into such simple categories. In preferring a dualistic approach, Slaughter also underestimates the problems which will arise because, in many respects, we now live in one world in which there are no 'others'. The cultural differences will not just be between those who are connected and those who are not.

Izumi Aizu: With the internet 'seemingly minor culture now has a place where it can exhibit'

Izumi Aizu, an intercultural communications specialist in Japan, argued that the internet creates a global arena for 'seemingly minor culture . . . that the mass media or the mass economy cannot pay attention to' (p. 473). In some developing countries, he continued, 'people are now jumping in to use the net, not only to absorb the knowledge or information from the advanced countries but to share their *own* with others' (p. 478).

Coming from a non-Western culture, Aizu seems to have a more subtle and theoretically sophisticated understanding of the interchange between the activities of, for example, Japanese artists on the web, and global influences. It is an interchange which is created by the active involvement of all those concerned. However, such a view tends to ignore the problem that the ability to use internet resources is unevenly spread. It does not confront the way in which the active involvement of those who are part of 'minor' cultures might unintendedly lead them to integrate their activities more closely, in some respects, with the asymmetries of autonomy and dependence of global internet use.

Karanja Gakio: 'We're trying to come up with . . . the tools for participating in this new universe'

Karanja Gakio, Vice-President of Africa Online, described his work as providing internet access in underserved areas of the world, particularly sub-Saharan Africa (p. 476). He is well aware that for most people in the developing world, the problem of survival is far more acute than the problem of being 'unconnected'. He recognized a certain moral responsibility in that the provision of internet access must not 'create conditions which further separate the elite and everybody else' (p. 470). He argued that far from being a free flow of information, 'a lot is dependent on economic realities' (p. 472). He explains that the same issues of 'getting culturally overrun on a global scale occur on a regional level as well' (p. 476).

Like Aizu's contribution to the panel debate, Gakio demonstrated that being heard on the internet does not come automatically, but involves an active struggle. However, while it involves complex local conditions and decision-making, this process is intricately. linked to processes of globalization.

Xiaoyong Wu: 'Policy of control is doomed to fail'

Xiaoyong Wu, an assistant chief executive of Phoenix Satellite Television Company in Hong Kong, commented on the role of government policy with regard to cultural imperialism and the internet, in particular the experience in China. He explained that government policy in China is very complex. 'On the one hand, it wants to continue to control the flow of information. On the other hand, China has a very dynamic economy which demands the free flow of information.' Wu argued that even in China, a policy of tight control is limited and ineffective, and ultimately doomed to fail (p. 471). Unlike Rushkoff, Wu sees this denudation as the work of global media organizations rather than as the inevitable consequence of the forces of technology.

What we must not conclude from Wu's comments is that nation-states have no role to play in creating policy and setting up agencies designed to impose some degree of regulatory control over the internet. It is in the interest of all users of the internet that any regulatory policy stimulates a global arena which is neither part of the state nor wholly dependent on the autonomous processes of the market.

The internet and the expansion of control over globalizing influences

We might ask if the relationship between the internet and globalization promotes the general good in any practical sense. Given that most debates about globalization stress the disruptive side of its developments, the internet has often been blamed for the deepening of world inequality.[35] Yet as a global arena of communication, the internet is shaking up existing institutions and ways of life no matter where we are or who we are.[36] Facing these challenges is not just a matter for those in 'poor' countries, as many commentators suggest. Even so, examples from these parts of the world are very illuminating because of the formidable challenges that those in non-Western countries face.[37] In this final section I want to examine some websites of organizations in countries where effective use of the internet might at first seem impossible, but where significant progress has nevertheless been made. Rather than throwing up our arms in despair, these examples begin to demonstrate that we should be looking to reconstruct our ways of life, together with our institutions, so that we might deal more effectively with the global challenges we face. The three websites I want to consider are (1) The 31st December Women's Movement of Ghana; (2) The Gatsby Marketing Centre; and (3) The Bombolulu Project. Each of these websites is hosted by Africa Online, a provider of internet services founded in 1994 by three Kenyans studying at MIT and Harvard University.[38] For many these websites might seem to fit Castells's description of being 'economically irrelevant'. Yet for those who have created these websites the content of such a discussion seems less important than their opportunity to make themselves visible by being connected.

The 31st December Women's Movement of Ghana

The First Lady and President of the 31st December Women's Movement of Ghana, H. E. Nana Konadu Agyeman Rawlings, sees their website as a way of informing the world about the aim of their movement, in the hope of developing 'meaningful collaboration with all progressive organizations who share its aspirations'.[39] Her desire is to see the 'emancipation of women at every level of development to enable them to contribute and benefit from the socio-economic and political progress of the country. Their participation will help to achieve the aims of the United Nations Declaration for Women: Equality, Development and Peace.'

This website demonstrates how such an organization is using the internet to tackle head on the problems that Ghanaian women face. The movement arose, the website explains,

> as the expression of the will of the women of the country to take themselves in hand, to have their role in society recognized and valorized. The aim of the Movement is that women should take responsibility for themselves instead of being 'assisted' persons . . . they are encouraged to organize themselves in order to find the means to settle urgent problems and, when conditions permit, to set up profitable economic activities.

The website lists programmes which the movement has developed where women are encouraged to 'participate in the decision-making process at the community, district and national levels'. These include literacy education, income-generating activities, daycare centres for children, environmental protection, health care, family planning and farm projects. Of course the website welcomes donations from agencies both local and abroad but this is no longer about aid being foisted upon those who are supposed to gain from it. It is about using the internet within generative programmes to empower women and foster their capability to take their own decisions regarding the problems they face. The internet is thus creating new opportunities for developing local sensitivity on a global scale, helping aid to remedy problems of global inequality rather than exacerbate them.

The Gatsby Marketing Centre

The Gatsby Marketing Centre is part of the Kenya Gatsby Trust, a non-profit organization engaged in 'improving and transforming the micro and small-scale operators to become commercial entrepreneurs ready for the market'.[40] At the marketing centre, design ideas are exchanged. Training is given in product design and development, environmental awareness and customer care. The organization also extends micro-credit to facilitate the finance of these small businesses.

The main aim of the Gatsby Marketing Centre website is to attract visitors to the market itself rather than to sell goods over the internet. Their activities do however support organic agriculture projects that export teas to Japan and Italy.

The Bombolulu Project

The Bombolulu Workshops for the Handicapped is located in Mombasa and operates sheltered workshops for a workforce of 160. The artisans making up the workforce, the website claims, aim 'to develop themselves as independent members of the wider community so they can acquire the respect and security they deserve'.[41] The artisans specialise in making jewellery, wood-carvings and leather items, and in tailoring. Many of the products they sell have evolved from designs developed by ancient tribes. The Bombolulu Project exports its products to twenty-two countries worldwide.

The Bombolulu website is a key innovation in the project's attempts to change 'from a charity to a project which more positively encourages the social and financial independence of its workforce'. The webpages list and describe the products that are made. There is a simple form allowing those interested in importing goods to request further information and make an order.

While nothing may come of these websites that can be reflected in the volume of world financial transactions, they do reflect in a fundamental way how organizations and individuals are attempting to use the internet to achieve greater control over globalizing influences. They demonstrate that it is not utopian to suppose that the internet can be used in projects to combat global inequality. However, it would be rather naive to suggest that a globally inclusive cosmopolitan society can rest on the enthusiasm of self-help groups on their own. As Giddens writes: 'Global problems respond to local initiatives but they also demand global solutions.'[42] The Africa Online website lists a great many more organizations than I have just described that have no e-mail address and no website. The rates for building and hosting websites are high, and what is the use of having a website that most people cannot visit anyway? Many hyperlinks connect South with North but few reverse the gesture. Wresch concludes in *Disconnected*: 'As we think more about information – where it comes from, where it goes, where it can't go, who gets it, who doesn't – we find a situation that is far more complicated than is usually described in the 'gee whiz' articles on the wonders of World Wide Web.'[43] The movement towards more inclusive information environments demands a parallel movement towards more global forms of governance – regulatory measures and policies that are more adept in facilitating global dialogue, empowerment and solidarity, and in coping with conflicts arising from inequalities on a global scale. As long as the internet helps us to increase our powers of perception and heighten our awareness of the consequences of our actions, I think that we should agree with a point also made by Wresch that there is still some hope that global inequality is not altogether beyond our control.

9

Regulation and the internet

The development and use of modern communication technologies have always been regarded by nation-states as being of prime relevance to their interests, and thus as demanding some form of regulation. This concern is not surprising, given the central role that the use of these technologies has played in bringing about the transition from traditional societies to modern nation-states. Technologies that can be used to transmit messages to relatively large audiences attract particular attention in this respect. This is because of their profound significance as a major factor in influencing the values and moral standards in modern society. In most democratic nation-states, and with varying degrees of success, policy-makers have attempted to secure frameworks for mass communication that reflect and accommodate cultural diversity and pluralism. This is in part due, as Giddens writes, to the 'generic association between the nation-state and polyarchy'.[1] Individuals are not just *users* of communication systems, they are also participants in political communities in which the competent formation of opinion and the making of decisions depend on the availability of information and the monitoring of the differing ideas of others. The internet, too, has come to play the role of a general public communication system. Nation-state authorities continue to be baffled by the problems that result from attempting to regulate it.

Opinions on how the internet should best be regulated have long been divided. Some argue that the internet is ungovernable and that the very idea of effective state policy is defunct. They base their opinions on what they see as the anti-authoritarian and liberating nature of the internet. Efforts to regulate the internet, they claim, are destined to flounder because cyberspace is inherently global and pliant, allowing individuals and organizations to evade authorities by slipping into anonymity and by retreating beyond the bounds of their jurisdictions. Yet, while there is certainly some truth in this, the internet has also affected the scope of the regulatory processes themselves. The internet is making possible more complex arrangements for monitoring, tracking down and identifying 'miscreants'. Long gone are the days when authorities had to rely on 'a good eye and retentive memory'.[2] Those using the internet for illegitimate purposes are still situated somewhere in time-space. In many respects, their doings are more visible and open to scrutiny than ever before.[3]

Others concerned with the regulation of the internet have argued that the idea of state policy is not so much impossible as strangely old-fashioned. They base their opinion on the idea that intervention contravenes freedom of information and expression, and is a preoccupation of the past. Yet even fervent supporters of free speech, cultural diversity and pluralism would agree that people should not be free to engage in activities such as inciting racial hatred or circulating images of child pornography.

Most observers of the development of the internet have come to accept that some degree of regulation is necessary and appropriate, yet few have remained unperturbed by some of the attempts to regulate the internet that have unfolded over its early years. Some of these, particularly those involving censorship, seem to have been more the result of 'moral panic' than the outcome of processes of careful and considered deliberation.[4]

In this chapter I want to critically examine the various alternative modes of internet regulation that have been developed and how they might affect cultural transmission. Government policy is affecting the internet, intranets and extranets in many ways. It has, for example, been directed at regulating the boundary lines between the internet and other media, or it can be aimed at stimulating economic development and jobs.[5] Here I shall examine the way in which policy attends to the internet as a general public communication system, focusing in particular on measures that attempt to regulate access and content. A major problem with internet regulation has been its tendency to focus more or less exclusively on what Castells has called 'perverse integration': the use of the internet for the transmission of harmful or illegal material.[6] Regulation therefore has tended to be designed to cope with such problems in a reactive way, combating them by attempting to block flows of information. I will argue, however, that more generative policies need to be initiated if nation-states are to mobilize the internet as a means for serving diverse goals. Based on a list of possible government achievements constructed by Giddens,[7] these goals may include:

1 Representing diverse interests.
2 Establishing a forum for the reconciliation of competing claims of these interests.

3 Creating an open public sphere, in which unconstrained debate can be carried on about policy issues.
4 Providing a diversity of public goods.
5 Fostering market competition.
6 Promoting social peace.
7 Actively developing human capital.
8 Sustaining the law.
9 Providing economic infrastructure.
10 Reflecting and shaping widely held norms and values.
11 Fostering local, regional and transnational alliances and pursuing global goals.

The nature of the internet coupled with the conditions of reflexive modernity demand new kinds of control. Developing and shaping these will require policy-makers to approach the internet as a modality of cultural transmission rather than simply as an alternative and dangerous channel for harmful or illegal material. Against the backdrop of my discussion in the preceding two chapters concerning the internet, publicness and globalization, my aim here is to discover how policy-makers might best pursue what Thompson describes as the *principle of regulated pluralism* within internet praxis.[8] Pursuing this principle is fundamental to what governments can achieve with respect to internet use.

First I shall argue that government regulation of the internet can be better understood if the conditions the regulator seeks to promote are properly systemized. This will involve critically elaborating the 'principle of regulated pluralism' within the context of the internet as a general public communication system. Second, I shall examine the various methods of internet regulation that governments around the world have sought to promote, and the kinds of problems they have encountered in applying them. This discussion will also bring to the fore some of the bodies that have been involved in regulating the internet, together with some of the main fields of attempted regulatory supervision. Third, I shall set out some possible ways forward.

Existing policies – those governing broadcasting, for example – have often been understood to offer little guidance to internet regulation. However, while internet regulation has raised many new concerns for governments, it has also intensified some old ones. Moreover, as communication technologies become increasingly integrated, the integration of policy measures becomes increasingly urgent. I therefore want to stress throughout this chapter that important lessons can be learned from the experience of regulating more 'conventional' forms of communication. During the late 1980s Jay Blumler, concerned about the developments taking place in broadcasting at that time, wrote: 'caught in a veritable blizzard of technological, economic, structural and legal change, all the societies of Western Europe are today grappling with profound and (for them) unfamiliar issues of electronic media policy.'[9] He might just as well have been writing about the internet in the late 1990s. Moreover, these recurrent problems in communication policy have not differed from chronic problems encountered in other fields of state supervision. Regulatory measures instituted by nation-states generally became more strained and ineffective under conditions of reflexive modernization.

Promoting the principle of regulated pluralism

Whatever views we might hold about society and the role of communication, one thing is clear: there remains, in most countries of the world, great uncertainty about how states can best regulate the internet in the interests of their citizens. This situation might be improved if we first try to stipulate what kind of conditions government policy-makers must seek to create. Given Thompson's 'principle of regulated pluralism' and the earlier discussion here about the renewal of public life and the expansion and consequences of globalization, government policy-makers should essentially seek to limit two important areas of uncertainty and risk in internet use.

First, government policy-makers must secure conditions that involve the deconcentration of resources. This means curtailing the excessive power of large conglomerates and other powerful constituencies in such a way that 'diversity and pluralism are not undermined by the concentration of economic and symbolic power.'[10] On the one hand, this will require imperative control, such as legislation to limit mergers and takeovers and the like. On the other hand, regulative measures cannot always simply be instituted from the top. More generative policy programmes are required that are aimed at creating conditions which are sensitive to local demands and protective of narrower interests. Policy must thus create a framework within which the risks associated with internet use can be approached both on an individual level and on more global levels.

Second, government policy must secure conditions that involve 'a clear separation of media institutions from the exercise of state power'.[11] The arguments of early liberal thinkers such as Jeremy Bentham, James Mill and John Stuart Mill still have relevance and urgency today. John Stuart Mill argued that

> the peculiar evil of silencing the expression of an opinion is, that it is robbing the human race, posterity as well as the existing generation, those who dissent from the opinion, even more than those who hold it. If the opinion is right, they are deprived of the opportunity of exchanging error for truth: if wrong, they lose what is almost as great a benefit, the

clearer perception and livelier impression of truth, produced by its colli-
sion with error.[12]

This need to separate institutions of mass communication from the
exercise of state power involves the creation of institutional frameworks
within which, for example, the press, radio and television broadcasting
organizations can operate independently. At the same time, it requires
various independent supervisory bodies to be created by government to
watch over the performance of these systems. These forums act as arenas
in which individuals and organizations involved in using or providing
these media can be held accountable for their activities. With democratic
nation-states having retreated from the day-to-day affairs of running
these media, censorship is a rare occurrence. Yet regulatory measures often
specify situations where direct control is justified, for example when
freedoms are abused or situations occur which threaten state security.

The twin aspects – the deconcentration of resources and the separation
from the exercise of state power – are encapsulated in the 'principle of
regulated pluralism'. When applied to the regulation of the internet as a
general public communication system, this means that government policy-
makers pursuing regulated pluralism must secure a broad institutional
space, regulated with a view to promoting diversity and pluralism. Given
the global nature of internet communication, they must do so at local,
national and international levels.

However, in applying this principle, policy-makers would not wish,
for example, to legitimize a webpage that contained illegal and harmful content on the grounds that such a page increased pluralism and
diversity. Regulation clearly has no rationale if it does not provide a
normative foundation for grounding accounts as to why certain forms of
diversity and pluralism are desirable while others are not. While such a
normative foundation will never determine cultural transmission via the
internet, it is informative of the policy-makers' intent as to the legitimacy
of particular forms of resource mobilization. The problems facing policy-
makers are therefore not just to do with learning about the capabilities
and limitations of different techniques of regulation, that is their design
and implementation. Nor are they merely about making the right decisions given the difficult lessons that policy-makers are learning about
recent changes and tensions in communication, polity and economy. The
problems faced by policy-makers in regulating the internet have to do
with a legacy of deeply ingrained assumptions about the proper control
of communication technology which they have seemed very reluctant to
abandon. Those who set out to isolate and solve the problem of how
best to control the use of the internet in the interests of its users, defining it as part of a crisis which occurred like a 'veritable blizzard', may
perhaps get lost in the snow. Internet users today are not waiting for fair

weather but for more positive arguments as to why certain forms of internet use are desirable while others are not.

While it is perfectly obvious that most of us would sympathize with an authority that requested the removal from the internet of a webpage that contained illegal and harmful content, such decisions are not always so clear-cut. To secure the conditions of regulated pluralism in internet regulation, therefore, authorities must open up their decision-making to 'arguments of principle' as well as 'arguments of policy'. As I explained in chapter 7, arguments of principle involve rights-based strategies concerned with the independence, rather than the conformity, of individual action. Arguments of policy involve goal-based strategies concerned with the following of rules which dictate a particular outcome. We can only pursue regulated pluralism if we have a more sophisticated way of recognizing legitimate moral positions. This in turn might favour the creation of more successful deliberative arrangements, which in turn may contribute to resolving some of the complex issues to which internet regulation gives rise.

Methods of internet regulation and their problems

An important source of frustration in facing the problem of internet regulation has been the clash of two distinct perspectives. Governments tend to approach the internet as a technology that facilitates the public circulation of material, and is therefore akin to broadcasting – an activity for which they have developed, albeit through independent bodies, a high degree of content regulation. Individuals, on the other hand, tend to approach the internet, sometimes even literally, as an extension of media such as the telephone which have been characterized by only a very marginal regulation of content. Neither of these perspectives is helpful on its own.

In this section I want to survey a broad array of different mechanisms to do with the internet regulation.[13] Some of these measures have been initiated by governments directly, while others have been merely encouraged by them. Yet while these measures have been presented in an attempt to regulate the new medium, the experience of their strengths and weaknesses in other areas of media regulation has commonly been ignored. Given the characteristics of the internet as a modality of cultural transmission together with the conditions of reflexive modernization, some of these weaknesses have become more pronounced. It is therefore difficult to envisage how some of these mechanisms might operate effectively and durably.

To begin with I shall consider the question of censorship, and go on to discuss the difficulties of negative regulation. Next, I shall consider the search for international frameworks for regulating the internet, and then examine the strengths and limitations of self-regulation. Lastly, I shall focus on some of the tribulations of the rating and filtering systems that have been developed.

The uncomfortable question of censorship

Until the 1990s there was little government-initiated regulation of internet access and content. Users belonged to a limited community of academics, government and commercial research institutions. From 1990 onwards, as the internet began to expand and to play the role of a general public communication system, nation-state authorities began to take more notice. Probably the most apparent form of internet regulation so far has been direct censorship, often motivated with reference to the unfathomable amounts of child pornography allegedly sent and received over the internet.

A major incident of direct censorship occurred in 1995, when the prosecuting attorney's office of Munich District Court in Germany ordered CompuServe, an internet service provider, to ban access to over two hundred Usenet newsgroups. Many upset users cancelled their CompuServe subscriptions. CompuServe, whose head office is in Ohio, protested that they were merely in the business of transmitting information, mostly created by individuals who resided in different countries and under different legal systems. Given the sheer volume of Usenet newsgroups, providers generally argued that they could not monitor the suitability of new documents posted each day.[14]

Another incident of direct censorship occurred in 1996, when the British police sent a letter to all internet service providers in the United Kingdom instructing them to ban over a hundred newsgroups because they were believed to contain pornographic material. The letter mentioned the necessity of 'moving quickly towards the eradication of this type of newsgroup from the internet'.[15]

In another incident involving German federal prosecutors in 1997, a German academic computer network serving over four hundred universities and research establishments blocked all six thousand webpages on the server of the Dutch internet service provider XS4ALL. The reason given was that 'Radikal', a left-wing magazine, was accessible through their network. A number of commercial organizations with websites on the XS4ALL server terminated their contracts because their German clients could not access them.[16]

While in democratic nation-states crude censorship was thought to belong to the past, this kind of intervention often reappears in some form when new technologies challenge existing patterns of control. Much can be learnt from the experience in television when video, cable and satellite television was first introduced. In this context, James Curran and Jean Seaton write of the 'closing of doors which many had regarded as permanently unlocked: the reimposition of censorship in a new form, made the more dangerous because it is occurring in response to a public mood that owes much to fear of the new technology itself'.[17] However, given the nature of the internet as a modality of cultural transmission and under conditions of reflexive modernization, the outrage caused by censorship has been particularly acute. This is because it stands in contrast to the high hopes many users entertained of it being a 'liberating' technology. Another aspect of censorship in relation to the internet is that it has global consequences affecting many people. Not only this, censorship decisions can be globally challenged. 'Radikal' magazine, for example, was available at forty other sites which were not blocked by the German authorities.[18] Moreover, with the decline of final authorities under conditions of reflexive modernization, who can legitimately claim to have the authority to censor? Many newsgroups affected by censorship later appeared not to have contained illegal, harmful or offensive content after all. Acts of censorship cannot be said to promote the *principle of regulated pluralism* in any way. The problems posed by these developments have served only to fuel the outlook of new cultural pessimists who see the internet as a threat to social order.

The difficulties of negative regulation

In most countries, internet regulation has been based on existing law which has sometimes been amended to take account of online communication. However, in most countries governments have also begun to realize that the capacity for the negative regulation of communication systems has gradually been slipping away.

In Great Britain, the Obscene Publications Act 1959 and 1964 applies to the creator of a website in the same way as it does to other forms of publication. Material is deemed to be obscene if it tends to 'deprave or corrupt' unless 'it is proved that publication . . . is justified as being for the public good . . .'[19] However, the 1998 enquiry of the Select Committee for Culture, Media and Sport into audio-visual communications and the regulation of broadcasting argued that while the internet will become a platform for audio-visual content barely distinguishable from broadcast content, this did not mean that it could be subject to regulation in the same way as broadcasting. 'We are far from persuaded', it concluded, 'that any particular legislative provision for regulation for internet content . . . is viable.'[20] It stated five reasons underpinning this conclusion.

This is first of all a matter of scale. Second, it is a matter of means of access: an audio-visual transmission over the internet could be one of millions of one-to-one transactions, over which there can be no legislative control. Third, it is a function of the internet's economic and social potential. The potential of the internet as an engine of economic growth and social progress is enormous; it would be an act of self-indulgence to purport to jeopardize this unique opportunity by means of a virtually unenforceable law. Finally, the internet is international; any framework for its regulation must equally be international.

In the United States, legislators have also been struggling with the problems and consequences of negative regulation. In 1996 a group of organizations forming the Citizens' Internet Empowerment Coalition filed a lawsuit challenging the Communications Decency Act which was contained in the Telecommunications Act 1996.[21] They claimed that the Act violated free speech and did not protect children from inappropriate material. Anyone using the internet to send or display material accessible to minors under eighteen years of age, and deemed as 'indecent' or 'patently offensive by contemporary community standards', could be prosecuted, imprisoned and fined. The Justice Department, however, did not enforce the law while the case was in progress.[22]

By 1997, the United States Supreme Court had ruled that the provisions of the Communications Decency Act regarding indecent content were unconstitutional, and that free speech on the internet merited the highest standards of Constitutional protection.[23] However, as Jonathan Weinberg explains, the plaintiffs 'relied heavily on the existence and capabilities of filtering software (also known as blocking software) in arguing that the Communications Decency Act was unconstitutional'.[24] A statement by the President remarked: 'With the right technology and rating systems – we can help ensure that our children don't end up in the red light districts of cyberspace.'[25]

In 1998, the American Civil Liberties Union, the Electronic Frontier Foundation and the Electronic Privacy Information Center joined together to file a lawsuit challenging the Child Online Protection Act, also known as 'CDA II'. They did so with the backing of a diverse group of internet users, including journalists, artists, booksellers, and gay and lesbian groups.[26]

Drafting legislation to regulate internet access and content was clearly proving very difficult for nation-states. The experience in the United States, Great Britain and in many other countries directed attention towards the need to craft international arrangements and resulted in a display of almost blind enthusiasm for self-regulation and rating systems. However, it is not clear how such measures might promote the *principle of regulated pluralism*.

The search for international frameworks

In many respects, international policy frameworks reflected national concerns writ large. Evidence of this can be gleaned for example from various publications of the European Commission at the century's end.[27] The European Commission recognized that the internet was renewing 'a number of economic sectors, with the emergence of a vibrant and fast-growing "internet economy"'. Simultaneously, the internet had also become 'a powerful influence in the social, educational and cultural fields – empowering citizens and educators, lowering the barriers to the creation and distribution of content, offering universal access to ever richer sources of digital information'. However, the Commission also listed a number of areas of concern: national security (bomb-making, drugs, terrorism); protection of minors (violence, pornography); protection of human dignity (racial hatred, discrimination); economic security (fraud); information security (hacking); protection of privacy (electronic harassment); protection of reputation (libel, comparative advertising); and intellectual property (copyright). Regarding these issues, the Commission recognized the need 'to strike the right balance between ensuring the free flow of information and guaranteeing protection of the public interest'.[28]

Overviews of the European Commission's ideas for regulation were contained in various action plans and included:

1 Creating a European network of hotlines to ensure Europe-wide coverage and stimulate the exchange of information and experience. An important aim of the Commission is to provide regulatory transparency and prevent a fragmentation of the European internal market.
2 Encouraging self-regulation and drawing up guidelines for codes of conduct.
3 Developing filtering and rating systems and ensuring that rating systems take European specificities into account.
4 Encouraging awareness actions drawing attention to hotlines, self-regulation and rating systems within the industry and among internet users.
5 Coordinating with similar international initiatives to ensure coherence between European action and activities in other parts of the world, for example, in cooperation with the OECD, the WTO and the UN.[29]

The Commission acknowledged the important role of internet service providers, but it stressed that it should not 'be forgotten that the prime responsibility for content lies with authors and content providers'. Similarly, it suggested that 'in the highly decentralized internet environment, internet users have a very important role to play in contributing to industry self-regulation.' In this respect, the Commission called for action which stressed parental responsibility rather than governmental intervention and action to improve the traceability of users. It disagreed with the kind of intervention that involved the blocking of providers: 'such a restrictive regime is inconceivable for Europe as it would severely interfere with the freedom of the individual and its political traditions.'[30] It also argued against drafting regulations too widely, for example, regulations resulting in an unconditional ban on using the internet to disseminate material that is freely available in other media; or resulting in situations in which information cannot be safely published at all.

Policy-makers at the European level were overly enthusiastic about the possibilities of self-regulation and rating systems. They described rating systems purely in terms of having the 'advantage of offering "bottom-up" rather than "top-down" solutions'.[31] Rating systems, they claimed, 'provide an effective technology for the indexing and screening of content – and a flexible and inexpensive solution to the differences of sensibilities between various families and cultures. Although the internet may have created new risks, these techniques also offer new opportunities'.[32] However, self-regulation and rating systems themselves also create risks, some of which I shall consider next.

The limitations of self-regulation

It is not just nation-states and international regulatory measures that have come to stress the possible role of self-regulation in internet praxis. A number of representatives of other groups, such as Jonah Seiger of the Center for Democracy and Technology, have also come to believe that 'the only way to control information on the web is to rely on end-users.'[33] Esther Dyson, the chairman of the Electronic Frontier Foundation, celebrated the striking down of the Communications Decency Act, commenting that 'the court's decision takes the responsibility for controlling and accessing speech on the net out of the hands of government and puts it back where it belongs: in the hands of parents and other individuals.'[34]

Self-regulation has been developed in many forms. It might consist of an interest group that sets up a hotline or a webpage that supports a particular cause. Women Halting Online Abuse, for example, describes its mission as 'to educate the internet community about online harassment, empower victims of harassment, and formulate voluntary policies that systems can adopt in order to create harassment-free environments'.[35] Another example of this kind of self-regulation is the CyberAngels initiative, which has developed what they call a 'net patrol programme'. In it, they claim to use their 'special knowledge of online harassment and crimes' to aid 'law enforcement in finding child pornography, sexual predators and other online criminal content and activities'.[36] The rules of their IRC division channel state that: 'coarse language . . . suggestive chat and any other unsuitable behavior (as determined by our Division Directors and Executive Staff) are unacceptable.' With almost religious conviction, they urge their individual community members to 'be an Angel!'[37]

Self-regulation can also be industry based and involve a provider drawing up codes of conduct which its members or subscribers must follow. In many cases, however, self-regulation has involved the setting up of broader independent supervisory bodies which claim to represent the interests and values of a wide range of different groups. An example of such a self-regulatory body is the Internet Watch Foundation which was established in Great Britain in 1996.[38] The IWF began as a hotline for receiving and processing complaints about child pornography and other illegal material on the internet, but rapidly expanded to take on other responsibilities. In 1997, for example, the IWF participated in European Commission consultations and in 1998 it produced a paper for the development of rating systems at a national level.

Self-regulation, like censorship, has often created a host of already familiar problems. The press, for example, has a long history of self-regulation and has created various councils dealing with complaints, standards, ethics and conduct. Yet, as Denis McQuail argues,

> attempts to codify press responsibility cannot overcome the fundamental differences of perspectives and interests between the various participants in the media institution and between the different social and political systems in the world. Nor, in practice, has it proved easy to reach effective self-regulation. Despite the variety of formulation and wide range of application, most codes of media ethics focus on a limited number of principles for good professional conduct.[39]

The problems of self-regulation that McQuail describes have, in many respects, only intensified in the case of the internet. The internet brings together many different cultural perspectives and creates many new opportunities for conflict. Moreover, the conditions of reflexive modernization severely challenge existing forms of self-regulation.

Some of these problems have become evident, for example, in the Cyber-Rights & Cyber-Liberties (UK) movement's criticisms of the IWF's activities as a quasi-governmental body. They have claimed that the IWF was essentially 'an industry based private organization with public duties'. They argued that because the IWF was so closely related to the Department of Trade and Industry and the Home Office, and to the internet industry in general, it did not constitute an independent body.[40] If authorities or bureaus like the Internet Watch Foundation are somehow perceived to be direct voices of government and industry, then it is difficult to see how they might further the *principle of regulated pluralism*.

The Cyber-Rights & Cyber-Liberties (UK) movement argued in favour of a very different initiative, which had been set up in the Netherlands and established what they call the 'Dutch model'. They claimed that this initiative has a much broader base than the British IWF because of the wider range of interests involved: the Dutch Foundation for Internet Providers, internet service providers, Dutch internet users, the National Criminal Intelligence Service, the National Bureau against Racial Discrimination and a number of other experts. However, a closer examination of the achievements of the Dutch hotline reveals that these have in fact been rather disappointing.[41] The creator of this Dutch initiative, Felipe Rodriquez, even claimed that the project had been a complete failure.[42] The hotline, he argued, had not reduced the amount of child pornography available on the internet and prosecutions were few. He argued that the internet had not only revealed the scale of the problem, it had also revealed the failure of police services to cooperate and tackle the problem effectively. Moreover, he warned that the processes of self-regulation were in danger of creating privatized systems of censorship, and environments where webpages could be removed and spirited away without recourse to any formal legal authority.

The tribulations of rating and filtering systems

Rating and filtering systems have developed from the idea of so-called 'safe portals' and from a variety of software filters. 'Safe portals' involve users installing a private gateway, for example a browser or a search engine, which allows them to strictly regulate which websites are accessed from the computer.[43] Software filters also allow users to block inappropriate material and limit the total time spent online.[44]

The possible role of rating and filtering systems received an important impetus with the development of the Platform for Internet Content Selection or PICS. This technique allows information to be filtered on the basis of electronic labels that can be attached to websites. It was developed by Paul Resnick and James Miller at the Massachusetts Institute of Technology's World Wide Web Consortium in 1996.[45] Resnick explains that 'labels can convey characteristics that require human judgement – whether the webpage is funny or offensive – as well as information not readily apparent from the words and graphics, such as the website's policies about the use or resale of personal data.'[46] The World Wide Web Consortium stressed that PICS in itself was merely a set of technical specifications that made it possible for 'independent entities' or authorities to do a number of things: first, to set labelling vocabulary and criteria for assigning labels; second, to assign labels; third, to distribute labels; fourth, to write filtering software; fifth, to set filtering criteria; and sixth, to instal and run filtering software.[47] PICS was thus not a rating system in itself but a technique that allowed rating and filtering systems to operate.

One of the most prevalent rating systems has been developed by the Recreational Software Advisory Council and is called RSACi. The RSAC described itself as 'an independent, non-profit organization that empowers the public'. In creating RSACi the council's aim was 'to provide a simple, yet effective rating system for websites which both protected children and protected the rights of free speech of everyone who publishes on the World Wide Web'.[48] Although the RSAC claimed to be an independent rating bureau, it received support from a number of corporate sponsors including CompuServe, PointCast, Dell, Disney Online and others. The most consequential of the RSAC's achievements, however, was the integration of its system into Microsoft's Internet Explorer browser. This allowed users to activate what Microsoft dubbed a 'content advisor' and set the level of sex, nudity, violence and offensive language they wished to tolerate. This then weeded out inappropriate webpages according to 'filtering rules'. Users could also choose to use a different rating bureau, but Microsoft included no others in its pull-down menu.

While systems like RSACi may offer many new advantages, both the labelling of content and the filtering systems themselves raised a number of social concerns which are capable of generating a significant degree of mistrust. Let us examine a number of these. First, certain browsers already have a particular rating system integrated into them. Downloading and installing browsers such as these privileges the labelling alternatives that the particular system offers, even though the user may also download other browsers.

Second, while organizations creating rating systems may claim to be 'independent', this will not in itself answer the enormous questions concerning their accountability and the transparency of their activities. Even the World Wide Web Consortium acknowledges the dangers if a particular labeller were to get too powerful. They explain: 'if a lot of people use a particular organization's labels for filtering, that organization will indeed wield a lot of power. Such an organization could, for example, arbitrarily assign negative labels to materials from its commercial or political competitors.'[49] The RSAC, on its part, attempted to ground the legitimacy of its system by claiming that RSACi was 'based on the work of Dr Donald F. Roberts of Stanford University, who has studied the effects of media for nearly 20 years'. This seems but a poor reflection of the intricate measures in place for underpinning the legitimacy of supervisory bodies that monitor other institutions, for example broadcasting.

Third, while creators of websites can label their websites themselves, anyone can create a PICS label that describes a website or even a complete provider's server. This means that one individual with a grudge against another can label the other's site or server without the other's approval. While the World Wide Web Consortium described this as 'analogous to someone publishing a review of your website', it is actually far more consequential.[50] Weinberg, for example, explains that 'the Christian Coalition, say, or the Boy Scouts – can seek to establish rating services reflecting their own values, and these ratings can be implemented by off-the-shelf blocking software'.[51] Once a website was blocked, the consequences would be much more far-reaching than the repercussions of a critical review that might appear in a newspaper. Once a website was blocked, those using a rating system such as PICS would not even know that the website had ever existed!

Fourth, while creators of websites can opt not to label them, users of the RSACi system could choose to uncheck a box so that all non-RSAC rated websites would be blocked. This could, RSAC advised, 'be very helpful given the nature of the web and how quickly new sites are being set up every day. Unchecking this box is your best bet for blocking unwanted content from your children!'[52] This meant that websites could be blocked for no other reason than that they had not been labelled. The Stonewall website, for example, which was discussed in chapter 5, was not RSAC-rated in 1998 and could not be viewed for this reason.[53] If the user's own website was not rated, the content advisor would not even have allowed them to view it themselves!

Fifth, rating and filtering systems will not allow total control of content access. Users can find ways of turning the system off. They may even attempt to instal another browser which does not have such controls integrated into it. They can also access the internet from a different computer. Moreover, rating systems are only applied to the WWW and do not yet include other internet environments such as IRC.

Sixth, rating and filtering systems can be implemented upstream from the end-user's computer, at the internet service provider or on an organization's firewall. Although this will not allow governments to create national firewalls, it does enable providers to comply with government requirements that prohibit access to specific websites. Moreover, individuals can subscribe to particular providers which filter out certain information. Governments might even compel providers to self-rate.[54]

Seventh, the accuracy of filtering systems is often poor. As Weinberg explains, 'sites discussing gay and lesbian issues are commonly blocked, even if they contain no references to sex.'[55] Jonathan Wallace, who created the website 'An Auschwitz alphabet' that also contains material on sexual torture, argues that he will not rate his site because filtering systems lump his page together with the 'Hot nude women' page.[56] The question of the accuracy of filtering systems is also raised with respect to organizations that run search engines. If they rate the websites which they include, this will undoubtedly raise questions concerning the consistency of their ratings.

Eighth, while rating and filtering systems have been ushered in to protect children, other adult users might not so easily disable them or alter the settings for their own use.

All these concerns call for the careful monitoring of the practices of labelling services and rating bureaus and the ways in which filtering systems are used. This issue was also raised in the Cyber-Rights & Cyber-Liberties (UK) movement's criticisms of the Internet Watch Foundation's involvement in developing a rating system at a national level in Great Britain. It stressed the importance of setting up 'an independent working group which would assess the real amount of problems and seek the best solutions'.[57] Given the nature of the internet as a modality of cultural transmission and the conditions of reflexive modernization, it will prove very difficult for agencies to design adequate rating systems and filtering rules governing information access. At the same time, if rating and filtering systems are to be more than just dumb mechanical nannies their creators will have to maintain active trust in their performance, and display levels of accountability and transparency far beyond what they are achieving at present.

Some possible ways forward

Internet regulation locks into the attributes of the internet as a technical medium of transmission and profoundly affects, in Thompson's terms, its 'channels of selective diffusion' and 'mechanisms for restricted implementation' of information and other symbolic content. In creating their policies, regulators recognize the cultural significance of the internet described in terms of its importance for social and economic progress. However, they have nevertheless initiated forms of regulation that may unintendedly endanger the potential of the internet as the deliberative mediated publicness upon which such progress depends.

I have already argued that internet regulation should strive to promote regulated pluralism. What possible ways forward are there, given the current developments? Rather than attempting to recapitulate ideas and criticism already elaborated on, I shall set out five ways forward in propositional form.

(1)   While censorship can sometimes be justified, the continual threat of censorship will prevent the internet becoming the powerful influence in

the economic, social, educational and cultural fields that many hope. Acts of censorship by the state fuse the gap distancing the institutions of communication from the exercise of state power. In the long term, such actions can only undermine the trust citizens vest in state authorities. Acts of censorship also continually display the inappropriateness of the 'public good' as a touchstone for the legitimacy of control. Under conditions of reflexive modernization, most individuals and organizations are now aware of the inadequacy of the circular reasoning which underpins decisions to ban certain internet content in this way. Policy must be designed to sustain an effective and positive system of legislation.

(2)   Given that the regulation of media content is becoming increasingly difficult, governments are promoting self-regulation and the activities of rating bureaus. While regulation must always attend to local or community needs, some of the examples of self-regulation and rating bureaus which I have discussed above clearly highlight problems arising from unacceptable concentrations of power. The 'independent' nature of the IWF and RSAC left many rather unimpressed. It must not be forgotten that providers which are encouraged to take on tasks of self-regulation are not public bodies. They are part of the internet industry and their prime interest is to keep their businesses profitable. If controversial content jeopardizes their businesses they will have their own private reasons for removing it. Their overall goal is not so much to further the 'public good' as to increase, on average, the satisfaction of their subscribers' preferences. The touchstone for the legitimacy of their decisions is the market. Rating bureaus and labelling and filtering services, together with the software producers that use them, may also have a profound impact on internet access and content. The overall goals they promote will be 'hardwired' into the very structure of the filtering rules that allow or block access to webpages. As Weinberg explained, RSACi

> classifies sexually explicit speech without regard to its educational value or its crass commercialism . . . A typical home user, running Microsoft Internet Explorer set to filter using RSACi tags, will have a browser configured to accept duly rated mass-market speech from large entertainment corporations, but to block out a substantial amount of quirky, vibrant individual speech from unrated (but child-suitable) sites. This prospect is disturbing.[58]

Governments have seemed oblivious to the dangers that concentrations of power in this area may have. There is clearly a case for more positive action on the part of the state to create institutional frameworks which allow for monitoring and supervision of these developments, promoting more inclusive forms of control on a participatory basis. Governments must actively create conditions which allow the internet to be used for unconstrained debate and as a forum for reconciling competing claims and interests. Moreover, it is not satisfactory to narrow this debate down to issues solely related to the protection of minors.

(3)   While it is important for governments to increase people's awareness of the existence of hotlines, filtering systems, etc., they should also take a more active role in educating individuals and organizations about their rights and responsibilities with respect to internet use. As Giddens writes: 'we all need protection against risk, but also the capability to confront and take risks in a productive fashion.'[59] Part of the problem of children accessing inappropriate material on the internet, for example, is to do with parents being unable to properly assess the opportunities and risks involved. Moreover, not enough is made of the distinction drawn for example by the British government's 1979 Report of the Committee on Obscenity and Film Censorship, which distinguished between material to which individuals are involuntarily exposed and material which they actively seek out.[60] If individuals, for example, do not wish to know about gay and lesbian lifestyles, then they should simply avoid using their search engines to find them and download their content onto their browsers.

(4)   Child pornography and abuse are indeed horrific problems. The internet has increased the visibility of such human suffering. However, it would be naive to suppose that if we were to ban all evidence of these problems from the internet, they would simply disappear. Instead governments should consider how the internet might be used to cope with such problems in a more generative fashion. The internet might be used, for example, to target certain individuals in order to prevent abuse taking place.

(5)   Globalization is not just a backdrop to internet regulation. National policies will only succeed in a context of active collaboration between states. While in some regions transnational alliances have been formed, global policies still remain underdeveloped and call for urgent attention. National policies are inherently bound up with global conditions.

These five possible ways forward might allow government policymakers to create the deliberative mediated publicness on which social and economic progress via the internet depends.

Concluding reflections

The impact of the internet on modern culture does not lend itself to a neat inventory of its effects. The ease with which writers of other studies shift from enthusiasm to pessimism, slipping sometimes into indifference, suggests that our theoretical frameworks for understanding the interactional impact of the internet are woefully inadequate. Modern culture is being transformed. But we need to think about this transformation in a different way. Let me attempt, in conclusion, to make a summary of the themes of this book.

Recent literature in social and cultural theory suggests that we are moving into a new age, the characteristics of which are summarized well in Bauman's *Life in Fragments* and in Giddens's *The Consequences of Modernity*, where they are also criticized.[1] Some of the characteristics of this new age, as Giddens sets out,[2] are very disturbing:

1 Social transformations have centrifugal tendencies and a dislocating character.
2 Individuals are dissolved or dismembered by the fragmenting of experience.
3 Individuals feel powerless in the face of globalizing tendencies.
4 The 'meaning' of day-to-day life is 'emptied' as a result of the intrusion of abstract systems.
5 Coordinated political engagement is precluded by the primacy of dispersal.

Such conditions seem to suggest that we have 'nothing to lose'. If that is true, it is not difficult to imagine that they promote the kind of fake culture of 'anything goes' as Lyotard describes.[3]

Some writers concerned with modern communication networks, most notably Castells, have tended to collapse the consequences of these new technologies directly into the fears that are thought to describe our modern age. He writes about 'dehumanization', 'marginalization', 'exclusion', 'disintegration', 'abduction of identity', 'polarization', 'dependency', 'multicultural syndromes', 'perverse integration and connections', 'war', 'network logic and geometry', 'the Fourth World', 'generic labor versus self-programmable labor', 'irrelevant humans', 'the space of flows that dominate the space of places of people's cultures', 'the end of history', 'the end of cities', 'the edge of forever', 'the architecture of nudity', and even 'hell'.[4] In many respects, Castells is continuing themes that have become prevalent in the studies of many other writers who attempt to understand the impact of the internet on modern culture. Here, forms of human association are deemed to appear like micro-organisms growing in petri dishes, and internet use is claimed to decentre a self that exists in many worlds and plays many roles at the same time.

While all these studies seem to lock the individual and the broader institutional contexts in which they exist into a rather ill-fated future, my hope is somewhat different. I have therefore focused on the new kinds of relations which the internet affords and how they might be placed in the service of coping with our modern experience, rather than becoming yet another source of anxiety and fear. This is not to say that we should not take the warnings of Castells and others seriously. We do indeed live in a world of great uncertainty and risk, yet these are for the most part socially manufactured risks. They are part and parcel of conditions to which we all contribute: consequently we all have a shared responsibility to try and do something about them.

The concept of reflexive modernization breaks the stranglehold the protracted debate about modernity versus postmodernity has tended to place upon conceptual innovation.[5] It helps to capture the possibility of risk understood as a core element of an innovative society rather than as a mostly negative feature that emerges mysteriously behind the backs of individuals and which they can do very little about. I have tried to explain that the internet did not emerge by accident under the conditions of reflexive modernization. It has been created and it has been continually developed with respect to very specific needs and interests. But as with all new technologies, its uses and consequences have not always been wholly foreseen.

I have argued that in order to understand more fully the new options and new burdens created by the internet, intranets or extranets, we need to approach these not as alternative channels of communication but, as Thompson stipulates, as modalities of cultural transmission.[6] Using his theoretical framework to create a theoretical approach to the internet allows us to understand more fully how, in the words of Williams, such technology 'can be used to affect, to alter, and in some cases to control our social process'.[7]

Using Thompson's arguments, concepts and ideas, I have examined a wide range of issues on which the internet is having a profound impact: forms of human association, modern forms of organization, the self and experience, publicness, globalization, and finally, what government might achieve through regulation. In each case, I have related internet use to key debates and ideas concerning these areas. More importantly, I have attempted to tease out and crystallize alternative, but positive, approaches to risk and uncertainty and relate these to new kinds of action and interaction using the internet. Together with examining new risks and new uncertainties created by the internet, I have written about concepts and ideas that celebrate 'clever people', 'intelligent relationships', 'cosmopolitan attitudes', 'opening out', 'active trust', 'inclusion', 'reflexive engagements', 'generative intervention', 'limiting damage', 'refashioning the self', 'negotiating experience', 'reappropriating knowledge and skills', 'forging commitment and mutuality', 'tracking risk and transcending conflict', 'rights of participants to equal concern and respect', 'deliberative mediated publicness', 'the reciprocity and interdependency connecting the local and the distant' and about 'regulated pluralism': concepts which I have drawn from the work of a wide range of social theorists.

Most of my themes, however, are not new. Their contours were laid down some while ago, and their consequences are not yet fully understood. If we put aside the pessimistic rhetoric in recent literature on social and cultural theory, then a very different picture of the impact of the internet on modern culture begins to emerge. It is one that suggests that we might in fact have 'a great deal to lose'. Resigning ourselves to living in a culture in which 'anything goes' is not a viable option – it is a very dangerous one. Giddens describes this era not as postmodernity but as 'radicalized modernity' in which the consequences of modernity become more pronounced than ever before.[8] While some of the characteristics of 'radicalized modernity' continue to be very disturbing, they will not necessarily overwhelm us. Some of these are presented by Giddens in the following way:[9]

1 Dispersal is dialectically related to profound tendencies towards globalization and integration.
2 The self is a site of intersecting forces; yet individuals might actively resolve 'dilemmas of the self'.
3 Experience and action involve a dialectic of powerlessness and empowerment.
4 Day-to-day life is an active complex of reactions, involving both appropriation and loss.

5   Coordinated political engagement is both possible and necessary on a local, regional, national and global level.

Within these developments, communication technologies such as the internet are an essential tool with which we might hope to minimize the dangers and maximize the opportunities. Clearly, as Castells warns, individuals, groups, and other forms of social organization, will remain endowed with varying capacities and resources on which they may draw. Here, we need again to be strongly reminded of Bauman's observation that

> what we and other people do may have profound, far-reaching and long-lasting consequences, which we can neither see directly nor predict with precision. Between the deeds and their outcomes there is a huge distance – both in time and in space – which we cannot fathom using our innate, ordinary powers of perception – and so we can hardly measure the quality of our actions by a full inventory of their effects.[10]

We need therefore to steer our culture not towards one in which 'anything goes' but towards one in which technologies such as the internet are used to reflect on our complex world, to gain a better understanding of it, and to intervene in it the best we can.

Notes

Introduction

1 J. B. Thompson, *The Media and Modernity: A Social Theory of the Media* (Polity Press, Cambridge, 1995), p. 10.

2 M. Castells, *The Rise of Network Society*, vol. 1 of *The Information Age: Economy, Society and Culture* (Blackwell, Oxford, 1996), p. 199.

3 N. Negroponte, *Being Digital* (Hodder and Stoughton, London, 1995), p. 6.

4 E. Ullman, *Close to the Machine: Technophilia and its Discontents* (City Lights Books, San Francisco, 1997), pp. 138–9.

5 C. Stoll, *Silicon Snake Oil: Second Thoughts on the Information Highway* (Macmillan, London, 1995), quotations pp. 4, 2, 4.

6 W. Wresch, *Disconnected: Haves and Have-Nots in the Information Age* (Rutgers University Press, New Brunswick, 1996), pp. 2–4.

7 A. Giddens, *The Third Way: The Renewal of Social Democracy* (Polity Press, Cambridge, 1998), p. 64.

8 J. B. Thompson, *Ideology and Modern Culture: Critical Theory in the Era of Mass Communication* (Polity Press, Cambridge, 1990).

9 M. Morris and C. Ogan, 'The internet as mass medium', *Journal of Communication* 46, no. 1 (1996).

10 H. Rheingold, *The Virtual Community* (Addison-Wesley, Reading, Mass., 1993).

11 W. B. Millard, 'I flamed Freud: a case study in teletextual incendiarism', in D. Porter (ed.), *Internet Culture* (Routledge, New York and London, 1997).

12 Thompson, *Ideology and Modern Culture*.

13 A. Giddens, *Beyond Left and Right: The Future of Radical Politics* (Polity Press, Cambridge, 1994), pp. 4–7.

14 G. Gilder, 'Feasting on the giant peach', Telecosm series, *Forbes ASAP*, 26 Aug. 1996.

15 List of issues based on A. Giddens's 'Framework for radical politics', in *Beyond Left and Right*, pp. 11–20.

16 See esp. J. B. Thompson, 'Mass communication and modern culture: contribution to a critical theory of ideology', *Sociology* 22 (1988), pp. 359–83; *Ideology and Modern Culture*; *The Media and Modernity*.
17 R. Williams, *Culture and Society* (Penguin, Harmondsworth, 1961).
18 R. Williams, *Television: Technology and Cultural Form* (Fontana, London, 1974).
19 A. Giddens, *Social Theory and Modern Sociology* (Polity Press, Cambridge, 1987), p. 155.
20 J.-F. Lyotard, *The Postmodern Condition: A Report on Knowledge* (University of Minnesota Press, Minneapolis, 1984).

1   Some developments that have transformed modern societies

1 F. Webster, *Theories of the Information Society* (Routledge, London, 1995).
2 M. Castells, *End of Millennium*, vol. 3 of *The Information Age: Economy, Society and Culture* (Blackwell, Oxford, 1998), pp. 340–51.
3 R. Williams, *Television: Technology and Cultural Form* (Fontana, London, 1974).
4 J. B. Thompson, *The Media and Modernity: A Social Theory of the Media* (Polity Press, Cambridge, 1995), pp. 44–80.
5 A. Giddens, *Beyond Left and Right: The Future of Radical Politics* (Polity Press, Cambridge, 1994).
6 M. Mann, *A History of Power from the Beginning to* AD *1760*, vol. 1 of *The Sources of Social Power* (Cambridge University Press, Cambridge, 1986), p. 431.
7 J. Kieve, *The Electric Telegraph: A Social and Economic History* (David and Charles, Newton Abbot, 1973).
8 R. Abler, 'Effects of space-adjusting technologies on the human geography of the future', in R. Abler et al., *Human Geography in a Shrinking World* (Duxbury Press, North Scituate, 1975).
9 I. de Sola Pool, *The Social Impact of the Telephone* (MIT Press, Boston, 1977).
10 D. G. Janelle, 'Central place development in a time-space framework', *Professional Geographer* 20 (1968); A. Giddens, *The Nation-State and Violence*, vol. 2 of *A Contemporary Critique of Historical Materialism* (Polity Press, Cambridge, 1985), p. 178.
11 M. McLuhan, *Understanding Media: The Extensions of Man* (McGraw-Hill, New York, 1964), p. 5.
12 Ibid.
13 U. Beck, *Risk Society: Towards a New Modernity* (Sage, London, 1992), p. 19.
14 Giddens, *Beyond Left and Right*, p. 4.
15 Z. Bauman, *Postmodern Ethics* (Blackwell, Oxford, 1993), p. 17.
16 J. Habermas, *The Theory of Communicative Action*, vol. 2: *The Lifeworld and System: A Critique of Functionalist Reason* (Polity Press, Cambridge, 1987), pp. 394–5.
17 A. Giddens, *The Consequences of Modernity* (Polity Press, Cambridge, 1990).

18 Ibid., p. 24.
19 Habermas, *Theory of Communicative Action*, vol. 2, p. 183.
20 G. J. Mulgan, *Communication and Control: Networks and the New Economies of Communication* (Polity Press, Cambridge, 1991), pp. 58–60.
21 Giddens, *The Consequences of Modernity*, p. 27.
22 Habermas, *Theory of Communicative Action*, vol. 2, p. 390.
23 Ibid.
24 Giddens, *The Consequences of Modernity*, pp. 26, 87.
25 Ibid., p. 137.
26 A. Giddens, *Modernity and Self-Identity: Self and Society in the Late Modern Age* (Polity Press, Cambridge, 1991), p. 112.
27 R. Sennett, *The Fall of Public Man* (Vintage Books, New York, 1978), pp. 282–4.
28 D. Dougan, 'Benchmarking the internet: reaching beyond the Bell curve', in *The Harvard Conference on the Internet and Society*, ed. O'Reilly & Associates (Harvard University Press, Cambridge, 1997), p. 38.
29 S. Lash and J. Urry, *Economies of Signs and Space* (Sage, London, 1994), p. 3.
30 U. Beck, A. Giddens and S. Lash, *Reflexive Modernization: Politics, Tradition and Aesthetics in the Modern Social Order* (Polity Press, Cambridge, 1994).
31 Giddens, *Beyond Left and Right*.
32 Beck, Giddens and Lash, *Reflexive Modernization*, pp. 2–3.
33 Ibid., pp. 56–7.
34 Habermas, *Theory of Communicative Action*, vol. 2, p. 395.
35 Thompson, *The Media and Modernity*, p. 209.
36 Beck, Giddens and Lash, *Reflexive Modernization*.
37 D. Held, 'Democracy, the nation-state and the global system', *Economy and Society* 20, no. 2 (1991), p. 161.
38 M. Castells, *The Power of Identity*, vol. 2 of *The Information Age: Economy, Society and Culture* (Blackwell, Oxford, 1997), p. 304.
39 J. Habermas, *Legitimation Crisis* (Polity Press, Cambridge, 1976); C. Offe, *Contradictions of the Welfare State* (MIT Press, Cambridge, Mass., 1984); C. Offe, *Disorganized Capitalism* (Polity Press, Cambridge, 1985).
40 C. J. Mulgan, *Communication and Control*, pp. 58–60.
41 Z. Bauman, *Postmodernity and its Discontents* (Polity Press, Cambridge, 1997), p. 203.
42 Giddens, *Beyond Left and Right*, pp. 12–20.
43 R. A. Dahl, *Polyarchy* (Yale University Press, New Haven, 1971), pp. 1–2.
44 Castells, *The Power of Identity*, p. 303.
45 Giddens, *Beyond Left and Right*, p. 15.
46 L. Hirshhorn and T. Gilmore, 'The new boundaries of the "boundaryless company"', *Harvard Business Review* (May–June 1992), p. 105.
47 J. Fulk and G. DeSanctis, 'Electronic communication and changing organizational forms', *Organization Science* 6, no. 4 (July–Aug. 1995).
48 C. Hecksher, 'Defining the post-bureaucratic type', in C. Hecksher and A. Donnellon (eds), *The Post-bureaucratic Organization: New Perspectives on Organizational Change* (Sage, Thousand Oaks, Calif., 1994), pp. 14–62.
49 V. P. Barabba, *Meeting of the Minds: Creating the Market-Based Enterprise* (Harvard Business School Press, Boston, 1995), p. 114.

50 M. Castells, *The Rise of Network Society*, vol. 1 of *The Information Age: Economy, Society and Culture* (Blackwell, Oxford, 1996), p. 163.
51 Habermas, *Theory of Communicative Action*, vol. 2, p. 395.
52 Giddens, *Modernity and Self-Identity*, p. 207.
53 Thompson, *The Media and Modernity*, p. 180.
54 Giddens, *Modernity and Self-Identity*, p. 3.
55 Ibid., p. 192.
56 Ibid., p. 189.
57 Hecksher, 'Defining the post-bureaucratic type'.
58 J. Fulk and G. DeSanctis, 'Electronic communication', p. 342.
59 Ibid., p. 343.
60 Beck, Giddens and Lash, *Reflexive Modernization*, pp. 66–74, 100–7.
61 Ibid., p. 67.
62 Ibid., p. 100.

2   The rise of the internet

1 K. Hafner and J. Markoff, *Cyberpunk: Outlaws and Hackers in the Computer Frontier* (Fourth Estate, London, 1991).
2 K. Hafner and M. Lyon, *Where Wizards Stay Up Late: The Origins of the Internet* (Simon and Schuster, New York, 1996), and P. H. Salus, *Casting the Net: From ARPANET to Internet and Beyond* (Addison-Wesley, Reading, Mass., 1995).
3 S. Zuboff, *In the Age of the Smart Machine: The Future of Work and Power* (Basic Books, New York, 1988).
4 V. Bush, 'As we may think', *Atlantic Monthly*, July 1945.
5 Hafner and Lyon, *Where Wizards Stay Up Late*, pp. 64–7.
6 P. Baran, 'On distributed communication networks', *IEEE Transactions of the Professional Technical Group on Communication Systems*, vol. CS-12, no. 1 (Mar. 1964).
7 Hafner and Lyon, *Where Wizards Stay Up Late*.
8 J. C. R. Licklider, 'Man–computer symbiosis', *IRE Transactions on Human Factors in Electronics*, vol. HFE-1 (Mar. 1960), pp. 4–11.
9 J. C. R. Licklider and W. Clark, 'On-line man–computer communication', paper presented at the Spring Joint Computer Conference of the American Federation of Information Processing Societies, Aug. 1962.
10 J. C. R. Licklider, 'The computer as a communication device', *Science and Technology* (Apr. 1968).
11 Hafner and Lyon, *Where Wizards Stay Up Late*, pp. 71–3.
12 Ibid., pp. 12–13.
13 Salus, *Casting the Net*, p. 57.
14 J. E. O'Neill, 'The role of ARPA in the development of the ARPANET, 1961–1972', *IEEE Annals of the History of Computing* 17, no. 4 (1995).
15 'The NSFNET backbone services acceptable use policy', National Science Foundation, June 1992, secs 10–11.
16 Zona Research, http://www.zonaresearch.com.
17 S. T. Walker, 'Completion report: ARPA network development', Defense Advanced Research Projects Agency, Information Processing Techniques Office, Washington DC, 4 Jan. 1978.

18 T. Berners-Lee, 'Information management: a proposal', Mar. 1989, http://www.w3.org/History/1989/proposal.html.
19 Ibid.
20 Ibid.
21 Enquiry into audio-visual communications and the regulation of broadcasting, House of Commons Select Committee for Culture, Media and Sport, 6 May 1998, http://www.parliament.the-stationery-office.co.uk/pa/cm199798/cmselect/cmcumeds/520-vol1/52002.htm.
22 Ibid.
23 J. Wallace, *Overdrive: Bill Gates and the Race to Control Cyberspace* (John Wiley, New York, 1997); Zona Research.
24 *Financial Times*, 19 May 1998.
25 J. Weinberg, 'Rating the net', *Hastings Communications and Law Journal* 19, no. 2 (1997), pp. 453–82.
26 Nua Internet Surveys, http://www.nua.net/; US Department of Commerce, 'The emerging digital economy', National Technical Information Service PB98–137029, 1998.
27 The estimates for the number of internet users vary depending on the source used. For a comprehensive and up-to-date overview see Nua Internet Surveys.
28 Ibid.
29 NAZCA, http://nazcasaatchi.com/.
30 Nua Internet Surveys.
31 K. Maney, 'China turns to internet: infant industry stirs passion and paranoia', *USA Today*, 14 Nov. 1997.
32 Nua Internet Surveys.
33 Russian Non-profit Center for Internet Technologies, http://koi.www.rocit.ru/.
34 Asia Biz Tech, http://www.nikkeibp.asiabiztech.com/Database/1999–Jan/13/Mor.04.gwif.html.
35 Nua Internet Surveys.
36 Graphic, Visualization and Usability Center, http://www.gvu.gatech.edu/user_surveys/.
37 T. P. Novak and D. L. Hoffman, 'Bridging the digital divide: the impact of race on computer access and internet use', Project 2000, 2 Feb. 1998, http://www2000.ogsm.vanderbilt.edu/.
38 Graphic, Visualization and Usability Center.
39 Find/SVP, http://www.findsvp.com/.
40 Graphic, Visualization and Usability Center.
41 SRI Consulting, http://www.sri.com/.
42 Graphic, Visualization and Usability Center.
43 Find/SVP.
44 RelevantKnowledge, http://www.relevantknowledge.com/.
45 Graphic, Visualization and Usability Center.
46 INTECO, http://www.inteco.com/.
47 AIMC, http://www.teleservicios.com/internet.htm.
48 CommerceNet, http://www.commerce.net/research/stats/wwwstats.html.
49 CyberAtlas, http://cyberatlas.internet.com/.
50 International Data Corporation, http://www.idc.com.
51 Durlacher Quarterly Internet Report 3, http://www.durlacher.com.
52 Department of Trade and Industry, 'Secure electronic commerce statement', 27 Apr. 1998, http://www.dti.gov.uk/CII/ana27p.html.

53 Booz.Allen & Hamilton, http://www.bah.com/press/internet_survey.html.
54 International Data Corporation.
55 G7 Government On-line Project, Project Definition Statement, http://www.open.gov.uk/govoline/10120_2.htm; G7 Government On-line Project, 'A review of progress and project status', Document 10143, version 1, 9 July 1996. The G7 countries are Canada, France, Germany, Italy, Japan, UK, US.
56 General Accounting Office, http://www.gao.gov.
57 Nua Internet Surveys.
58 *The Guardian*, 7 Oct. 1997; Enquiry into audio-visual communications and the regulation of broadcasting.
59 S. Zuboff, *In the Age of the Smart Machine*.
60 Government Direct: A Prospectus for the Electronic Delivery of Government Services, http://www.open.gov.uk/citu/gdirect/greenpaper/index.htm.
61 Ministry of Transport, Public Works and Water Management, http://www.dgv.minvenw.nl/home/categorie.asp?categorie=dvp.
62 Boeing Company, http://www.boeing.com/.
63 J. E. Fook, 'Boeing's intranet flies high', *Internet Week*, 24 Jan. 1997.
64 Ford Motor Company, http://www.ford.com/global/index-d.html.
65 M. J. Cronin, 'Ford's intranet success', *Fortune*, 30 Mar. 1998.
66 Internet relay chat channel #Gay.nl can be found on EF-net using the following servers: irc2.sci.kun.nl, or irc.sci.kun.nl, irc.xs4all.nl or stealth.net.
67 #Gay.nl home page, http://www.gaynl.demon.nl/.
68 M. Castells, *End of Millennium*, vol. 3 of *The Information Age: Economy, Society and Culture* (Blackwell, Oxford, 1998).
69 A. Giddens, *A Contemporary Critique of Historical Materialism*, vol. 1: *Power, Property and the State* (Macmillan, London, 1981), p. 19.
70 Ibid.
71 A. Giddens, *The Constitution of Society: Outline of the Theory of Structuration* (Polity Press, Cambridge, 1984), p. 16.
72 R. E. Walton, *Up and Running: Integration, Information Technology and the Organization* (Harvard Business School Press, Boston, 1989), pp. 26–8.

3 Cultural transmission and the internet

1 D. Porter (ed.), *Internet Culture* (Routledge, London, 1997), p. xi.
2 Ibid.
3 B. Latour, 'Thought experiments in social science: from the social contract to virtual society', Virtual Society?, first annual public lecture, Brunel University, 1 Apr. 1998, http://www.brunel.ac.uk/research/virtsoc/events/latour2.htm.
4 J. B. Thompson, 'Mass communication and modern culture: contribution to a critical theory of ideology', *Sociology* 22 (1988), pp. 359–83; J. B. Thompson, *Ideology and Modern Culture: Critical Theory in the Era of Mass Communication* (Polity Press, Cambridge, 1990); J. B. Thompson, *The Media and Modernity: A Social Theory of the Media* (Polity Press, Cambridge, 1995).
5 A. Giddens, *The Constitution of Society: Outline of the Theory of Structuration* (Polity Press, Cambridge, 1984), p. 110.

242 Notes to pp. 56–67

6   A. L. Kroeber and C. Kluckhohn, *Culture: A Critical Review of Concepts and Definitions* (Harvard University Press, Cambridge, 1952).
7   R. Williams, *Culture* (Fontana, London, 1981), p. 10.
8   Kroeber and Kluckhohn, *Culture*, p. 77.
9   Thompson, *Ideology and Modern Culture*, pp. 122–45.
10 Kroeber and Kluckhohn, *Culture*, p. 31.
11 J. G. Herder, *Reflections on the Philosophy of the History of Mankind* (Chicago University Press, Chicago, 1968); Kroeber and Kluckhohn, *Culture*, p. 38.
12 Thompson, *Ideology and Modern Culture*, p. 126.
13 G. Klemm, *Allgemeine Cultur-Geschichte der Menschheit* (B. G. Teubner, Leipzig, 1843–52).
14 Kroeber and Kluckhohn, *Culture*, pp. 44–6.
15 Ibid., p. 287; E. B. Tylor, *Primitive Culture: Researches into the Development of Mythology, Philosophy, Religion, Art, and Custom*, vol. 1 (John Murray, London, 1891), p. 1.
16 Thompson, *Ideology and Modern Culture*, p. 129.
17 See also A. Giddens, *New Rules of Sociological Method: A Positive Critique of Interpretative Sociologies* (Hutchinson, London, 1976), p. 119.
18 Thompson, *Ideology and Modern Culture*, p. 130.
19 Ibid., p. 132.
20 Kroeber and Kluckhohn, *Culture*, p. 86.
21 R. W. Sellars, V. J. McGill and M. Farber (eds), *Philosophy for the Future* (New York, 1949), p. 363.
22 R. Bain, 'A definition of culture', *Sociology and Social Research* 27 (1942), p. 87.
23 K. Davis, *Human Society* (Macmillan, New York, 1949), pp. 3–4.
24 Thompson, *Ideology and Modern Culture*, p. 132.
25 C. Geertz, *The Interpretation of Cultures: Selected Essays* (Basic Books, New York, 1973).
26 Thompson, *Ideology and Modern Culture*, pp. 132–5.
27 Ibid., pp. 136, 146.
28 Ibid., pp. 164–71.
29 H. A. Innis, *Empire and Communications* (Oxford University Press, London, 1950) and *The Bias of Communication* (University of Toronto Press, Toronto, 1951); M. McLuhan, *The Gutenberg Galaxy: The Making of Typographic Man* (Routledge and Kegan Paul, London, 1962); *Understanding Media: The Extensions of Man* (Routledge and Kegan Paul, London, 1964).
30 Ford Motor Company, http://www.ford.com/global/index-d.html.
31 British Broadcasting Corporation, http://www.bbc.co.uk/.
32 A. Giddens, *Modernity and Self-Identity: Self and Society in the Late Modern Age* (Polity Press, Cambridge, 1991), p. 26.
33 Ibid., pp. 146–7.
34 Thompson, *Ideology and Modern Culture*, p. 167.
35 A. Giddens, *Central Problems in Social Theory: Action, Structure and Contradiction in Social Analysis* (Macmillan, London, 1979), p. 66.
36 Universidade de São Paulo, http://www.usp.br/.
37 Thompson, *Ideology and Modern Culture*, p. 168.
38 The Digital City Amsterdam, http://www.dds.nl; information in various languages: http://www.dds.nl/dds/info/english/.

39 Thompson, *Ideology and Modern Culture*, p. 168.
40 Ibid., p. 169.
41 Giddens, *The Constitution of Society*, pp. 68–73.
42 Innis, *The Bias of Communication*, pp. 33–60.
43 Ibid., p. 33.
44 Giddens, *The Constitution of Society*, p. 135.
45 B. Sherman and P. Judkins, *Glimpses of Heaven, Visions of Hell: Virtual Reality and its Implications* (Hodder and Stoughton, London, 1992), p. 127.
46 S. Plant, 'Beyond the screens: film, cyberpunk and cyberfeminism', *Variant* 14 (1993) p. 14.
47 D. Boden and H. Molotch, 'The Compulsion of Proximity', in R. Friedland and D. Boden (eds), *NowHere: Space, Time and Modernity* (University of California Press, Berkeley, 1994), p. 258.
48 R. D. Sack, 'The consumer's world: place as context', *Annals of the Association of American Geographers* 78 (1988), p. 642.
49 M. McLuhan, 'Effects of the improvement of communication media', *Journal of Economic History* 20 (1960), pp. 566–75.
50 M. Morris and C. Ogan, 'The internet as mass medium', *Journal of Communication* 46, no. 1 (1996), pp. 39–50.
51 Thompson, *Ideology and Modern Culture*, pp. 218–19.
52 Ibid., p. 219.
53 J. Habermas, *The Structural Transformation of the Public Sphere: An Inquiry into a Category of Bourgeois Society* (MIT Press, Cambridge, Mass., 1991).
54 J. Habermas, *The Theory of Communicative Action*, vol. 2: *The Lifeworld and System: A Critique of Functionalist Reason* (Polity Press, Cambridge, 1987), p. 390.
55 Thompson, *Ideology and Modern Culture*, pp. 114–21; Thompson, *The Media and Modernity*, pp. 71–5.
56 R. Dworkin, *Taking Rights Seriously* (Duckworth, London, 1987), pp. 22–8.
57 Thompson, *The Media and Modernity*, pp. 74–5.
58 Ibid., pp. 260–1.
59 P. Bourdieu, *The Field of Cultural Production: Essays on Art and Literature* (Polity Press, Cambridge, 1993).
60 Thompson, *The Media and Modernity*, p. 85.
61 Bourdieu, *The Field of Cultural Production*.
62 T. Hägerstrand, 'The domain of human geography', in R. J. Chorley (ed.), *Directions in Geography* (Methuen, London, 1973).
63 T. Hägerstrand, *Innovation as a Spatial Process* (Chicago University Press, Chicago, 1967), p. 332.
64 Thompson, *The Media and Modernity*.
65 Giddens, *The Constitution of Society*, p. 164.
66 Bourdieu, *The Field of Cultural Production*.
67 Thompson, *The Media and Modernity*, pp. 91–3.
68 S. Johnson, *Interface Culture: How New Technology Transforms the Way We Create and Communicate* (HarperCollins, New York, 1997), p. 6.
69 Ibid., pp. 18 and 25.
70 Ibid., p. 77.
71 Ibid., pp. 77–8.
72 Ibid., p. 128.
73 Thompson, *The Media and Modernity*, p. 8.

4 The internet and forms of human association

1 H. Rheingold, *The Virtual Community: Homesteading on the Electronic Frontier* (Addison-Wesley, Reading, Mass., 1993).
2 Ibid., p. 3.
3 Ibid., p. 4.
4 Ibid., pp. 1–16.
5 M. Poster, *The Second Media Age* (Polity Press, Cambridge, 1995), p. 35.
6 Rheingold, *The Virtual Community*, p. 1.
7 Ibid., p. 2.
8 B. Anderson, *Imagined Communities: Reflections on the Origin and Spread of Nationalism* (Verso, London, 1983), pp. 13–14.
9 Poster, *The Second Media Age*, p. 34.
10 M. Nash, *The Cauldron of Ethnicity in the Modern World* (University of Chicago Press, Chicago, 1989), pp. 128–9.
11 F. Tönnies, *Community and Association (Gemeinschaft und Gesellschaft)*, trans. C. P. Loomis (1887; Routledge and Kegan Paul, London, 1955).
12 Anderson, *Imagined Communities*.
13 Z. Bauman, *Intimations of Postmodernity* (Routledge, London, 1992), p. xix.
14 Anderson, *Imagined Communities*, pp. 15–16.
15 A. Giddens, *The Nation-State and Violence*, vol. 2 of *A Contemporary Critique of Historical Marxism* (Polity Press, Cambridge, 1985), pp. 192–7.
16 J. Nancy, *The Inoperative Community* (University of Minnesota Press, Minneapolis, 1991), p. xxxviii.
17 R. Dworkin, *A Matter of Principle* (Clarendon Press, Oxford, 1986), p. 2.
18 M. Oakeshott, *On Human Conduct* (Clarendon Press, Oxford, 1975), p. 112.
19 Ibid., pp. 315–16.
20 Ibid., p. 316.
21 A. Giddens, *Beyond Left and Right: The Future of Radical Politics* (Polity Press, Cambridge, 1994), p. 67.
22 H. C. Lucas, *The T-Form Organization: Using Technology to Design Organizations for the Twenty-First Century* (Jossey-Bass, San Francisco, 1996).
23 J. Habermas, *The Theory of Communicative Action*, vol. 2: *The Lifeworld and System: A Critique of Functionalist Reason* (Polity Press, Cambridge, 1987), p. 395.
24 Bauman, *Intimations of Postmodernity*, pp. xvii–xix.
25 Z. Bauman, *Postmodernity and its Discontents* (Polity Press, Cambridge, 1997), p. 196.
26 Giddens, *Beyond Left and Right*, p. 124.
27 Bauman, *Postmodernity and its Discontents*, p. 196.
28 Bauman, *Intimations of Postmodernity*, pp. 138–9.
29 Ibid., pp. 134–5.
30 Bauman, *Postmodernity and its Discontents*, p. 203.
31 M. Castells, *The Information Age: Economy, Society and Culture*, vol. 3: *End of Millennium* (Blackwell, Oxford, 1998), p. 352.
32 A. Giddens, *The Constitution of Society: Outline of the Theory of Structuration* (Polity Press, Cambridge, 1984), pp. 184–95.

33 C. Fischer, *To Dwell Among Friends: Personal Networks in Town and City* (University of Chicago Press, Chicago, 1982).

34 A. Giddens, *The Consequences of Modernity* (Polity Press, Cambridge, 1990), p. 116.

35 Giddens, *Beyond Left and Right*, p. 94.

36 Giddens, *The Consequences of Modernity*, pp. 18–20.

37 Oakeshott, *On Human Conduct*, p. 112.

38 Giddens, *Beyond Left and Right*, p. 130.

39 Oakeshott, *On Human Conduct*, p. 122.

40 J. Dewey, *Democracy and Education* (Macmillan, New York, 1917), p. 120.

41 Giddens, *Beyond Left and Right*, p. 131.

42 Ibid., p. 130.

43 J. B. Thompson, *The Media and Modernity: A Social Theory of the Media* (Polity Press, Cambridge, 1995), pp. 8–9.

44 F. Barth (ed.), *Ethnic Groups and Boundaries: The Social Organization of Culture Difference*, the results of a symposium held at the University of Bergen, 23–6 Feb. 1967 (Allen and Unwin, London, 1969).

45 Bauman, *Intimations of Postmodernity*, p. xx.

46 See Giddens, *Beyond Left and Right*, pp. 124–5.

47 J. Lyotard, *Peregrinations: Law, Form, Event* (Columbia University Press, New York, 1988), p. 38.

48 See Giddens, *Beyond Left and Right*, pp. 124–5.

49 Rheingold, *The Virtual Community*, p. 14.

50 Giddens, *The Nation-State and Violence*, pp. 181–92.

51 Giddens, *Beyond Left and Right*, p. 125.

52 Bauman, *Intimations of Postmodernity*, p. 135.

53 See Giddens, *Beyond Left and Right*, pp. 124–5.

54 See ibid.

55 J. B. Thompson, *Ideology and Modern Culture: Critical Theory in the Era of Mass Communication* (Polity Press, Cambridge, 1990), p. 120.

56 Z. Bauman, *Life in Fragments: Essays in Postmodern Morality* (Blackwell, Oxford, 1995), p. 275.

57 E. Reid, 'Electropolis: communications and community on Internet Relay Chat', electronically distributed version of honors thesis for the Department of History, University of Melbourne, 1991.

58 In order to understand the extracts of IRC dialogue that appear here it might help to know that if someone with the nickname 'saro' says 'hello' it will appear as '<saro> hello' for everyone else in the channel to see. Nicknames like 'Wes20' often communicate a person's claimed age. If capital letters are used, for example 'HELLO', it usually means that a person wants to convey that they are shouting. If questions are repeated or are followed by a series of question marks, it often displays that a person is getting impatient. Asterisks are sometimes used to denote descriptions of emotion, or to show that a person is doing something rather than saying something, or passing a comment that is not directly relevant to the discussion at the time. For example: '<saro> *feels sick*' or '*saro has gone to make a pot of tea'. Some lines in the dialogue are inserted by the IRC system itself. For example '***saro has quit IRC (Leaving)' shows that 'saro' has left both the channel and IRC altogether. Participants can also send each other private messages that are invisible to others.

59 Rheingold, *The Virtual Community*, pp. 300, 14.
60 S. Turkle, *Life on the Screen: Identity in the Age of the Internet* (Simon and Schuster, New York, 1995).
61 S. Turkle, 'Virtuality and its discontents: searching for community in cyberspace', *American Prospect* 24 (Winter 1996), p. 57.
62 Turkle, *Life on the Screen*, p. 268.
63 Ibid., p. 262.
64 Bauman, *Postmodernity and its Discontents*, pp. 194–5.
65 A. Giddens, *A Contemporary Critique of Historical Materialism*, vol. 1: *Power, Property and the State* (Macmillan, London, 1981), p. 18.
66 Turkle, *Life on the Screen*, p. 180.
67 Bauman, *Intimations of Postmodernity*, pp. vii–viii.
68 Rheingold, *The Virtual Community*, p. 3.
69 L. Wittgenstein, *Philosophical Investigations* (Blackwell, Oxford, 1972).
70 A. Giddens, *Central Problems in Social Theory: Action, Structure and Contradiction in Social Analysis* (Macmillan, London, 1979), p. 71.
71 E. Goffman, *Forms of Talk* (Blackwell, Oxford, 1981), pp. 70–1.
72 Giddens, *The Constitution of Society*, p. 171.
73 M. Castells, *The Rise of Network Society*, vol. 1 of *The Information Age: Economy, Society and Culture* (Blackwell, Oxford, 1996), p. 199.
74 Ibid., p. 362.
75 Giddens, *The Consequences of Modernity*.
76 Giddens, *Beyond Left and Right*, p. 130.
77 Bauman, *Postmodernity and its Discontents*, pp. 102–3.
78 Thompson, *Ideology and Modern Culture*, p. 120.

5 Organizations and the internet

1 A. Giddens, *Beyond Left and Right: The Future of Radical Politics* (Polity Press, Cambridge, 1994).
2 H. C. Lucas, *The T-Form Organization: Using Technology to Design Organizations for the Twenty-First Century* (Jossey-Bass, San Francisco, 1996); M. J. Earl, *Management Strategies for Information Technology* (Prentice Hall, New York, 1989); S. Zuboff, *In the Age of the Smart Machine: The Future of Work and Power* (Basic Books, New York, 1988).
3 J. M. Juran, *Juran on Planning for Quality* (Free Press, New York, 1988).
4 M. Hammer and J. Champy, *Reengineering the Corporation* (Harper Business, New York, 1993).
5 T. Davenport, *Process Innovation: Reengineering Work through Information Technology* (Harvard Business School Press, Boston, 1993), pp. 37–66.
6 T. H. Davenport, R. G. Eccles and L. Prusac, 'Information politics', *Sloane Management Review* (Fall 1992).
7 S. Davis and J. Botkin, *The Monster under the Bed: How Business is Mastering the Opportunity of Knowledge for Profit* (Simon and Schuster, New York, 1994), pp. 109–31.
8 C. W. Choo, *The Knowing Organization: How Organizations Use Information to Construct Meaning, Create Knowledge, and Make Decisions* (Oxford University Press, Oxford, 1998).
9 V. Barabba, *Meeting of the Minds: Creating the Market-Based Enterprise* (Harvard Business School Press, Boston, 1995), pp. 109–10.

10   Ibid., p. 114.
11   T. N. Warner, 'Information technology as a competitive burden', in T. Forester (ed.), *Computers in the Human Context: Information Technology, Productivity and People* (Blackwell, Oxford, 1989), p. 274.
12   The failure of some information systems has resulted in law suits, see for example P. Key, 'SAP America hit with a $500m suit', *Philadelphia Business Journal*, 2 Nov. 1998.
13   M. Castells, *The Rise of Network Society*, vol. 1 of *The Information Age, Economy, Society and Culture* (Blackwell, Oxford, 1996), pp. 168–9.
14   A. Giddens, *The Third Way: The Renewal of Social Democracy* (Polity Press, Cambridge, 1998).
15   Z. Bauman, *Life in Fragments: Essays in Postmodern Morality* (Blackwell, Oxford, 1995), p. 103.
16   A. Giddens, 'Time and social organization', in *Social Theory and Modern Sociology* (Polity Press, Cambridge, 1987).
17   Ibid., p. 155.
18   Ibid., pp. 153–62.
19   Ibid., p. 152.
20   Ibid., pp. 162–5.
21   Ibid., p. 162.
22   See J. B. Thompson, *The Media and Modernity: A Social Theory of the Media* (Polity Press, Cambridge, 1995), ch. 1, note 6.
23   Giddens, 'Time and social organization', p. 157.
24   Castells, *The Rise of Network Society*, p. 168.
25   U. Beck, A. Giddens and S. Lash, *Reflexive Modernization: Politics, Tradition and Aesthetics in the Modern Social Order* (Polity Press, Cambridge, 1994), p. 44.
26   Ibid., p. 88.
27   Key, 'SAP America hit with a $500m suit'.
28   For example, Independent Counsel Kenneth Starr's report into the conduct of President Clinton over Lewinsky matter: Referral to the United States House of Representatives pursuant to Title 28, United States Code, §595(c), Submitted by The Office of the Independent Counsel, September 9, 1998, http://icreport.house.gov/icreport/.
29   D. Ernst, 'Inter-firms networks and market structure: driving forces, barriers and patterns of control', Berkeley Roundtable on the International Economy research paper, University of California at Berkeley 1994, pp. 5–6.
30   Castells, *The Rise of Network Society*, p. 420.
31   Ibid., p. 375.
32   D. Harvey, *The Condition of Postmodernity: An Enquiry into the Origins of Cultural Change* (Blackwell, Oxford, 1990), p. 294.
33   F. Jameson, *Postmodernism, or the Cultural Logic of Late Capitalism* (Verso, London, 1991), pp. 38–45.
34   H. Voss, 'Virtual organizations: the future is now', *Strategy and Leadership* (July–Aug. 1996).
35   T. Davenport and K. Pearlson, 'Two cheers for the virtual office', *Sloan Management Review* (Summer 1998), p. 52.
36   Ibid.
37   British Airways, Public Relations Archive, 20 July 1998, http://www.british-airways.com.
38   Castells, *The Rise of Network Society*, p. 420.

39 A. Giddens, *The Consequences of Modernity* (Polity Press, Cambridge, 1990), p. 19.
40 Davenport and Pearlson, 'Two cheers for the virtual office', p. 56.
41 U. Karmarkar, 'Getting control of just-in-time', *Harvard Business Review* (Sept.–Oct. 1989), pp. 122–31.
42 Beck, Giddens and Lash, *Reflexive Modernization*, pp. 37, 186.
43 Giddens, *The Third Way*, p. 102.
44 Ibid., p. 42.
45 Giddens, *Beyond Left and Right*, p. 42.
46 Beck, Giddens and Lash, *Reflexive Modernization*, p. 96.
47 Giddens, *The Third Way*, p. 65.
48 R. Dworkin, *Taking Rights Seriously* (Duckworth, London, 1977), pp. 248–53.
49 Harvey, *The Condition of Postmodernity*, p. 294.
50 I base these traits on ideas put forward by Giddens in *Beyond Left and Right*, pp. 159–63.
51 See for example S. Telleen, 'IntraNet methodology, concepts and rationale', http://www.amdah1.com/doc/products/bsg/intra/concepts1.html.
52 L. Garton and B. Wellman, 'Social impacts of electronic mail in organizations: a review of research literature' in *Communication Yearbook*, vol. 18, (Sage, London, 1995), p. 441.
53 Giddens, *The Third Way*, p. 63.
54 E. M. Hallowell, 'The human moment at work', *Harvard Business Review* (Jan.–Feb. 1999).
55 Singapore government's website, http://www.gov.sg/.
56 United Kingdom government's 10 Downing Street website, http://www.number-10.gov.uk/index.html.
57 J. Reith quoted in A. Briggs, *The Birth of Broadcasting*, vol. 1 of *History of Broadcasting in the United Kingdom* (Oxford University Press, London, 1961), p. 256.
58 Giddens, *The Third Way*, p. 71.
59 Nua Internet Surveys, http://www.nua.net/.
60 Best of Italy, http://www.best-of-italy.com/.
61 R. Cowe, 'Workers go desktop shopping', *The Guardian*, 10 July 1998.
62 A. Abela and A. Sacconaghi, 'The secret of building customer relationships on line', *McKinsey Quarterly*, no. 2 (1997), pp. 216–19.
63 Blackwell's Online Bookshop, http://www.blackwell.co.uk/.
64 J. M. Jordan, 'Organizing for electronic commerce: toward lightweight decentralization', Version 1.0, The Ernst & Young Center for Business Innovation, July 1998.
65 British Petroleum's website is at http://www.bpamoco.com/.
66 'BP and Amoco merge to enter global top trio of oil majors', BP press release, 11 August 1998 and http://www.bpamoco.com/.
67 R. Newing, 'BP introduces its $250m digital nervous system', *Financial Times*, 10 July 1998.
68 The Internet Applications Group, http://www.intapps.com.
69 V. Houlder, 'Far-flung workers find it's good to talk', *Financial Times*, 4 Apr. 1997.
70 The Internet Applications Group.
71 Microsoft UK, http://www.eu.microsoft.com/uk/it_managers/Solutions/backoffice/d_cstudy_kmanagement.htm.

72 The Internet Applications Group.
73 Shell, http://www.shell.com./.
74 See for example Friends of the Earth website, http://www.foe.co.uk/.
75 Shell, 'Profits and principles – does there have to be a choice?', London, 1998, http://www.shell.com/shellreport/index.html.
76 Family Research Council, http://www.frc.org/.
77 Ibid.
78 M. Castells, *The Power of Identity*, vol. 2 of *The Information Age: Economy, Society and Culture* (Blackwell, Oxford, 1997), pp. 134–56.
79 Thompson, *The Media and Modernity*, p. 191.
80 A. Giddens, *Modernity and Self-Identity: Self and Society in Late Modern Age* (Polity Press, Cambridge, 1991), p. 182.
81 Stonewall's website is at http://www.stonewall.org.uk/.
82 S. Hall, 'Thatcherism today', *New Statesman and Society*, 26 Nov. 1993, p. 16.
83 Giddens, *Modernity and Self-Identity*, p. 175.

6   The internet, the self and experience in everyday life

1 U. Beck, A. Giddens and S. Lash, *Reflexive Modernization: Politics, Tradition and Aesthetics in the Modern Social Order* (Polity Press, Cambridge, 1994), p. 13.
2 J. B. Thompson, *The Media and Modernity: A Social Theory of the Media* (Polity Press, Cambridge, 1995), p. 207.
3 Ibid.
4 A. Giddens, *Modernity and Self-Identity: Self and Society in the Late Modern Age* (Polity Press, Cambridge, 1991), p. 187.
5 Z. Bauman, *Life in Fragments* (Blackwell, Oxford, 1995), p. 99.
6 Ibid., p. 103.
7 Thompson, *The Media and Modernity*, p. 210.
8 Giddens, *Modernity and Self-Identity*, p. 75.
9 Bauman, *Life in Fragments*, p. 82.
10 Giddens, *Modernity and Self-Identity*, p. 156.
11 Thompson, *The Media and Modernity*, p. 208.
12 Giddens, *Modernity and Self-Identity*, p. 168.
13 Thompson, *The Media and Modernity*, p. 212.
14 Giddens, *Modernity and Self-Identity*, pp. 189–201.
15 R. Kraut et al., 'Internet paradox: a social technology that reduces social involvement and psychological well-being?, *American Psychologist* 53, no. 9 (1998), pp. 1017–31.
16 D. Morley, *Television, Audiences and Cultural Studies* (Routledge, London, 1992).
17 J. Lull, *Inside Family Viewing* (Routledge, London, 1990), p. 36.
18 I. de Sola Pool, *The Social Impact of the Telephone* (MIT Press, London, 1977).
19 D. Chandler, 'Personal home pages and the construction of identities on the web', http://www.aber.ac.uk/~dgc/webindent.html.
20 A. Giddens, *New Rules of Sociological Method: A Positive Critique of Interpretative Sociologies* (Hutchinson, London, 1976), p. 92.
21 Ibid., p. 51.
22 Thompson, *The Media and Modernity*, p. 228.

7 Publicness and the internet

1 J. B. Thompson, *The Media and Modernity: A Social Theory of the Media* (Polity Press, Cambridge, 1995), p. 245.
2 A. W. Gouldner, *The Dialectic of Ideology and Technology; The Origins, Grammar, and Future of Ideology* (Macmillan, London, 1976), p. 102.
3 Z. Bauman, *Life in Fragments: Essays in Postmodern Morality* (Blackwell, Oxford, 1995), pp. 44–71.
4 Thompson, *The Media and Modernity*, p. 236.
5 Ibid., p. 247.
6 Ibid., p. 255.
7 K. Sontheimer, 'La responsibilitad de la television ante la sociedad', *Folia Humanistica* 15 (1979), pp. 745–50.
8 Thompson, *The Media and Modernity*, p. 257.
9 J. Habermas, *Communication and Evolution of Society* (Heinemann, London, 1979), p. 186.
10 J. Habermas, *Legitimation Crisis* (Heinemann, London, 1976); J. Habermas, *Reason and the Rationalization of Society*, vol. 1 of *The Theory of Communicative Action* (Heinemann, London, 1984); J. Habermas, 'Discourse ethics: notes on a program of philosophical justification', in Seyla Benhabib and Fred Dallmayr (eds), *The Communicative Ethics Controversy* (MIT Press, Cambridge, Mass., 1990), pp. 60–110.
11 Habermas, *Reason and the Rationalization of Society*, pp. 273–344.
12 S. Benhabib, 'Afterword: communicative ethics and current controversies in practical philosophy', in Benhabib and Dallmayr, *The Communicative Ethics Controversy*, p. 343.
13 T. McCarthy, *Ideals and Illusions: On Reconstruction and Deconstruction in Contemporary Critical Theory* (MIT Press, Cambridge, Mass., 1993), p. 199.
14 Thompson, *The Media and Modernity*, p. 261.
15 M. Castells, *The Rise of Network Society*, vol. 1 of *The Information Age: Economy, Society and Culture* (Blackwell, Oxford, 1996), p. 199.
16 A. Giddens, *New Rules of Sociological Method* (Hutchinson, London, 1976), pp. 81–6.
17 U. Beck, A. Giddens and S. Lash, *Reflexive Modernization: Politics, Tradition and Aesthetics in the Modern Social Order* (Polity Press, Cambridge, 1994), pp. 82–5.
18 R. Dworkin, *Taking Rights Seriously* (Duckworth, London, 1977), p. 82.
19 Ibid.
20 J. Slevin, 'The normative foundations of television culture, a critical account of the conceptualization of moral responsibility in Dutch and British state broadcasting policy', Ph.D. diss., King's College, Cambridge, 1993.
21 R. Dworkin, *A Matter of Principle* (Clarendon Press, Oxford, 1986), p. 338.
22 Ibid., p. 336.
23 Slevin, 'The normative foundations of television culture', and Tweede Kamer (second chamber of the Dutch houses of parliament), 1974–1975, 13353.
24 Dworkin, *Taking Rights Seriously*, p. 233.
25 Ibid., p. 26.
26 Ibid., p. xi.
27 Ibid., pp. 248–53.
28 Ibid., p. 249.

8 Globalization and the internet

1 A. Giddens, *Beyond Left and Right: The Future of Radical Politics* (Polity Press, Cambridge, 1994).

2 U. Beck, A. Giddens and S. Lash, *Reflexive Modernization: Politics, Tradition and Aesthetics in the Modern Social Order* (Polity Press, Cambridge, 1994), p. 95.

3 Ibid.

4 J. B. Thompson, *The Media and Modernity: A Social Theory of the Media* (Polity Press, Cambridge, 1995), p. 150.

5 Z. Bauman, *Life in Fragments* (Blackwell, Oxford, 1995), p. 24.

6 Beck, Giddens and Lash, *Reflexive Modernization*, p. 96.

7 Ibid., pp. 96, 95.

8 Bauman, *Life in Fragments*, p. 251.

9 A. Giddens, *The Third Way: The Renewal of Social Democracy* (Polity Press, Cambridge, 1998), pp. 28–33.

10 A. Giddens, *The Consequences of Modernity* (Polity Press, Cambridge, 1990), p. 65; D. Bell, 'The world and the United States in 2013', *Daedalus* 116 (1987).

11 Thompson, *The Media and Modernity*, pp. 119–48; Beck, Giddens and Lash, *Reflexive Modernization*, p. 97.

12 Bauman, *Life in Fragments*, p. 251.

13 M. Castells, *The Rise of Network Society*, vol. 1 of *The Information Age: Economy, Society and Culture* (Blackwell, Oxford, 1996), p. 428.

14 Bauman, *Life in Fragments*, p. 252.

15 Castells, *The Rise of Network Society*, p. 428.

16 M. Horkheimer, *Sozialphilosophische Studien: Aufsätze, Reden und Vorträge, 1930–1972*, ed. Werner Brede (Athenäum Fischer Taschenbuch, Frankfurt, 1972).

17 T. Adorno, 'The stars down to earth: the Los Angeles Times astrology column', *Telos*, no. 19 (Spring 1974), pp. 88–9.

18 T. Adorno, 'Culture industry reconsidered', *New German Critique* 6 (Fall 1975), p. 19.

19 M. Horkheimer and T. Adorno, *Dialectic of Enlightenment* (Continuum, New York, 1997), p. 120.

20 J. B. Thompson, *Ideology and Modern Culture: Critical Theory in the Era of Mass Communication* (Polity Press, Cambridge, 1990), p. 100.

21 H. I. Schiller, *Communication and Cultural Domination* (International Arts and Sciences Press, New York, 1976), p. 5.

22 Ibid., pp. 5–6.

23 H. I. Schiller, *Mass Communications and American Empire* (Beacon Press, Boston, 1971).

24 Ibid., p. 98.

25 H. I. Schiller, *The Mind Managers* (Beacon Press, Boston, 1973), p. 1.

26 Ibid., p. 3.

27 Ibid., p. 186.

28 H. I. Schiller, 'A quarter-century retrospective', in *Mass Communications and American Empire* (Westview Press, Boulder, 1992), pp. 11, 12–15.

29 E. G. Wedell, *Broadcasting and Public Policy* (Michael Joseph, London, 1968), p. 297.

30 D. Kellner, 'Network television and American society', *Theory and Society* 10, no. 1 (Jan. 1981).
31 Thompson, *The Media and Modernity*, pp. 169–73.
32 T. Liebes and E. Katz, *The Export of Meaning: Cross-Cultural Readings of Dallas* (Oxford University Press, Oxford, 1990).
33 A. Giddens, *A Contemporary Critique of Historical Materialism*, vol. 1: *Power, Property and the State* (Macmillan, London, 1981), p. 63.
34 *The Harvard Conference on the Internet and Society*, ed. O'Reilly & Associates (Harvard University Press, Cambridge, 1996).
35 M. Holderness, 'Falling through the net: developing nations lack internet access', *New Statesman and Society*, 13 Oct. 1995, p. 24.
36 This point has been emphasized by a growing fear of US domination even in Europe, see V. Smart et al., 'Lost in cyberspace: Europe's failure to prevent the US from dominating the Internet', *The European*, 11 Sept. 1997, p. 8.
37 'The race for cyberspace: inequality of information technology resources among countries', *Asian Review of Business and Technology*, no. 3 (Mar. 1998), p. 24.
38 Africa Online, http://www.africaonline.com.
39 31st December Women's Movement of Ghana, http://www.africaonline.com.gh/31dwm/index.html.
40 Gatsby Marketing Centre, http://www.africaonline.com.ke/gatsby/index.html.
41 Bombolulu, http://www.africaonline.co.ke/bombolulu/us.html.
42 Giddens, *The Third Way*, p. 153.
43 W. Wresch, *Disconnected: Haves and Have-Nots in the Information Age* (Rutgers University Press, New Brunswick, N.J., 1996), pp. 246–7.

9 Regulation and the internet

1 A. Giddens, *The Nation-State and Violence*, vol. 2 of *A Contemporary Critique of Historical Materialism* (Polity Press, Cambridge, 1985), p. 199.
2 P. Priestley, *Victorian Prison Lives: English Prison Biography 1830–1914* (Methuen, London, 1985), pp. 11–12.
3 See for example 'Table of UK cases involving child pornography on the internet', in Cyber-Rights & Cyber-Liberties (UK) Report, 'Who watches the watchmen: internet content rating systems, and privatised censorship', Nov. 1997, http://www.leeds.ac.uk/law/pgs/yaman/watchmen.htm.
4 S. Cohen, *Folk Devils and Moral Panics: The Creation of The Mods and Rockers* (MacGibbon and Kee, London, 1972).
5 S. Braman, 'Policy for the net and the internet', *Annual Review of Information Science and Technology* 30 (1995).
6 M. Castells, *End of Millennium*, vol. 3 of *The Information Age: Economy, Society and Culture* (Blackwell, Oxford, 1998), pp. 74–5.
7 List of possible government achievements adapted from A. Giddens, *The Third Way: The Renewal of Social Democracy* (Polity Press, Cambridge, 1998), pp. 47–8.
8 J. B. Thompson, *The Media and Modernity: A Social Theory of the Media* (Polity Press, Cambridge, 1995), pp. 240–3.
9 J. Blumler, 'Introduction: current confrontations in West European television', in J. Blumler (ed.), *Television and the Public Interest: Vulnerable Values in West European Broadcasting* (Sage, London, 1992), p. 1.

10 Thompson, *The Media and Modernity*, p. 241.
11 Ibid.
12 J. S. Mill, *On Liberty and Other Writings* (Cambridge University Press, Cambridge, 1989), p. 20.
13 See Y. Akdeniz, 'Internet law related news', Cyber-Rights & Cyber-Liberties (UK), http://www.leeds.ac.uk/law/pgs/yaman/netlaw.htm.
14 'The CompuServe incident: chronicle of events', 13 Mar. 1996, http://www.uni-konstanz.de/~dierk/censorship/compuserve/chronik.html.
15 Letter from the Metropolitan Police to the UK ISPs, Aug. 1996, made available by Cyber-Rights & Cyber-Liberties (UK), http://www.leeds.ac.uk/law/pgs/yaman/themet.htm.
16 'German academic net blocks Dutch site', *Wired News*, 18 Apr. 1997, http://www.wired.com/news/print_version/story/3265.html?wnpg=all.
17 J. Curran and Jean Seaton, *Power without Responsibility: The Press and Broadcasting in Britain*, 3rd edn (Routledge, London, 1988), p. 217.
18 'German academic net blocks Dutch site'.
19 See Obscene Publications Act 1959, secs 1 and 4, HMSO.
20 Enquiry into audio-visual communications and the regulation of broadcasting, House of Commons, Select Committee for Culture, Media and Sport, 6 May 1998, http://www.parliament.the-stationery-office.co.uk/pa/cm199798/cmselect/cmcumeds/520-vol1/52002.htm.
21 Telecommunications Act 1996, http://www.technologylaw.com/techlaw/act_index.html.
22 The Blue Ribbon Campaign for Online Free Speech, http://www.eff.org/blueribbon.html.
23 Electronic Frontier Foundation, 'Supreme Court victory for free speech: CDA ruled unconstitutional', press release, 26 June 1997.
24 J. Weinberg, 'Rating the net', *Hastings Communications and Law Journal* 19, no. 2 (1997), pp. 453–82.
25 The White House Office of the Press Secretary, Statement by the President, 19970626, 26 June 1997.
26 Blue Ribbon Campaign for Online Free Speech.
27 European Commission, Green Paper on the Protection of Minors and Human Dignity in Audiovisual and Information Services, Brussels, Oct. 1996, http://www2.echo.lu/legal/en/internet/gpen-txt.html and European Commission, 'Illegal and harmful content on the internet', Communication to the European Parliament, the Council, the Economic and Social Committee and the Committee of the Regions, Brussels, 11 Oct. 1996, http://www2.echo.lu/legal/en/internet/communic.html and European Commission, Working Party on Illegal and Harmful Content on the Internet, Report, Brussels, Nov. 1996, http://www2.echo2.lu/legal/en/internet/wpen.html and Report on the Commission Communication on Illegal and Harmful Content on the Internet, Committee on Civil Liberties and Internal Affairs, Rapporteur Mr Pierre Pradier, 20 Mar. 1997 and 'Action plan on promoting safe use of the internet', Annex 1: Summary of Action Lines, Brussels, 1997, http://www2.echo.lu/legal/en/internet/actpl-al.html.
28 European Commission, 'Illegal and harmful content on the internet'.
29 European Commission, 'Action plan on promoting safe use of the internet', and 'Illegal and harmful content on the internet'.
30 European Commission, 'Illegal and harmful content on the internet'.

31 European Commission, Green Paper on the Protection of Minors and Human Dignity in Audiovisual and Information Services.

32 European Commission, 'Illegal and harmful content on the internet'.

33 J. Seiger quoted in A. Penenberg, 'The evolving legal tack in Germany', *Wired News*, 17 Apr. 1997, http://www.wired.com/news/print_version/story/3219.html?wnpg=all.

34 Electronic Frontier Foundation, 'Supreme Court victory for free speech'.

35 Women Halting Online Abuse, http://whoa.femail.com/.

36 CyberAngels, Mission Statement, http://www.cyberangels.org/about/mission.html.

37 CyberAngels Channel Rules, http://www.cyberangels.org/ircdivision/rules.htm.

38 The Internet Watch Foundation, http://www.internetwatch.org.uk.

39 D. McQuail, *Mass Communication Theory: An Introduction* (Sage, London, 1994) p. 126.

40 Cyber-Rights & Cyber-Liberties (UK) Report: 'Who watches the watchmen. Part II: Accountability and effective self-regulation in the information age', Sept. 1998, http://www.cyber-rights.org/watchmen-ii.htm.

41 M. Oostveen, 'Kinderen voor het Grijpen', *NRC Handelsblad*, 20 June 1998.

42 F. Rodriquez, 'Column Felipe: zelfregulering op het Internet Werkt niet', *Planet Multimedia*, 17 July 1998, http://www.planet.nl/computer/multim/17-7-98/mm17-7-98a.html.

43 European Commission, 'Safe portals', under 'Promoting best use, preventing misuse', http://www2.echo.lu/best_use/portals.html.

44 European Commission, 'Software filters', under 'Promoting best use, preventing misuse', http://www2.echo.lu/best_use/software.html.

45 P. Resnick and J. Miller, 'PICS: internet access controls without censorship', *Communications of the Association for Computing Machinery* 39, no. 10 (1996), pp. 87–93.

46 P. Resnick, 'Filtering information on the internet', *Scientific American*, Mar. 1997, pp. 106–8.

47 World Wide Web Consortium, 'PICS, censorship, and intellectual freedom FAQ', http://www.w3.org/PICS/PICS-FAQ-980126.html.

48 Recreational Software Advisory Council on the Internet, http://www.rsac.org.

49 World Wide Web Consortium, 'PICS, censorship, and intellectual freedom FAQ'.

50 Ibid.

51 Weinberg, 'Rating the net'.

52 Recreational Software Advisory Council on the Internet.

53 Stonewall, http://www.stonewall.org.uk/.

54 Weinberg, 'Rating the net'.

55 Ibid.

56 J. Wallace, 'Why I will not rate my site', http://www.spectacle.org/cda/rate.html.

57 Cyber-Rights & Cyber-Liberties (UK) Report: 'Who watches the watchmen. Part II'.

58 Weinberg, 'Rating the net'.

59 A. Giddens, *The Third Way: The Renewal of Social Democracy* (Polity Press, Cambridge, 1998), p. 64.

60 Report of the Committee on Obscenity and Film Censorship, Cmnd 7772, HMSO, London, 1979.

Concluding reflections

1 Z. Bauman, *Life in Fragments* (Blackwell, Oxford, 1995), pp. 105–25; A. Giddens, *The Consequences of Modernity* (Polity Press, Cambridge, 1990).
2 The following list is adapted from A. Giddens, *The Consequences of Modernity* (Polity Press, Cambridge, 1990), p. 150, Table 2: A Comparison of Conceptions of 'Post-Modernity' (PM) and 'Radicalized Modernity' (RM).
3 J. Lyotard, *The Postmodern Condition: A Report on Knowledge* (University of Minnesota Press, Minneapolis, 1984), p. 76.
4 These are some of the descriptions and concepts used by Castells to approach communication networks in our modern age: M. Castells, *The Information Age: Economy, Society and Culture* (Blackwell, Oxford, 1996–8), vol. 1: *The Rise of Network Society*; vol. 2: *The Power of Identity*, and vol. 3: *End of Millennium*.
5 U. Beck, A. Giddens and S. Lash, *Reflexive Modernization: Politics, Tradition and Aesthetics in the Modern Social Order* (Polity Press, Cambridge, 1994).
6 J. B. Thompson, *Ideology and Modern Culture: Critical Theory in the Era of Mass Communication* (Polity Press, Cambridge, 1990); J. B. Thompson, *The Media and Modernity: A Social Theory of the Media* (Polity Press, Cambridge, 1995).
7 R. Williams, *Television: Technology and Cultural Form* (Fontana, London, 1974).
8 Giddens, *The Consequences of Modernity*.
9 Adapted from ibid., p. 150, Table 2.
10 Z. Bauman, *Postmodern Ethics* (Blackwell, Oxford, 1993), p. 17.

Index